1989

# CONSERVATION AND PRACTICAL MORALITY

# CONSERVATION AND PRACTICAL MORALITY

*Challenges to Education and Reform*

Les Brown

*Formerly Professor of Education*
*University of New South Wales*

St. Martins Press   New York

© Leslie Melville Brown, 1987

All rights reserved. For information, write:
Scholarly & Reference Division,
St. Martin's Press, Inc., 175 Fifth Avenue, New York, NY 10010

First published in the United States of America in 1987

Printed in Hong Kong

ISBN 0–312–16272–3

Library of Congress Cataloging-in-Publication Data

Brown, Les, 1914–
    Conservation and practical morality.

    Bibliography: p.
    Includes index.
    1. Ethics. 2. Social ethics. 3. Conservation of natural resources—
    Moral and ethical aspects.
    I. Title
    BJ1031.B74   1987        170        86–1795
    ISBN 0–312–16272–3

# Contents

vi                                Contents

# Preface

In broad terms this book may be considered a companion to *Justice, Morality and Education*, since each traverses similar territory in moral theory and the associated area of distributive justice, as well as in fundamental educational theory. In other respects the two books diverge, with quite different complexities in each. Moral theory now widens from individuals in relation with others to a more general viewpoint on the well-being or quality of life of all persons, wherever they may live, constituting their *common good*. This clearly gives it a utilitarian flavour, but utilitarianism – in any of its varying formulations – is shown to be inadequate for a normative theory of the common good.

The book will be seen to fall roughly into two parts, though a formal organizational structure has seemed to be unnecessary. In the first two chapters fundamental theoretical distinctions are made. Succeeding chapters have a more practical orientation, including the last which, apart from bringing into focus some of the main preceding emphases, considers the high demands placed on *education*, in conjunction with social and political reform.

The argument begins with an essential basis of moral theory in order to show what a moral problem is. In the second chapter it is shown that some problems of conservation are also moral problems, but that some others are *not*. The criteria for these distinctions are a set of moral principles which are found to be common ground in contemporary moral philosophy. As standard moral principles they are compatible with much of continental philosophy, such as existentialism, and also with most of the major religious traditions throughout the world. At specific points certain religious doctrines are in conflict with the principles, as in the respective interpretations of 'person', and in the attitude to sentient animals. It is preferred, therefore, to rely on moral principles which are common to the various forms of moral philosophy in English-speaking countries, viewing moral philosophy as an academic discipline, and its principles as justified by reason with the support of common moral values. Beliefs in the continuous efficacy of intellectual or religious traditions may be based on different assumptions and may lead to different arguments and judgments from those expressed in this book.

An attempt is made to encourage critical and reflective reader participation by interleaving philosophical ideas from time to time, both to sharpen the particular ideas being introduced and to stimulate further thought, sometimes by contrast. Chapter summaries are designed with the same end in view, putting the complexity of ideas in perspective before proceeding to further complexities. The final pattern is one of relationships between conservation and practical morality which draw together a diversity of disciplines and social concerns.

Without critical reader-involvement there is a danger that some of the ideas which are developed will become ends in themselves, such as the historical perspective on philosophers' (and others') notions of the common good in Chapter 1; or on decision-making and the law in Chapter 3; or on practicalities of Commissions in Chapter 5. The exploration of viewpoints on the common good shows their consistent connection with social circumstances, pointing to conservation as a relatively recent moral concern. Decision-making has a clear relationship with the question of *who* is to make the judgements on the large moral and social questions of our time, such as conservation in some of its aspects, leading to a positive suggestion for political reform. The law draws attention to particular relationships between practical morality and conservation, sometimes negatively, or by contrast, at other times positively in its influence on quality of life. The same practical relationships depend partly on the administrative feasibility of Commissions.

Since the book is concerned with practical morality, the judgements made depend on asking at many points, What is the case? There is therefore more factual information provided than is usual in a book of ideas on conservation and morality which links moral theory with social and political theory. The Selected Bibliography is itself an indication of the wide social ramifications of the conservation issue, the need to explore viewpoints in many areas other than in moral or political philosophy in order to avoid ungrounded enthusiasms or superficial judgements. Some of the books and articles included express views which the author does *not* support; they are not all of equal intellectual rigour; but together they do help to make up a complex picture of some of the ideas and information relevant to the making of practical judgements on conservation as a moral question.

It is difficult enough for most persons to live a practical morality in relation to persons in the family and the immediate circle of acquaintances; harder by far to live a practical morality which brings in the suffering of people of other countries; highly improbable, without much better education, for wide practice of a morality that includes weighing the probable needs of unborn kin in the next century or so; and almost impossible, it would seem, in the light of the considerations of this book, to improve the quality of life of persons everywhere – the common good of people of the habitable earth – without fundamental social and political reforms, initiated and sustained by unprecedented changes in public education. The moral face of conservation is indeed complex, but it is genuine. It presents an enigmatic or a false face mainly to those with insufficient knowledge and understanding of moral, social and political complexities, and of the prospects for improvement through education.

L.M.B.

# 1 Morality, the Common Interest and the Common Good

The central concern of this book is the problem of whether conservation may be regarded as a practical moral activity, but like morality and education (as well as many other activities in which we engage in relation with others, such as politics, business administration, law and so forth) there is always a body of theory to enlarge our understanding of practice and in some ways to guide it. We therefore begin by asking in the widest sense what *morality* means, and what its purpose is. In this undertaking we shall be setting certain boundaries of moral activity. The need to do this may not be immediately obvious, but will be made so as soon as the understanding of morality is applied to a specific problem such as conservation where vaguenesses and misunderstandings are not uncommon. To use the customary language of moral philosophy, our approach will be both normative and meta-ethical: that is, we shall propose a coherent moral outlook as a system of ideas, beliefs or judgements to use as a standard in subsequent discussions; and we shall enquire into the nature of our thinking as we make our moral judgements, decisions or conclusions prior to moral action. The meta-ethical explanation we make is independent of the normative position we take on morality, but by throwing light on mental states and processes during and preceding our practical judgements on what we ought (morally) to do, we have an opportunity to increase self-understanding and thereby facilitate moral relationships with others. Before we consider conservation as a moral problem, therefore, it is necessary to understand what a moral problem is.

Our starting point is the very assumption that our morality is concerned with our relationship with others. In pursuance of the general intentions we have stated, the plan will be gradually to

1

expand understanding of the common interest from a moral standpoint in these ways: first, by bringing the nature and purpose of moral living into sharper focus, such as by enquiring into the relevant characteristics of *others* with whom we relate; second, by considering the social context of morality, enquiring into community relations of a closely integrated kind and then into extensions from these into national and international relations of a looser and less binding kind; third, by considering a fundamental notion of morality related to individual *interests* in particular, then by widening this reference to explain the moral nature of the common interest and the *common good*.

Since we are concerned with giving moral direction to problems of conservation, the next task is to choose and justify the use of a particular moral compass to give us dependable bearings. Shall it be based on utility (or maximizing satisfactions), or rights of individuals, or simply on imperatives of duty? And finally, to give the kind of understanding needed on common interests which are central to the study of a morality of conservation, we shall consider the possible influence of attitudes and values in our moral thinking, in this way using meta-ethical explanations to throw light on how we make our practical judgements. These various considerations have a direct relevance to conservation and common interests, though there is much more to be said on morality than these alone suggest.

## NATURE AND PURPOSE OF MORALITY: PERSONS

Some of the intuitions of what is good or bad, right or wrong, we carry with us from childhood through our active relationships with others in the family circle. In this first society we live in we may be selfish or unselfish, helpful or unhelpful, cooperative or uncooperative, benevolent in our attitudes to others or spiteful, malicious, unkind, destructive. One pattern of behaviour is commended by parents, the other reprimanded, yet parental praise may be for no better reason than that, to them, harmony is more tolerable than disharmony. To impart a conviction that unselfishness, helpfulness and so forth are morally *good*, parents themselves need to believe that they are good, and not merely a means to a preferred end that is prudent, or expedient, or comfortable to live with. Children who break the peace may do so for a good reason: they may be pursuing

activities providing individual benefit and satisfaction – one ham-
mering in nails while another is practising at the piano. Why should
not each pursue his or her own *interests* in this sense? Why should
piano-playing take precedence over carpentry? In such cases of
conflict of interests the wise parent organizes time and opportunity
for each to be satisfied, at the same time demonstrating that
personal interests are to be respected by others, not disrupted. Here
are the rudiments of a morality that is learned in childhood. One's
own interests are not to be sacrificed, but the important lesson is
that others have interests too, and rights, and the moral task is to
try ever harder to rise above a fundamental impulse to do whatever
one wants to do, regardless of others – following exclusively, that is,
the path of *self*-interest. For reasons that are sometimes complex,
many adults have never taken the first step towards practical
morality, have never voluntarily *considered* the interests of others
but have conceded to them – when they have had to – because of
external constraints of laws, regulations and social disapproval. In
this sense they have remained a-moral throughout their lives,
despite increase in understanding which permits them to use others
towards their own ends, or if beyond manipulation, to ignore them
totally. The egoist remains morally ignorant as long as he closes his
mind completely to others' interests. With all his knowledge of
human manipulability, or simply of human strengths and weaknesses, his insights may not extend to an understanding of *persons*,
and his will certainly does not bend to accepting membership of a
community of persons, or to perceiving any interests held in
common with others. To consider others' interests in a moral sense
is not a process of calculation or of weighing advantages but rather
of disciplining oneself to relax self-interest in an attempt to assume
others' standpoints.

To achieve this understanding is not simply a matter of reaching
human maturity, or of attaining, from a natural development from
childhood, an adult perception of others as having individual
outlooks, interests, desires, motives or intentions, attitudes and
values, and goals. That perception is not confined to adults: some
children may have it more clearly than some adults. The insight into
others' standpoints as we step out of our egoism and consider
others' interests is fundamental to living morally with others, but it
is a variable among human capacities. Even with the clearest
perspicacity, it does require an effort. The notion of personhood is
not egalitarian in any assumed equality of individual empathic

understanding, and it is not egalitarian in any assumption that persons are of equal worth, for they are clearly not by any moral norms that may be used. Equality of persons in a moral sense is rather an equality of consideration both *as* persons, and with respect to their individual interests. It is only in a loose and vague way that we may speak judgementally and literally of equality of respect for all persons. Inevitably as moral agents we will respect those making the greatest effort to live morally, above those who are hardly making an effort at all. Practical morality comes naturally to no one. Yet those making a minimum moral effort within their respective social environments are equally deserving of *consideration as persons* with their unique patterns of individual interests: prior consideration does not go to the person making the maximum moral effort. The weaker moral agent is not to be dismissed as a non-person, or retributively as one who should receive no more consideration than he gives. But in the consideration of interests again there is no egalitarian implication, for equal moral consideration does not imply equal moral worth. Once there is agreement on judgemental criteria, a motive to become wealthy, for instance, is not likely to be judged as equally commendable as a motive to prevent suffering: indeed, it would be difficult to justify the first as moral at all. One thing is beyond question: we are fortunate to have the general human powers we do have for living rationally and morally in association with others, a good fortune which comes sharply to mind as we contrast our powers with those of non-human animals. Beyond that, we must give equality of consideration of interests to all individuals who have interests, and in the loose sense of respect for persons we must respect individuals morally as persons when we recognize that they have interests. But these interests, as well as their motives and goals, must have some kind of moral tenor, otherwise we would find ourselves respecting as persons those who murder, plunder, seek to destroy others even, simply because we recognize that they have interests. We have yet to explain what we mean by 'moral tenor'.

To this point we have considered persons as abstractions – as members of the human species endowed with a mental life characterized by common attributes of desires, motives, aspirations, goal-seeking and so forth. We could give substantive weight to this abstraction by filling it out as particular *personalities*, but that would be to give it too much content – to include items irrelevant to morality such as details of physique, sociability, volubility or reticence, and so forth. To recognize a person is to move distinctly from the abstract to the concrete: it is to perceive the dynamic emotional and conative life of a particular individual, to stand at his centre so closely that his purpose and striving can be understood as very similar to our own in their fundamental states; or his satisfactions and frustrations, his envy and anguish, his ambitions, goals, delusions, anxieties, his loves and hates, all in the particular fabric of a life being lived. With this grasp of the concreteness of a person we are in a position to concede that if we are to live morally in association with him, we can no longer be impelled exclusively by self-interest; his interests must be taken into account for the simple reason that to ignore them would be a selfish and contradictory denial of the personhood we have perceived in him. We are not persuaded by the extrinsic and pragmatic consideration that we each have to yield to the other at times for the sake of social harmony. The appreciation of person at once enables us, with effort and occasional self-sacrifice, to live morally with others, and denies the achievement to the lower animals. *Part* of our good fortune is that we are rational, with variable dual powers of introspection and reflection.

We shall return to the question of interests when we have given further shape to the formal notion of morality, noting that one of the central moral interests individuals have is to be viewed by others as *persons*: as moral subjects, each with an active self-and-other orientation to the world, rather than as objects to be ignored, or used as ends, or ruthlessly destroyed. And purely *as* persons (which is to say nothing of human variability in capacity for moral conduct) all persons are equal, none to be accorded precedence in moral consideration on the basis of family connections, official positions, representation of associations such as trade unions or employers; or on grounds of race, religion or sex, or demeaned as inferior through slavery, feudalism, colonialism or any other subject–overlord relationship, or victor–defeated relationship as might exist in occupation of enemy territory during or after war. The two fundamental impediments to equality of consideration of persons in practical morality, apart from ignorance and obtuseness, are *status* and *presumption*. In the most favourable light, status-seeking is an attempt to improve in self-confidence and self-respect, believing in one's ability to fill a position both competently and responsibly. In its worst light, status-seeking is a primitive urge to dominate, to win power and influence over others, regardless of competence or responsibility to others. Apart from these extremes, in all hierarchical organizations with stratified promotion positions, as well as in simpler structures of administrator and staff, employer and employee, professor and lecturer, officer and other ranks, however mixed and complex the motivation may be to improve one's own position in relation to others' (economic, social, interpersonal rivalry and so forth) the common tendency is for power to corrupt perceptions of others as persons in the moral sense – each with his own outlook on the world, his own satisfactions to fulfil and obstacles to overcome. When vain and insensitive persons achieve high status, presumption may aggravate an unfortunate moral condition as they increasingly alienate themselves from ordinary people and indulge in self-aggrandizement (such as by clamouring for public acclaim or political honours). In varying degrees, indeed, status has a strong inclination to mask perceptions of persons, as presumption leads to the judging of others with inferior status to be in fact inferior, and therefore demanding no more than summary consideration. A common tendency is thus for the alliance of status and presumption to result in a degree of moral deterioration through the very loss of focus in the perceptions of persons.[1]

The moral claim to equality of consideration of all persons *as* persons, and of their interests, is a much stronger claim than one which asserts equality of all human beings in dignity and rights simply because they belong to 'a common stock', as one of the United Nations declarations has expressed it.[2] This is a family or species view. Individuals are not born as persons in the moral sense, merely as human beings: their peculiar *moral* personhood (as distinct from legal personhood or a particular religious personhood, for instance) becomes evident at some time after infancy, when through the gradual development of rational powers they become at the same time capable of moral choices. Similarly the perception of personhood in others is an understanding that develops after early childhood: it is learned, as practical morality is learned with respect to dispositions and reasoning.

## SOCIAL CONTEXT OF MORALITY

Learning to be moral occurs in a social setting, beginning normally in the home. The fundamental idea of morality is that we ought to consider others' interests, that we ought not to remain entirely self-interested as very young children are. There is no question of the practicability of total egoism: it is demonstrated every day by some adults. For them egoism pays, and what serves their own interests is given the highest value and exclusive attention: other individuals are to be used, manipulated, exploited or avoided. For total egoists of this kind a society of people is necessary: alone their lives would be unrewarding. By contrast, those who have acquired sufficient insight into others' desires and motives, their strivings to make a place for themselves in the world, to perceive the elements of a shared person-hood with them, also need a society of people; again alone their lives would be unrewarding, but in a very different sense. For the moral person who lives in a perceived community of persons with some common interests, shares with others an understanding that there are others apart from himself who are making their way in the world, and fundamentally with similar outlooks, but above all, who are *rational*. So in a very broad sense only, a community of persons is a rational–moral community (a description which is not always supportable, as we shall see, from the standpoint of reciprocity). There is a third group to be considered, namely, recluses. These have no urge to turn others to advantage: by definition they stand alone. Is theirs a special kind of morality, one requiring no social context? In the contemporary world the position of the recluse is largely theoretical, for it is difficult for anyone to exist without any contact with the outside world, or without external sustenance of any kind. Certainly those who assume the position even temporarily may claim obligations to no one else. Having withdrawn from a supposedly rational–moral community, they may believe themselves in no way responsible for others' well-being. From an existentialist stance, some may believe their responsibility is solely to themselves, to show the world through creative activity the pitch of their abilities. But the recluse is fundamentally an egoist. He must have known something of the world of joy and of suffering before he withdrew from it. However unsullied his moral motives, however much he refrains from harming others in any way, the fact that he makes no effort to help those in his original community who may be in need of help, and shuns benevolence as he turns inwardly and exclusively to his own interests, leaves him in an a-moral condition. Practical morality requires not only the effort to get inside the lives of others as much as we can to a perception of personhood; it requires the further effort to act in their interests when reason and moral attitudes compel us to a conviction that we ought.

In Part I of *The Descent of Man* Charles Darwin approached the
question of how it is that human beings have a moral sense or
conscience, in this respect marking them off more distinctively than
in any other respect from the lower animals (pp. 108–9).[3] He
deigned to be the first to approach the question from the side of
natural history, contending that any animal endowed with clear
social instincts would also develop a moral sense as soon as its
intellectual powers developed to a sufficient level. So in his view the
necessary conditions for a moral sense, common to the animal world
in general including the human, are social instincts and a social
context in which they might be expressed, together with *intellect*.
The social instincts lead to pleasure in the company of others of
one's species, and importantly to a measure of sympathy with them,
both greatly strengthened by habit (p. 109). Darwin justified the
moral sense partly on pragmatic grounds: moral conduct is
necessary for social cohesion (pp. 129, 146). When asked how a
large number of members of the one tribe could become endowed
with social and moral qualities, he suggested as a 'low motive' the
expectation that a good deed for a person would be returned,
followed by the development of a habit of performing benevolent
actions, suggesting that such habits after many generations might
even become inherited. Social reputation, or the praise and blame
of fellow-men, he considered a much stronger stimulus to moral
development (p. 147).

Darwin was relying not merely on observation of animal
behaviour, filling in where necessary with a naturalistic speculation,
but also on a background of moral thought carried forward to
his time from the eighteenth century: there was then a strong
predilection for the idea of a moral sense or sentiment as *natural*
to man. Thus in social interaction individuals were believed to
express a certain sympathy for others and a general tendency
towards benevolence,[4] a viewpoint which is to be weighed in the
context of a partly instructional purpose. Certainly morality then
had a social significance – it was man in relation to his fellows that
mattered morally – but with more candour and insight Hume saw,
as Darwin did, that structures of social rules or laws are contrived
for the mutual benefit of members of a social group, so that to him
practical morality had both a *natural* impulse stemming from
the moral sentiments and virtuous motives that are part of our
natures, and an *artificial* impulse stemming from a consideration of
the social circumstances of the time and place: these included the

'scanty provision nature has made for his wants' which is part of the general human condition, along with 'selfishness and confin'd generosity'.[5] And if these were to Hume as 'natural' as the moral sentiment, to him practical morality obviously calls for an effort before egoism can be suppressed in relevant situations. Beyond that, in practice a morality does not flow naturally from sympathy or a moral sense: it needs to be worked out, and so in that sense is a contrived notion, taking into account both psychological and sociological considerations.

Both Hume's and Darwin's observations on morality find some confirmation in empirical research on moral development in children, not so much with very young children, when rule-following is necessarily for reward or for penalty avoidance because of their inability to reason, but rather, as understanding grows and children comply with rules in the family or the school, to earn social praise or to avoid social blame. For it is that limited understanding of moral rules which characterizes as well much of practical morality among adults.

If it is true that part of our practical morality is derived from a common moral sense which includes sympathy or benevolence, and that it is directed towards a relaxation of our egoism in relevant situations and a practical consideration of others' interests, we may wonder whether the boundaries of our moral community ought to be confined in any way. What indeed *is* the social context of morality? It would be contradictory to espouse a practical morality that is plainly unattainable, yet the capacity to live morally by comprehending the personhood of others and considering their interests in a practical way may be as variable as any other human capacity. Thus while some adults' relationships with others may extend no wider than the family and the workplace, other adults may be morally moved by the unsatisfied interests of people in acutely underprivileged countries. For some, undoubtedly, such people are remote and different: their basic needs and interests are so vaguely apprehended as to leave no moral stirring. For others, perception of the tragedy of starvation comes in a flash: to them it is *persons* who face a predicament of family disintegration, death and disease which compels a practical moral attention. Is each moral agent then to adopt a social and moral community that matches the narrowness or breadth of his 'confin'd generosity' as attributed to us by Hume? Such a solution would be no more than an adaptation to a social situation, not a normative account of what one ought to do.

If a global morality is attainable by some, and can be justified on moral grounds, it becomes at once a normative prescription for all. Practical impediments such as ingrained self-interest, inadequate knowledge of life in other countries, a simple failure of imagination, are tasks for *education*, whose goal is not perfection but increasing improvement.

The strongest moral motivation to answer the call of persons in other countries comes during national disasters such as the plight of millions facing starvation in sub-Saharan African countries, or victims of earthquake, hurricane or tidal wave disasters.[6] This itself presents a difficulty in our practical morality, inasmuch as we tend to generalize the impact without an opportunity to perceive its particular effects on individuals – their ambitions, frustrations and losses, fears for the future, anxieties about rebuilding their lives. But the perception we do have of shattered families is a sufficient beginning to a morality with wider boundaries than merely political or geographical ones. The opportunities for moral motivation and moral action within it are apparent. We shall return to this notion of an unrestricted moral community of persons when we consider conservation in the next chapter. As for the directness or physical immediacy of our perception of person, this we regard as no more necessary to a knowledge of suffering than it is to observe a cavity in a tooth to claim knowledge that a person has toothache. Empirical knowledge of the misery of starvation and disease is not dependent on taking the pulse or analysing a blood sample.

## THE FUNDAMENTAL IDEA OF MORALITY

On the nature and purpose of morality the most prominent considerations to emerge are these: first, practical morality is learned; second, it functions in a social context; third, the perception of others as persons enables us to come to grips with their *interests*, which compel our attention; fourth, moral persons all are equal, in the sense of deserving equal consideration *as persons*; fifth, morality is practised as we resist the inclination of self-interest and in relevant situations act towards the interests of others; sixth, among some of the reasons people may have for living by moral rules is to win social approval or to avoid social disapproval.

One of the recurring and underlying ideas of morality is that it is a consideration of the interests of other persons. But this will not do as it stands as a statement of morality's fundamental notion. While it enables us to exclude some things from the category of the moral, it fails to take account of other relevant things. Similarly the notion of a rational–moral community of interacting persons, bound to observe an unwritten contract of moral rules for their mutual benefit, does not cover all cases. As a moral idea it can be clearly justified, since however short of it the practice of moral living may fall in any society of the past or the present, it may be defended not as a statement of the *is*, but as a projection from it to the way things *ought to be*. We may argue, within limits, that the extension of moral rules and values on the one hand, and of rationality on the other, is a task for education. In other respects our intuitive convictions may be that personhood excludes some objects of our moral consideration, and some of our intuitions are not easily dismissed even though we may reject their claims to direct knowledge, and may view intuitions generally with some suspicion when we find that on occasion they happen to clash. Thus intuitively we may find that we are not able to exclude from our moral attention those who do not live by moral rules at all, because they cannot, and similarly are not rational in conduct because they simply cannot be. There are the severely intellectually retarded, young children, seniles, for instance, those who are comatose, or in a state of prolonged sleep, and those who are anencephalic, with no awareness of the world about them. Intuitively we believe that all of these have to fit into a moral scheme: we care for them as a matter of imperative duty. Then there are foetuses, and children of the future who have not even been conceived – our posterity. Not least of all there are sentient animals whose species still suffer at the hands of man. Of imbeciles, young children and seniles we may say that they experience pleasure and pain, and on these grounds alone that they have interests to be considered, although we may question whether they are persons in the *moral* sense. More positively we may say that the anencephalic and the comatose are not persons, yet they demand protection and care. They do not *have* interests in the literal sense since they cannot experience them, though their nervous systems may respond to stimuli as do some of the lower animals which we may hesitate to classify as sentient. More positively still, unborn generations do not *have* interests, since they do not exist. Sentient animals can experience pain, and some of them can enjoy an emotional life in play, or in caring for their young, or in gregarious living. The case of future generations is of particular interest to conservation and will be discussed in the next chapter. Some argue that foetuses have a place in a moral scheme through human potentiality – a stronger claim at least than might be made for unborn generations of the future, for since the latter have not been conceived we cannot be sure that they will be. The only claim we can make for them is on the basis of the future being like the present and the past.

We shall test the statement that morality is a consideration of others' interests, where the others in question refer to certain non-persons including sentient animals, as well as to persons, acknowledging that we have moral obligations as well to human beings outside this category of persons who literally have interests, such as to victims of accidents who remain in prolonged comas. But there is another consideration to be weighed.

There have been many individuals who have led unblemished moral lives, but have been in a sense *morally* recluse. While their moral ideas may have been impeccable, and they may have had good moral intentions in their relations with others, they have been ineffectual in practice. It would be contradictory to speak of a practical morality that was never practised, or was confined exclusively to the promotion of self-interest. In impulse such people are to be distinguished from those who have no concern whatever for others' interests, whose thoughts and actions are entirely for their own. But benevolent thoughts which lead to no moral action in considering others' interests are inconsistent with practical morality. The statement of the fundamental idea of morality must therefore be amended: morality is a *practical* consideration of others' interests. As with all such formal statements, further explanation is necessary to an understanding of its wider meaning. We have to ask what we mean by a *practical* consideration, for instance. In particular situations, judgements will be made on moral intentions or motives which are clearly oriented towards action, but in which the act is unmistakably thwarted by circumstances. Such a person is as much a moral agent in practice as the one who performs the moral act intended. There may be warranted exceptions to a universal conclusion of benevolent intentions with moral acts oriented towards others: in some situations a decision *not* to act may be justified. There may be situations, too, where stronger reasons can be adduced to support acting in one's own interests rather than in another's: seeking shelter from flying bullets rather than exposing oneself to almost certain death.

Another explanation needed to give fuller meaning to the fundamental idea of morality is that in considering *interests* of all those in the moral category, including persons and non-persons, there is a need to acknowledge the place of *rights*. In the wider application of interests which we have now adopted, only *some* interests will be regarded as rights, which is both a stronger and more restrictive notion than that of interests. In a theory of rational reciprocity, moral rights invoke a community of rational persons who may claim, assert and even waive their rights, with an expectation of reciprocal duties or obligations on others to respect the rights. Animals, the severely intellectually retarded, young children and others we have included as having *interests*, do not have moral rights. The assigning of rights to them is a legal rather than a moral matter. To have rights is to be able to understand the mutuality of rights and duties: if someone asserts a right, to expect others as a matter of moral duty to respect it.

In a community of rational persons, some moral rights demand corresponding moral duties: not to be cheated, for instance; not to be discriminated against on entirely irrelevant grounds such as race or sex. On such matters we have a moral conviction of duty, with the force of Kant's categorical imperatives.[7] In some situations this command of moral duty does not require that recipients have any rights claims against us, so that the right–duty reciprocity notion is not universally relevant. Moral persons may feel themselves compelled to act, for instance, when confronted with cases of dire poverty in their own neighbourhood, or with social dislocation and degradation from famine thousands of miles away. The notion of a rational–moral community of persons may be a practicable morality in some associations of peers who have a mutual willingness to conduct their affairs by commonly accepted rules, and in a wider sense it is suitable as a moral prescription, or an ideal towards which individuals might aspire both at home and internationally. But situations where there is the command of moral duty towards others with no specific rights claims against the moral agent (except those of a general humanitarian kind) demonstrate again that the area of practical morality is much wider than one of rational–moral group interaction. On the other hand, the extension of the boundaries of practical morality can be too wide for internal consistency. Those who defend as a moral notion that of *artificial persons* (referring to states, corporations, banks and other special groups whose members do have moral dealings with clients) are swayed by legal interpretations. The notion of *artificial person* in this sense is metaphorical, with application to the law, business administration and government rather than to practical morality. No persons are artificial in practical morality: by contrast, the moral notion of person will be shown, especially in Chapters 4 and 5, to have wide application.

There is more to be said on rights and interests, especially in the context of a coherent viewpoint to give direction to practical morality. In the meantime the discussion of interests raises a question of vital concern to the relationship between morality and conservation in the following chapter. That is the question of whether practical morality can justifiably include a wide and to some extent a nebulous area, called the *common interest*.

## THE COMMON INTEREST AND THE COMMON GOOD

To this point the emphasis has been on practical morality as it relates to individuals – whether persons (rational to a degree), or non-persons (incapable of rational conduct), who are nevertheless objects of our moral obligations and therefore present a conflict with any attempt to base practical morality entirely on reciprocal individual relationships. In principle, practical morality requires that persons be true to their own moral convictions as they relate to other persons or to non-persons. Moral lapses are to be expected of all, but moral persons are characterized by their consistency to the rules they regard as for them and for others with whom they interact. This individual morality of persons was contrasted by Sidgwick in *The Elements of Politics* with a public morality of rules governed by sanctions. The former he called a *true* morality, the latter *positive* morality, but positive morality lacked the definiteness of a true morality.[8] This was taking the idea of morality as a practical consideration of others' interests into a wider area of society than that of interacting rational persons, but it was an area also where moral values are apt to lose their edge as they merge with social values which are not necessarily moral at all, such as allegiance to union principles in opposition to those of employers or vice versa. In Sidgwick's *positive* morality, the consideration of others' interests is inclined towards the prudence of acting to win social praise or to avoid social blame. It is quite another step from a morality of individual persons (interacting rationally on agreed moral rules) to *a practical consideration of common interests*. Here the person is compelled by moral duty, as he is in considering the interests of those non-persons to whom he has moral obligations. Attention to common interests is therefore a higher morality than Sidgwick's positive morality, but it shares with positive morality a similar indeterminacy.

In a theory of common interests the assumption is made that in some matters there are interests in common to all members of a specified society, interests which we all have, or ought to have, such as security or a healthy environment. To regard these as interests is to see them from the viewpoint of the moral agent who includes among the others, whose interests he considers, both those capable of experiencing them and those – such as infants – who are not, but over whom he accepts a custodianship with moral obligations. To remove some of the vaguenesses associated with *common interest*, one question to be asked concerns the size of the population or society which is in mind; a second is what makes the common interest a *moral* matter, rather than a political matter, or an economic matter, or an administrative matter.

Some have seen the common interest as the national interest, but nations vary in strength from a million or two million to over a billion, and difficulties of identification, cohesion and a perceived commonalty must increase with numbers as one attempts to ascertain what is in fact the common interest for all individuals. That interest is nothing if it is not perceived by its members as one shared among them. Those who think of the common interests of smaller societies or groups within states, on the other hand, tend to see them rather as sectional interests, and therefore in political or economic rather than in moral terms. Yet the size of the population is irrelevant to a perception of a common interest from a moral standpoint. By conventional usage the expression refers to political organizations of nations or states, but logically it is applicable to the *world* population, as we shall see in connection with conservation, or it may be used to refer to relatively small populations such as those of universities or schools, or even families. The question of what makes a common interest a moral one rather than a political or economic one is much more difficult: there are organizations of nations such as the European Economic Community and NATO where on the face of it the common interest is fundamentally economic or political, and any moral connection would have to be argued for. This question will be explored from an historical perspective, showing, among other things, how a distinction may be made between the *common interest* and the *common good* as a way of clarifying the peculiarly moral standpoint.

## Historical Perspectives: The Common Interest and the Common Good

It is philosophers who have been interested throughout history in the notion of the *common good* as distinct from the *public interest* (or the *common interest*) which political leaders sometimes profess to be serving. It is philosophers also who – in seeking a common good of people – have been generally dissatisfied with forms of government, and some have been dissatisfied too with the kinds of persons attracted to government, believing that government should be in the hands of the very best persons the state can produce. As will be discussed more fully in Chapter 3, politicians' pronouncements on the public interest may conceal the fact that it is their own interests which they are mainly serving, and in some circumstances they may have no thought of a common good. Political confusion between the public (or common) interest and the common good may then be deliberate, but it is not always so.[9] The people themselves may not be clear on a distinction between the public interest and the common good. Indeed history has shown many instances where there has been a massive national support for what people have believed to be their shared *common interest*, while misconceiving their *common good*. The surge of enthusiasm for national socialism in Germany is a case in point.

In the views of selected philosophers on the common interest and the common good, Plato stands preeminently. In *The Republic* he set out to give an account of a social organization of all classes of people – workers, soldier auxiliaries and philosopher–rulers – in which the interests of the city-state were the common interest, safeguarded by those few in the highest group who also, by rigorous preparation, would be able consistently to put the common interest above all else, to perceive, in fact, a *common good*. Those men selected for the ultimate task of ruling were to be those already distinguished in 'doing zealously whatever they thought was for the citizens' interests' (412, p.97).[10] The position of the rulers may appear élitist, but Plato's point was that no other citizens were indeed *capable* of perceiving the interests of the city-state as the common interest of all. That common interest was one of social stability or harmony and justice to all (519–20, p.213) against a background, which Plato probably experienced, of both external threat and internal dissension. To pursue *self-interest* would be out of the question for the highly selected rulers: their vision and purpose were of 'making the whole city happy', not of making happy a few citizens only(420, p.104). (It is worth observing that at about the same time in history Eastern thought on the common good was similar to Western. Writing also against a background of social disharmony, Confucius asserted that government should operate for the good of the people 'just as parents affectionately care for their children'.)[11]

Aristotle continued Plato's concern for good government, in more specific references to the 'common interest'. In the *Politics*(1282[b]) he dignified political science as 'the most authoritative' of all the sciences and arts, and its good, he said, is 'justice, in other words, the common interest'.[12] He had begun the *Politics* with the explanation that every state is a community, every community is established with some good in view, and the state – aiming at the highest good of all – embraces all other goods(1252[a]). The *common good* is thus the good of every member of the state, and it is to be achieved – as Plato had said – by having a government of virtuous men who would be able to perceive the common interest as 'constituted in accordance with strict principles of justice'. Despotism comes when rulers ignore the common interest and have a regard only for their own interests(1279[a]).He understood, as Plato did, the political discord which frustrated attempts to fulfil the common interest and the common good.

The Romans were always mindful of the common interest, particularly when it was under challenge from arbitrary rule. In their public utterances they reflected the skill of a persuasive oratory (acquired in their higher education), yet some, such as Cicero, conveyed a genuine concern for the security of the state equally as strong as the Greeks had professed for their own city-state. The *common good* was clearly freedom from the tyranny and subversion which had challenged the integrity of the Roman state. Thus Cicero eulogized Marcus Antonius for eliminating dictatorship from the Roman constitution.[13]

From the Marcus Antonius of Cicero to Shakespeare's Mark Antony in *Julius Caesar* was a span of fifteen centuries, yet

Shakespeare's Mark Antony expressed, in his eulogy of Brutus, the Roman spirit of concern for the *common good* of all citizens as though he were both an honourable state-loving Roman and a politically perceptive Elizabethan as well. All the conspirators except Brutus had acted dishonourably in plotting Caesar's downfall. Such attacks, stemming from envy, had undermined the state on a number of occasions. But now, 'in a general honest thought And common good to all',[14] Brutus had honoured both the state and its citizens with a sincerely moral purpose. Shakespeare's political acumen was evident in his Histories and elsewhere, and it would be highly improbable that the despotism of the Tudors, including Elizabeth I, had escaped his moral attention. The only significant common interest that could be espoused in the Elizabethan era was security from invasion. Internal security might have been seen by some as a common interest, but its connection with despotic government which gave security to some only, though preferable to unconstrained lawlessness, could hardly be called a *common good*.

Already there is a consistency emerging in the notions of the common interest and of the common good. In the seventeenth century many writers referring to the common interest (usually designated by them 'the public interest') were strongly individualistic, with an overriding concern for securing individual property against the rapacity of rulers. In the climate of uncertainty during the Stuart kingships and the crushing retributive measures of Cromwell following the Civil War, security of property rights was a predominant common interest. Part of the *common good* was a strong state that could repel invasion and quell disorder at home. Peace was desired for stability and predictability, but also there was a desire for freedom from unwarranted taxation by the state which cut into private property, and freedom from any other unconstitutional attacks on individual rights, including the right to extend one's property legitimately as the law allowed.[15] The common interest was given unity and cohesion by the threat of Stuart despotism, and for a period by Puritan despotism, but it was passive rather than militant – an expression of the need for vigilance rather than a call for action. Since in this predominant seventeenth-century view a community was an association of *individuals*, the common interest and the common good were both to be promoted by protecting the interests of individuals, in particular their property interests. From this would flow a sense of sharing in the common interest.

Hobbes however had a different view. Individuals do not share any common interests, he believed. They are fundamentally *self-interested* and derive their satisfaction from fulfilling their individual desires, not in sharing in any common good. ' . . . whatever is the object of any man's Appetite or Desire; that is it, which he for his part calleth *Good*' (Leviathan, p. 120).[16] But if individuals lack a moral point of view in considering others' interests as well as their own, social circumstances compel them to come together in a primitive contractual state for their mutual security. This is clearly contrary to natural inclinations, thought Hobbes, and 'the concord of many persons is not constant enough for lasting peace' among them. 'Somewhat else must be done', he realised, 'when their private interest shall appear discrepant from the common good' (*De Cive*, p. 66).[17] For men are not like bees for which there is no natural separation of private interest and public good. ' . . . They desire the common good, which among them differs not from their private' (p. 67). Not so with man, a creature of entirely self-centred appetite or desire. Hobbes endowed man with prudence, but not with moral values. In the final paragraph of *Leviathan* he claimed that his discourse was completely impartial, 'occasioned by the disorders of the present time' (p. 728). He too was writing in an imperfect political society prone to tyrannical rule and civil unrest. Certainly the natural state of each man fending for himself was not reasonable. It was far more advantageous for men to come together *as individuals* for their mutual safety and security. And as they so contracted, giving up some of their power to a sovereign, they had a right to expect 'safety' in return. This safety was not mere preservation of life. Hobbes explained in *Leviathan*, but everything a man acquired by 'lawfull Industry' and without 'hurt to the Commonwealth': in other words, his property or personal possessions. In this settled state, with each man living to himself, lay the fundamental 'contentments of life' (p. 376). What then, was the *common good*? In Hobbes' view it was prudence and convenience for all the separate members of the community, an abstraction formed by summing individual situations, not an enjoyment of shared community relations involving a perception of common interests and a *common good* transcending individual self-interest. To Hobbes that was asking too much of human nature.

In contrast with Hobbes, Rousseau had notions of a social contract whose foundation was moral, not merely prudent. Like Hobbes he used the state of nature from which to launch a contract theory, but his social contract was very different from that of

Hobbes inasmuch as it opened the possibility for man to live *morally*
in a civil state which was impossible for him to achieve in a state of
nature. It was this very ingredient of *morality* which gave a
characteristic stamp to his perception of the common interest and
the common good. But as he developed his theory he moved ever
further from Hobbes until he finished with a rational and a moral
ideal: to a view, that is, that people would have if they were totally
rational, disinterested, benevolent, with complete command of their
self-regarding impulses. It was a theoretical enlightenment matching
that attributed by Plato to his philosopher–rulers. Rousseau
formulated his social ideal in terms of a *general will*, whose unifying
force is always the *common interest* of members. The general will is
'an institution in which each necessarily submits himself to the same
conditions which he imposes on others'. From such a voluntary
submission there comes at once an 'admirable harmony of interest
and justice'. This it is that gives to social deliberations 'a quality of
equity' simply through the perception of a common interest (*The
Social Contract*, p. 76).[18] The social contract is equitable 'because it
is common to all', and useful, but its only end is 'the common good'
(p. 77). Yet individuals must be rational, subordinating the
individual will to reason and the *common good*, and leading to
public enlightenment with a perfect 'union of understanding and
will' (p. 83). Otherwise the general will may be readily disturbed by
the individual will: indeed 'nothing is more dangerous in public
affairs than the influence of private interests' (p. 112). Rousseau
never overlooked the possibility of the general will being defeated:
the common interest is corruptible by both 'particular interests' and
'sectional societies' (p. 150). Thus even though the general will is
morally 'indestructible' and a moral authority to those living
together under a social contract of common interests, understanding
of the common interest and loyalty to the general will demand the
kind of perfection which Hobbes could never grant of human
nature: consistent rationality and mastery of self-interested impulses.
While Hobbes' perspective was on social realities and human
limitations, Rousseau's continued to be a vision of a rational and
moral idea, for the general will remained to him 'incorruptible and
pure' even when 'the meanest interest impudently flaunts the sacred
name of the public good' (ibid.).

The notion of a general will Rousseau left in a state of confusion
and contradiction. When he spoke of men coming together in civil
society he attributed to them 'only one will, which is directed

toward their common preservation and general well-being' (p. 149). Is this fundamentally different from Hobbes' position? Is it not the individual interest in preservation and well-being that he has in mind, with community interest no more than a sum of individual interests? There can be no dynamic will beyond the will of each individual, and the notion of a unifying *general* will which comprehends all individual wills and speaks for them in some kind of superordinate relationship to individual wills is either a flight of fancy or a purposely metaphorical use of language. Certainly it has no independent capacity to express an attitude to any object to which individual wills might themselves be directed. In so far as the notion of a will can be justified at all, it applies to individuals, not to communities or societies.[19] It remains to note that Rousseau wrote against a background of intense social unrest in France, shortly before the revolt against despotic monarchy.

No one was more scathing of the notion of a general will (which had been carried forward to the French Revolution in the Declaration of the Rights of Man) than Jeremy Bentham, who reacted sharply to the very idea of the people of France – in their widespread ignorance – being able to think at all about the matter.[20] The idea of a community as a sum of individuals, which in principle applied equally to wills (as in Rousseau) or to desires (as in Hobbes), had already been applied by Hume to the 'public good'. The idea of the *public (or common) good* 'is indifferent to us', he commented, 'except so far as sympathy interests us in it'. Justice (like all other virtues) is approved of 'for no other reason, than because it has a tendency to the public good'. In speaking of these virtues, he explained, we have in mind the advantages which individuals have gained from them (*A Treatise of Human Nature*, p. 618).[21] Their tendency towards the *public good* is a combination of our sympathies with these individuals. Indeed it is sympathy towards our fellows in society which gives us 'a general sense of common interest', the sort of feeling experienced by two rowers in a boat (pp. 490, 617). Now Bentham was to go much further in the notion of a community as a sum of individuals, and a common interest as no more than a sum of individual interests. The community is a 'fictitious body', he explained, and its interest is 'the sum of the interests of the several members who compose it' (*Principles of Morals and Legislation*, p. 2).[22] Interest cannot in the ordinary way be defined, he said (p. v, fn). A thing promotes the interest of an individual 'when it tends to add to the sum total of his pleasures: or, what comes to the same thing, to diminish the sum total of his pains' (ibid.). In his *Manual of Political Economy* he asserted that the end in view of government, in all its legislation, is none other than 'the maximum of happiness in a given time in the community in question'.[23]

Despite certain attacks on Hobbes, most eighteenth-century moralists supported the idea of the *public good* as the sum of individuals' good.[24] But the forward-looking benevolence which they saw in man's nature meant that maximizing pleasure or happiness was not enough for their morality. Hutcheson claimed that 'there can be no Right . . . inconsistent with, or opposite to the greatest publick Good' (p. 173). Love or benevolence he explained as the foundation of the finest in social virtues: all we need do is 'to enquire whether this Conduct, or the contrary, will most effectively promote the publick Good' (p. 99). And this comes naturally to many as we desire the happiness of others without any selfish intention. That benevolence is the core of a 'Publick Sense' (p. 398). Between private interest and public interest Shaftesbury saw a two-way flow of benevolence. It is to everyone's good to work towards the general good: indeed, the person who ceases so to act is wanting in himself, and at the same time ceases to promote his own happiness and welfare. No one can serve self-interest who does not continue to serve the interests of society, the common interest, or the '*Whole* of which he is himself a *Part*' (p. 65). Here was a more explicit statement than in Bentham of practical morality as a consideration of others' interests as well as one's own, even if the psychological assumptions were not always supportable.

To move now to our own times, in *A Theory of Justice* and in previous articles such as 'Justice as Fairness'[25] Rawls explains his theory that justice depends – as Plato and others had said – on the basic structure of society, with an appropriate distribution of fundamental rights and duties. The moral demands on individuals are high, as Rousseau found them to be in *The Social Contract*, and Rawls' theory is largely ideal theory, as Rousseau's was, with human imperfections glimpsed only cursorily as an attempt is made to justify a position in which rational persons are bound by a duty of fair play to follow rules which they have previously accepted as equitable. Being rational, they also accept limitations on their pursuit of self-interest as they realise that the contract of fairness is not unduly harsh on any single member, but imposes the same conditions on all. There are benefits for everyone in such an arrangement: in that sense all share a common interest. 'The duty of fair play stands beside other *prima facie* duties . . . as a basic moral notion' ('Justice as Fairness', p. 146). That is because there is an acknowledgement of the personhood of others participating in a common practice, a 'recognition of the aspirations and interests of the others to be realized by their joint activity' (p. 147). The common interest is thus in the realization of individual interests through a mutual understanding of others as persons and a recognition that the interests of everyone may be realized when rational and self-interested parties are related and constrained by a system of rights and duties already accepted as fair to all (p. 148). In *A Theory of Justice* Rawls explains that the principle of the common interest is applicable to matters which concern the interests of everyone, and to which the question of distributive effects is either irrelevant or immaterial. The principle of the common interest requires institutions to provide conditions that will enable all to further their aims equally and to share equally in the benefits of whatever ends are sought in common. Shared ends are such as *public order* and *security, public health and safety* (p. 97).[26] Rawls thinks of the *common good* as 'certain general conditions that are . . . equally to everyone's advantage' (p. 246). He notes the political convention of democratic societies to appeal to the common interest, and the reluctance of any political party openly to acknowledge that its legislation is likely to disadvantage any particular social group. But it will be justice, though still imperfect, if government policies tend in the direction of furthering the long-term prospects of the least advantaged according to principles of equal liberties and fair opportunity (p. 319).[27]

Ideal theory such as Rawls' establishes a model of rational and moral conduct similar to Rousseau's in its demands on personal high-mindedness and integrity once the terms of fairness are understood between the contracting parties. The link between justice and the common interest is Rawls' special contribution to the present enquiry. His references to political parties and policies provide a bridge to the final group to be considered for their views on the common interest and the common good. These are not philosophers, but a variety of *public interest groups*, each of which purports to be serving a *common good* among citizens by pursuing ends which are in the common interest. Such ends are above the interests of any of the group members, whose activities do not return to them any preferential or selective material rewards. Public

interest groups of this kind claim to be pursuing policies where
benefits are shared equally by all people, whether they are
supporting the group or not. They see as collective goods
(contributing to a common good) such things as consumer welfare,
conservation, world peace.[28] Their main relevance in the present
context lies in popular movements which claim to be disinterested in
their pursuit of a common interest and a common good which not all
people perceive, and on which governments also need to be
instructed. While politicians and political parties may be frequently
discredited in their vaunting of the 'public interest', public interest
groups are much more widely accepted in some countries for
integrity of moral purpose. They are distinct from anti-discrimination
groups, which aim at justice for a selective group of the population,
and distinct from public pressure groups, which aim to serve their
own interests rather than the common interest or the common good.
They are possible in our time as never before in history through the
extension of education. Their fundamental weakness is that they
presume to speak for the people, to know better than many of the
public do what their common interest is. It is easier to justify them
as fulfilling a function of heightening public awareness rather than as
dependably articulating the common interest of the population at
large, much less as perceiving the *common good*.

## The Viewpoints in Retrospect, and Further Reflections

The main historical and contemporary references to the common
interest and the common good will now be used to bring into focus
first, their similarity in objects or ends-in-view; second, individual
interest and its relationship with the common interest; and third, the
relationship between the common interest and the common good.
Further reflections will be included on the contemporary situation.

Mill called *security* 'the most vital of all interests' – something
which 'no human being can possibly do without.' It becomes a claim
on our fellows to join with us in ensuring this 'very groundwork of
our existence' (*Utilitarianism*, pp. 327–8).[29] That was precisely the
central thought of almost all of the philosophers and others whose
views have been summarized, including Plato, Aristotle, Cicero, the
Elizabethans, seventeenth- and eighteenth-century thinkers to the
time of Rousseau and the threshold of the French Revolution. But
then, following the moralistic tenor of Hutcheson and Shaftesbury,

when the benevolent serving of the common interest was held to give benefits to the individual, thereby indirectly serving his own interests, there came a new moral thrust, especially in the nineteenth century, when Bentham argued for the common interest being served by maximizing the well-being of everyone in the community. In our time Rawls has linked the common interest to an ideal theory of justice in which rational people recognize others' interests as well as their own as they pursue shared ends such as security and public health. With the same genuine moral purpose, public interest groups have expressed the common interest, again advocating ends that cause them deep concern, prominent among them both security and public health. Nothing has moved persons more in their various accounts of the common interest than a *threat to security*. That observation is of relevance to *conservation* as one of the outstanding public interest issues of our time, as will become evident in the next chapter.

On *individual interest*, and its relationship with the *common interest*, the first point to observe is that there is little reason to denigrate self-interest as such. It was not Hobbes so much as his critics who established it in mean and selfish terms. (It tends always to be debased as well in totalitarian ideologies where it suffers by contrast with a postulated supremacy of state interests.) But self-interest, without the overtone of selfishness, is the beginning and the end of all interests when we eliminate from our thinking all figurative projections of superordinate entities in the name of the state, or even comprehensive collectives of individuals. These abstractions are all indeterminate. To give concreteness to interests is to begin with the source, which is the individual person.

Second, when the individual *does* contemplate collectives of persons his thinking is both normative and variably rational. That is, he reasons that one of his own perceived interests – such as personal health and safety – is good for him and has application to all others in a specified community. Therefore he makes prescriptive statements such as, 'It is in the common interest to ban all nuclear weapons.' His attitude is moral to the extent that he has genuine concern for the interests of other individuals who are 'in the same boat', to borrow Hume's expression. In this case it is sympathy or benevolence which directs the person from his own interests (the *beginning*) to the interests of others about him. Unthinking creatures of instinct such as bees, Hobbes noted, appear at once to identify self-interest and the common interest: or, more accurately, they have *no* self-interest, but only an instinctual community interest, which is the health and well-being of the hive.

Third, the interests which the individual has, and which he may sympathetically extend to others as he imagines them in a group with like interests, are not merely *wants*, for the very reason of the human rational capacity. Though he may not always have articulated a justification for the interests he has, he is able to do so on demand if they are to be distinguished in any way from the raw matrix of wants.[30] In accounting for interests in this way, it is worth observing that the reasons adduced may sometimes be tentative or unconvincing, and that in this respect the rational justification of interests is sometimes not as strong as that of rights. It does not need to be in most circumstances. Common interests cannot be independently justified, since there is no common mind to justify them. They are justified in the only way possible, by an individual giving reasons on the basis of his personal interests.

Fourth, in the extrapolation from an individual interest to a common or public interest, for the normative inclination to prescribe a good for a wide range of others on the basis of the good already perceived as a self-interest, the others are invariably seen in at least national dimensions, reflecting the influence of political thought on moral thought. The quantitative strength of the common interest imposes a limitation on conceptual precision, for not only is it empirically impracticable to guarantee beyond doubt what the common interest of a nation is, but also there is no clear cut-off point for determining what proportion of agreement to disagreement is needed for a common or public interest to be claimed or verified.

In turning next to the relationship between the *common interest* and the *common good*, we consider first their similar usages, suggesting an interchangeability of the two concepts; then the respects in which the two are distinct. On their apparent synonymity, the first point to note is that the *common good* is no more precisely determinable than is the common interest. The criterion of a simple majority would not be an appropriate measure if nuclear power were claimed to be (or not to be) a factor in the common good. (On controversial matters such as this, majority opinion may change with further evidence, or it may be simply ill-informed.) On this basis alone the two concepts are similarly limited.

Second, the instance of nuclear power suggests that the common interest and the common good have identical ends, and that such ends relate to a few of the largest social and moral concerns. Rawls has suggested a restricted number, and philosophers and other thinkers over the centuries have generally focused, as we have seen, on *security*, or an end related to it, with the exception of Bentham who favoured an all-inclusive *well-being*. There is clearly no place in either the common interest or the common good for idiosyncratic fancies, or even for perhaps well-justified interests of particular *sections* of the community such as rail-travellers, shop-keepers or pensioners.

Third, politicization of the common interest and the common good leaves an impression of a common identity. The not unusual assertion by members of governments that their programmes or policies are both in the common interest and to the public good have the effect of obscuring important conceptual distinctions between them.

Other considerations suggest that the common interest and the common good are not synonymous. The common interest may be widely perceived as a shared interest in security by progressively building up arms to surpass those of a rival power but, in ways which will be discussed in Chapter 4, this would almost certainly be to the detriment of the common good of each nation. It is sometimes explained that where the common interest is involved, such as in national security or conservation, wide public participation is required, for in the last analysis, the public interest *is* the individual interest. But under present social conditions, and in the present state of public education, no matter how wide the public participation, it is not obvious that it will attain any better view of the *common good*. It is for other reasons that public participation is desirable, as will be explained in Chapter 3.

The conclusion to which these considerations lead is that in relevant situations the common good needs to be distinguished from the common interest. The fundamental point is that it is only in *ideal theory* that the common interest is seen as the common good: that is, with reference to situations where perfectly rational and perfectly moral persons make practical judgements of the common interest, disinterestedly and benevolently, and with all relevant knowledge at their command.[31] The gap between imperfect moral practice and ideal theory, as in Plato and Aristotle, Rousseau and Rawls, is very wide, as will become evident in subsequent chapters.

The limits of rationality and of practical morality impose constraints on individual capacities to perceive the common good to such an extent that Plato's ideal of the philosopher–ruler is a model to jolt us back to reality and may – as some believe – have been intended for that purpose. The notion of the common good is still a useful one in practical morality, as long as it is recognized as within the capacities of a few exceptional persons only both to perceive and to pursue, and never with infallibility. This question will be considered further in Chapter 3.

With this perspective on self-interest, the common interest and the common good, the next task is to examine briefly the major trends of moral theory to serve as a basis for working out a set of moral principles, or our own coherent moral point of view, which will constitute stable criteria as we consider moral questions relating to conservation. We shall examine in particular two of the foremost sets of moral theories of our time which have been seen by some as in conflict: utilitarianism and rights-based theories; with some attention to imperatives of duty as well, and the relationship to them of meta-ethical questions of attitudes and values. 'Common good' will be used when the end sought is *moral*, regardless of the accuracy of the perception (as may become evident in retrospect).

## MORAL POINTS OF VIEW

### Utilitarianism and the Common Good

Bentham's concern for maximizing happiness or well-being in the entire community has been found to be unique among the various contributions to notions of the common interest and of the common good. Yet the end in view is so comprehensive that some have reacted to the very practicability of more than a few exceptional individuals being able to perceive it. By contrast Marx and Engels held that individual interests develop into general or common interests as a matter of course, as no more than a 'personal development of people'.[32] The *common good* was presumably the end of this process.

There has probably never been a period in the history of mankind when, because of human limitations, the common interest has been perfectly perceived, merging, that is, with the moral and rational *common good*. Rawls' account of rational and self-interested persons working out the terms of their association 'behind a veil of ignorance' (before they become aware of what their interests are), brings to our notice the demands on anyone who attempts to determine what the common good is. For as soon as self-interest intrudes, the perfect impartiality of an entirely rational position vanishes, as Rousseau realised in his vision of a General Will. The notion of the common good as something people would perceive if they were perfectly rational, and perfectly benevolent, and which presumably no one can actually perceive, is not a suitable basis, though, for a *practical* morality.[33]

In the classical utilitarianism of Bentham and Mill, the notion of the well-being of all affected by an act, or by a general rule of conduct guiding moral action, is open-ended and imprecise, as is the notion of the common interest or of the common good. But it does give some moral bearings in the very few areas where the common interest is not confused by overspecification, politicization or conflicting sectionalization. Mill's addition of *quality* to quantity of happiness to be weighed at any one time did nothing to remove the enormous problem of calculation which Bentham faced.[34] But in two important explanations he cleared the way for a wider acceptance of utilitarianism: first, he emphasized at the centre the self-conscious, observing person who experiences his own quality of well-being and extends that experience as a normative prescription for all mankind 'to the greatest extent possible' (*Utilitarianism*, p. 186); second, he explained that in relating his own well-being to that of others, the individual is required to be 'as strictly impartial as a disinterested and benevolent spectator' (p. 291). In this moral ideal the task was to place 'the interest of every individual as nearly as possible in harmony with the interest of the whole' (p. 292).[35] In this vein both Moore and Sidgwick continued to remove some of the earlier misgivings, Moore stating as 'the natural meaning' of utilitarianism that 'the standard of right and wrong in conduct is its tendency to promote the interest of everybody' (or what a man 'commonly desires for himself'), and the theory was so named 'merely to emphasize the fact that right and wrong conduct must be judged by its results', as opposed to intuitionist views that certain conduct is right or wrong regardless of its consequences (*Principia Ethica*, pp. 105–6).[36]

The most recent of the major reformulations of utilitarianism is Preference Utilitarianism, which is based on weighing the desires or preferences of all persons likely to be affected by an act, and attempting to satisfy them, thereby returning to the idea of promoting interests, as Moore had explained. It is from this transformed perspective, since it widens into a possible theory of the common good, that the main challenges to classical utilitarianism have been answered.

First, the notions of sums, aggregates and balances of pleasure over pain or vice versa, are now dismissed, and the impracticability of calculating the happiness of the greatest number is freely recognized. What is called for is rather a practical judgement, a general assessment – imprecise but usable – based on an impartial consideration of individual interests which enlarge into a community interest, perceived morally as the common good.[37]

The second objection to be dismissed is that if the common good is viewed from the perspective of the end result of maximized community well-being, rather than from the perspective of the *individual* well-being, it leaves open the possibility of 'sacrifices and trade-offs', as they have been called, involving some individuals for the sake of a collective end.[38] This objection has been raised frequently in the belief that under utilitarianism individuals are not necessarily treated with equal concern and respect. Bentham had not drawn out the full moral implications of his notion of 'everyone to count for one, nobody for more than one', but recent Preference Utilitarians assert that equal concern and respect is precisely what he meant. By conjoining the fundamental moral principles of impartiality as one considers the interests of others in relation to one's own, equal consideration and respect for persons, and universalization as one prescribes what one finds relevant to others from one's own individual interests, R. M. Hare concludes his recent *Moral Thinking* (p. 228)[39] with the claim that in making our preferences as moral and rational persons we necessarily 'accommodate ourselves to the preferences of others'. In that position on all matters affecting others, individuals will prefer the same moral prescriptions. This 'rational *universal* prescriptivism', as he calls it, has immediate application to the common interest and the common good, for there is no restriction on the numbers we are to include in our moral outlook. Moral thinking cannot be undertaken by the individual alone: each must play his part, but it is 'something we have to do in concert' (ibid.). That is of fundamental significance to the common interest as part of practical morality, but it does not imply that the common good is perceived by all persons who share a common interest.

Hare is not troubled by the scepticism of knowing other minds: fundamentally we can regard others' experiences as analogous with our own (p. 127). We need to be impartial in giving equal weight to all preferences (those of others are equal, and our own equal to them (p. 129)), as long as they do not defy either logic or the facts (p. 180). The equal weight principle applies because the universal prescriptions of our moral judgements apply to all situations of an identical kind, and who the persons are who happen to be involved in the situations is immaterial.[40]

While Hare's version of Preference Utilitarianism is consistent with moral principles already proposed, it has turned out to be rather an accommodation of utilitarianism to already widely accepted moral principles (on equal consideration of the separateness of persons, for instance) than a novel source of further *prima facie* principles of relevance to a morality to the common good.

In this connection several further points on utilitarianism call for comment. First, suggestions of some that utilitarians should stress a *minimization of suffering* rather than a maximization of happiness or well-being is not appropriate generally for a moral theory of the common good, which is fundamentally concerned with positive prospects for quality of life.[41] Second, consequentialism (or the view that the rightness or wrongness of acts lies in their consequences, as utilitarianism holds) is not always relevant to the common interest or the common good in a practical morality. Just as one may act spontaneously out of a sense of duty in one's personal morality (in truth-telling or promise-keeping, for instance), so there may be situations of the common interest or common good where it would be inappropriate to weigh consequences for individuals making up the community. If members of a government are pledged by treaty to honour international obligations, by keeping faith they may be responding to moral responsibilities without necessarily considering consequences at all. In fact international law is based on moral assumptions and moral demands. Third, the quality of personal morality as practised in everyday living is not necessarily affected by an individual's attention to a common interest.[42] Fourth, very considerable practical difficulties must be conceded in ascertaining what in fact individuals' present preferences are at any one time, and it is true that some responses of individuals to what their preferences are may be transient, ill-informed and made with unawareness of consequences.[43]

As the last consideration suggests, Preference Utilitarianism does not satisfy all the requirements of a common good theory. What is needed in practice is a judgement of the common good which is not merely one of temporary all-round benefit (as might be made from individual preferences at any one time), but rather one which has the highest possible degree of dependability and durability. Of course mistakes may be made, but the judgement of the common good needs to be made on some occasions even with posterity in mind, calling for far-reaching enquiry. Procedurally therefore, the common good is to be ascertained by considering individual interests with stringent demands on research methodology. The facts must be known if public policies and acts based on them are to be consistent with moral principles. It is not being simple-minded to consider this as practicable in a computer age.[44]

**Rights-based Theories and the Common Good**

Rights-based theories are considered with a similar end in view, the formulation of *prima facie* moral principles for a moral theory of the common good. The general characteristics of moral rights have been discussed under the fundamental idea of morality. Individual well-being is certainly in mind in all rights-based theories as it is in Preference Utilitarianism, but the accent is different: in the former it is on individual interests, in the latter on collective interests. Further, through the expansion of rights there is a greater analysis and specification of *well-being* than there is in utilitarianism, including considerations of a quality of life. In this specification there is direct relevance to some aspects of the common good such as those relating to conservation. To illustrate, rights are said by some moral philosophers to include the right to share equally in all natural resources, or to have equal access to them, though with a *prima facie* rather than an absolute status.[45] Some of the rights held to be basic are similar to elements of the common interest, such as the health and safety of the individual, and the security of his property. Some of these rights are related in turn to the individual's quality of life: in particular his right to education so that selectively he might realize at least those potentialities likely to contribute to his well-being or satisfaction in life. His right to be respected by others as a person in the moral sense, when recognized, also contributes to his well-being, as it does to the well-being of other persons to whom he has reciprocal obligations: in a practical morality of respecting persons a major source of obstruction to the fulfilment of life plans is overcome. One of a person's rights is to elemental justice or to fair treatment[46] by governments, courts and administrative agencies of various kinds, whenever there is power exercised by some individuals over other individuals. In particular this has a distributive application to all social goods which enhance the quality of life. All persons have a right to an appropriate share in aspects of the good life consistent with their respective capacities and needs, including cultural aspects of the national heritage, and material conditions of life which allow them equal opportunities to formulate life-plans of their own, and the motivation to pursue them. In practical morality, the specification of rights has the advantage of calling to attention sensitive areas of distributive justice where there is discrimination or some form of unfairness in the treatment of persons or groups of persons.

Yet in none of these points is there a fundamental moral difference between rights-based theories and Preference Utilitarianism of the kind espoused recently by R. M. Hare. Differences are differences of approach, perspective or emphasis: they do not represent incompatibilities between the theories. There is in each an acknowledgement of common requirements of morality, including equal consideration of others as persons. Preference Utilitarianism is not inconsistent with distributive justice. There is no disagreement in the theories on the *prima facie*, or defeasible, nature of the principles underlying practical morality.

The recent debate between representatives of rights-based theories and Preference Utilitarianism[47] has not yielded further principles to guide practical morality. Rights-based theories are also found to be linked to the moral principles already discussed. As a Preference Utilitarian, Hare claims to recognize similar rights to those recognized by his opponents. But in fact rights assertions and explanations do not figure prominently in his theory, and practical morality requires that they be frequently asserted and defended against contrary influences or counter-assertions. There is a third viewpoint to be considered before summarizing a set of principles for a common good theory. This will also, by its nature, raise the meta-ethical question foreshadowed initially as the last to be considered in this chapter.

## Deontic Theories and the Common Good

Deontology merits brief mention only in the present context, but its emphasis on obedience to *duty* (from which, in Greek, it derives its name) is relevant for two reasons: first, to show that with respect to fundamental moral principles relating to person, it is not incompatible with either Preference Utilitarianism or rights-based theories; second, to show that it has no distinctive contribution to a theory of the common good except in so far as it leads to a better understanding of the nature of moral thinking.

Invariable obedience to the dictates of categorical imperatives, such as Kant's, has few adherents in our time because of the conflicts between moral principles in particular cases. By contrast with this degree of flexibility required in practical morality through the defeasibility of moral principles, Kant held that the Rational Will leads directly to categorical imperatives (*The Analytic of Pure Practical Reason*, p. 131).[48] 'Rational beings . . . are persons', he explained, 'because their very nature points them out as ends in themselves.' What is in contention is the notion that reason consistently prescribes for the Good Will what is to be done as a matter of duty: that all principles or rules commanded by it have something more than a *prima facie* status. We frequently *do* act out of duty, or so it seems to us, from a moral conviction of what is right in the circumstances. It is necessary for us to explain the nature of this area of our moral conduct with its strong element of habit. From this it may follow that our moral convictions are not consistently expressing the voice of reason, in Kant's sense, but that sometimes they *ought* to be subjected to the light of reason when they are not.

While a number of moral philosophers have criticised classical utilitarianism for its supposition that it is only consequences, and consequences for total happiness, that matter in moral conduct, pointing out that we often act from *intuitive convictions* that breaking promises, for instance, is wrong, there is no incompatibility in moral principles between deontic theories (acting out of duty or obligation) and either Preference Utilitarianism or rights-based theories. A consequentialist of any kind could judge an act or rule of promise-keeping as good for its positive contribution to an end of well-being – both individual and collective. A deontologist's support of promise-keeping would be as a response to moral duty. One of the fundamental rights in rights-based theories, the right to equal consideration as persons, leads to a justification of promise-keeping by reference to person (with exceptions always to be argued for). In moral practice, there is probably no one who is consistently consequentialist, or exclusively concerned with rights in his moral conduct, or consistently deontic. Where a deontologist faces moral complexities he may be obliged to take account of consequences, and a consequentialist may find himself frequently acting out of moral duty, or according to his moral convictions, in situations where he finds no reason to consider consequences. A deontologist may be strongly rights-inclined, giving to a right something of the authority of law. In one view 'the assertion of a right is categorical'; it simply must be respected.[49] But when we speak of moral duty being intuitional, or dispositional, or an expression of a moral conviction, what do we have in mind? Why is it said, from a deontic standpoint, ' . . . there are some things which a moral man will not do, no matter what' – including such things as harming innocent people, telling lies, enslavement and degradation?[50] It is to the character of our moral thinking that we now turn.

## Intuitions, Attitudes and Values

R. M. Hare describes two distinct levels of moral thinking – the *intuitive* and the *critical* (*Moral Thinking*, ch.2, pp. 25ff). A third is the meta-ethical. The intuitive gives us certain *prima facie* principles or dispositions, but critical thinking is necessary to resolve conflicts that are liable to occur at times between or among them (p. 40). He sees them as elements in a common structure of moral thinking, rather than as rivals (p. 44). While the explanation is at times misleading inasmuch as it aims to contrast the two, leaving the impression that much of the time they proceed independently of each other though permitting us the power to change from the intuitive to the critical as required by circumstances (pp. 45–50), it succeeds in drawing attention to the habitual aspect of our moral thinking which has come to us from Aristotle and Plato, as well as to the need to be critical.

A fuller account of this aspect of our moral thinking can be offered by considering various influences which *predispose* a person to think in a certain way by interacting with reason. In this explanation, dispositions and reason are concurrent, with dispositions sometimes supportive of reason, sometimes otherwise. It is thus a one-level moral thinking that we have in mind, not a two-level as suggested in Hare's account. Some can, of course, by education, effort and motivation, discipline themselves at times into critical thinking, but that does not imply that in the process they can totally cut off their dispositional influences. We shall confine ourselves to attitudes and values, though there are other dispositional influences such as motives or intentions which sometimes have a part to play.[51] Attitudes and values are used in combination because to value an object signifies a strongly favourable attitude towards it, and it is the two in unison which constitute the strongest dispositional influence on reason in some circumstances. Together the two have an action orientation, with emotion providing a strong cohesive impulse. They have a cognitive component as well, made up of various ideas, beliefs or opinions relevant to their object. They are difficult to change but not unchangeable, durable but not permanent, generally characterized by stubbornness to opposing tendencies, even to reason itself if initially they are inclined away from it. Above all, they are habitual, *learned* in some way, and therefore centrally important in any programme of public education, such as in matters relating to the common interest perceived morally as the common good. When there are unfavourable, or only mildly favourable, attitudes to objects, those objects are simply not valued, and the attitude–value nexus is not made. Then attitudes exist separately, as in the case of our prejudices. As we shall see in subsequent chapters, attitudes and values are related to interests. Values have characteristics which are not shared by attitudes, except in dynamic situations of attitude–value combination. In some circumstances values may be organized into systems, all related to matters of broad community concern such as protection of the environment. They express preferences – either personal or social. As personal standards they are given a normative bent as we extend them to relevant others. On broad questions of conservation, for instance, our values may incline us towards persuading others to adopt positions similar to our own. The values of public pressure groups are evidently values which members wish others in the community to share with them. (Then the attitudinal aspect is evident also.) While some objects are valued intrinsically, such as a poem, other things are valued instrumentally, such as a recreational activity for its contribution to health; but in the latter case the initial object normally becomes valued for its own sake as well, with the development of strongly favourable attitudes to it.

   Attitudes and values are best understood in practical situations and for that reason will be further explained in subsequent chapters. At this point one matter of overriding importance to moral thinking has emerged: since these dispositional tendencies and influences are of an *habitual* kind, and habits form a large proportion of moral thinking in most people's lives, it is of fundamental importance that they be learned with as much understanding as possible of the ideas or beliefs which constitute their cognitive core. It is also of fundamental importance to understand as clearly as possible the *nature* of attitudes and values as they function in moral thinking. To give an account of this non-rational part of our moral thinking, which some refer to as 'intuitional' – an account which is strongly supported by empirical evidence – is to offer the best account available to us, rather than leaving intuitions as poorly comprehended if not incomprehensible. There are occasions when attitudes and values are supportive of reason in their action-tending directiveness. Attitudes and values form part of our rational–dispositional thinking; they are together in all practical thinking when we deliberate on what we ought to do. When something is valued there are *some* reasons for valuing already there, for no act of preferring occurs without comparison among various options. Moral attitudes and values in combination, and in conjunction with reason, characterize most of our moral thinking. It is when they express habitual responses without engaging reason that attitudes and values need to be exposed in discussion.

In turning now to a summary of the significant points of this chapter, we move from the personal morality of a practical consideration of others' interests towards a *common good* morality which will engage our attention increasingly in subsequent chapters. In the summary the moral point of view will be presented which will give direction to the subsequent discussions.

## SUMMARY

Morality is a practical consideration of the interests of others from a disinterested and benevolent standpoint, in which moral intention leads to action (unless thwarted by circumstances). The connection between intention and action is certain predispositional tendencies interacting with reason: attitudes and values in particular. It is these that give us our moral convictions. Moral thinking is appropriately described as both dispositional and rational, a more accurate account than one which refers to intuition and critical thinking. The end of practical morality is the well-being of others, which implies not merely minimization of suffering, but also, and more positively, a concern for quality of life. It is important to note that in exceptional cases our moral obligations are rather wider than this interest-based practical morality, since our moral obligations extend to some incapable of experiencing interests.

This moral stance is consequentialist in the main but not utilitarian. Although Preference Utilitarianism answers most of the standard objections to classical utilitarianism, it is not itself totally acceptable for a theory of the common good because of the nature of preferences and desires. Rights-based theories support the same fundamental moral principles as does Preference Utilitarianism in their common concern for the interests of others regarded as persons. In practical situations, depending on circumstances, moral conduct may be consequentialist, or it may find rights justifications more appropriate, or it may express moral convictions in terms of moral duty. With respect to the fundamental moral principles there is no incompatibility between the three, and in a practical morality there is no rational requirement of consistency to one only.

From an ideal rational and moral standpoint the common interest is the common good, but in a practical morality the two concepts need to be kept distinct, even though they are used interchangeably in some circumstances without confusion. The need to separate the two arises from the Platonic judgement that the majority of persons have not the combined rational and moral capacity to perceive the common good. The best they can achieve is a shared perception of *common interests*, which in some circumstances may conflict with their unperceived *common good*.

The notion of the common good is more than the well-being which may be mentally summed or generalized from individual desires or preferences – more indeed than any utilitarian end so far stated. This is the most far-reaching practical judgement to be made in practical morality, and some individual preferences and desires, especially those of an ephemeral and unstable nature, are unlikely to point clearly to it. Quality of life criteria in making this judgement will relate to such things as equity in the distribution of both material and cultural goods, opportunities to develop at least selected potentialities by means of education, and a range of civil liberties including freedom of speech and assembly – all relevant to conservation from the standpoint of practical morality.

Philosophers' views on the common interest and the common good from Plato to Aristotle, to Hobbes and Hume, Rousseau, Mill and on to Rawls in contemporary thought, have directed attention to the very few objects of the common good so far defended. A unique contribution is that of Bentham with his reference to a non-specific common end of *well-being*. But the historical survey has not been fruitless. It has provided an opportunity to examine the notions of the common interest and the common good on which much of the subsequent argument depends. It is not surprising that aspects of conservation such as access to nature in some form are almost entirely a moral concern for our own period.

It is in this social context that conservation will be related in the next chapter to a *quality of life* for all people as the firmest specification of the *common good*, going much further than the historical attention to security, though in some respects still related to it.

# 2 Conservation and the Common Good

From the moral foundations of the previous chapter we may now consider first, whether conservation may be regarded as a moral question; and if it is, second, if it may be justified as part of the *common good*. The plan is first to explain the meaning of conservation; second to explore the kind of well-being or quality of life of particular relevance to conservation; third, to examine and expose some of the loose applications of morality to conservation which lack moral connections; fourth, to consider aspects of conservation which relate to distributive justice; fifth, in relation to conservation, to consider in turn the justification of a global morality, the moral responsibility of present generations to posterity and the morality of animal interests.

## THE MEANING OF CONSERVATION

Conservation is a composite notion referring both to the literal sense of *conserving*, or preserving as far as practicable a state of nature as we find it, and also to *protecting* it from wastage or unnecessary damage. Different interpretations of conservation are offered depending on whether the viewpoint is economic, legal or moral. From a moral standpoint, conservation is usually applied to a relationship between man and nature which is believed to promote his well-being (or improve the quality of his life) by first, preserving selected natural features; second, by protecting natural resources from both over-use and wanton destruction – mindful of both present and future interests; third, by restoring what has been temporarily impaired by use (but which is no longer needed to sustain human life according to moral standards accepted for quality of life); fourth, by enhancing the environments of human settlements so that they do not conflict sharply with the aesthetic appeal of the natural environment. Only part of the literal use of *conserving* natural resources is from an economic standpoint with reference to non-renewable sources of energy in coal, oil, natural gas, uranium and so forth; part is from a *moral* standpoint as the possible needs of future generations are considered. It is not contrary to this moral standpoint on conservation for man to use natural resources according to need, and it is neither a moral nor a rational view that nature should be preserved unchanged as far as possible. There is nothing intrinsically sacrosanct about nature as it is, for nature is itself in a constant state of change. Sometimes its change is sudden and destructive of living things, as in the case of earthquakes, volcanic eruptions, cyclones, tornadoes and floods. 'You cannot step twice into the same river', said Heraclitus, 'for other waters are continually flowing on.'[1] Like fire, to him the flowing of rivers symbolized constant change in all things.

Conservation from a moral standpoint is not confined to nature, though nature has been its primary focus. It applies also to the preservation and maintenance of objects of historical and cultural value as part of a national or world heritage, to buildings or monuments of various kinds. The generalization that conservation is 'a state of harmony between men and land'[2] is unhelpful to the moral perspective on conservation through its wide-sweeping applicability to a range of economic and social considerations.

In deciding whether conservation contributes to a common good and, prior to that, whether it is a moral matter at all, we find – like John Passmore – no need to construct a special environmental ethic, but for a different reason from his:[3] namely, in our view, that these questions are resolvable within the framework of moral principles agreed upon in contemporary moral philosophy, even though the ethical systems from which they are drawn may be in conflict on some matters which are not relevant to these questions.

## CONSERVATION AND QUALITY OF LIFE

The dual rational–dispositional character of our moral thinking applies as we consider those elements of our personal well-being which we classify as *quality of life* and which, through benevolence, sympathy and understanding, we prescribe for others. If we begin with personal values it is clear that our quality of life depends partly on good health, and partly too on safety from bodily harm, and as we value the same for others, these may be justifiably regarded as part of the composite common good from a moral standpoint. But not all our personal values are oriented in this way towards others' well-being as well as our own. If one values one's Japanese garden, for instance, it is not something one would wish all others to have too, and even if one did, there is no clear connection between a common valuing of such an object, and a common well-being through a universal improvement in quality of life.

The basic and indisputable elements in quality of life – health and security – were appreciated by the Greeks as their common interests: to these Aristotle added *aesthetic* appeal. To satisfy these common interests was to promote the common good, the happiness of all (*Politics*, 1332$^a$). For instance, the health of citizens was to be considered by situating the city with regard to healthy prevailing winds (1330$^a$) and by ensuring a good supply of fresh drinking water (1330$^b$), especially to cope with times when the city was under siege. Both in the arrangement of houses and in the ornamental construction of city walls there was to be thought for the visually appealing (1330$^b$–1331$^a$). It was one of the most fundamental perceptions of the Greeks that some, and only some, were able to understand the *common good*, for not all had the appropriate combination of 'nature, habit and rational principle' that makes men 'good and virtuous' (1332$^a$). Translated to our industrialized and technological societies, the question of aesthetic enjoyment contributing to quality of life, or to the common good, needs to be examined more closely. So few could find aesthetic satisfaction in a slag-heap, a quarry filled with rubbish, or in rusting cars abandoned by the roadside, that on such matters it may be assumed that the common interest is to have these removed or concealed from view, and that such action would add to the general quality of life, thereby serving the common good. Similarly, pungent or choking air is *generally* objectionable, and so is the taste of muddy or contaminated drinking water. On the assumption that action to improve the situation in these respects increases the quality of life generally, it becomes moral action. On the other hand, individuals value particular objects aesthetically in many different ways (objects such as rivers, rocks or trees), so that these preferences must be regarded as lying outside the moral sphere. Individual values they may be, and there may be individual values pertaining to abstractions such as solitude, or conviviality, which express strong preferences in matters of social relations. There is nothing extraordinary in this situation, for many values which individuals have are of a non-moral kind: values in areas of recreation, housing and so forth, all of which may contribute to *individual* enjoyment of life without in any sense relating to the interests of others, or to quality of life generally, or the common good. Happiness or contentment in a hedonistic sense is not a criterion for moral values, otherwise temporary pleasures of many kinds would qualify as moral, such as drug addiction, or car-stealing, where the interests of others are ignored. Valuing solitude as a temporary escape from busy social interaction is morally neutral, and so is conviviality for personal pleasure: in neither case is there the practical consideration of others' interests which is one of the *prima facie* principles of morality to be used as a normative reference. To value a wilderness, a tropical forest, an Antarctic wasteland of ice and snow may each yield peace of mind, but the value is not a moral value. Individual interests and values qualify as moral only when they accord with the moral principles stated in the first chapter, in particular when there is an orientation towards considering others' interests. Similarly the common interest is moral for the very reason that it begins with an individual interest which is extended morally to others' interests, or to a well-founded belief in the *common good*. To qualify as moral, the common interest must be more than an empirical quantification of individuals' interests, whether summed or averaged.

## INADEQUACIES IN ENVIRONMENTAL ETHICS

Some of the confusions in attempts to formulate a distinctive *environmental ethic* stem from a simple failure to clarify in the first instance what is a *moral* concern, issue, interest or value, as distinct from each as non-moral. It needs to be emphasized that our defence from charges of stipulativeness in defining moral boundaries is the reference to central agreement on the moral principles which we have reviewed in contemporary moral philosophy. By contrast, some of the theories proposed as *environmental ethics* do not subscribe generally to any such agreed principles, nor do they have any other clear connection with moral philosophy as a distinctive discipline.

We shall now illustrate certain environmental concerns which are *not* moral concerns, contrasting them with some that *are*. This will serve as a preparation for an examination of widespread claims in the last two or three decades for a separate environmental ethic.

One frequently-repeated claim is that we ought not to exploit stocks of animal and plant life to the extent of destroying their capacity for renewal, as in instances of overfishing or of the destruction of certain forest timbers. On the face of it this is a question of *prudence* rather than of morality, but it becomes a moral matter when there are no substitute foods or material resources available, and the interests of others *are* concerned, including those of posterity. A second fundamental concern is reflected in the view that industrialization is interfering with basic life-sustaining processes, such as a suitable level of oxygen in the atmosphere. Again, if it is so serious as to impair the interests of others, it needs to be argued for with clear supporting evidence before it can be regarded as a moral matter: if at the present stage of knowledge it is a matter of taking precautions, it is once again prudence rather than morality that we have in mind. A third widespread concern is at the extinction of species and the consequent reduction in the diversity of life-forms. But this in itself is not clearly a moral question since the interests of others are not involved. (The question of preventing suffering by sentient animals *is* a moral one, as we shall see, but this is not at issue in the present case.) For millions of years some species have been dying out. On the other hand, the present concern becomes a moral one if it can be established, with evidence, that in the loss of diversity of living things there is a loss in the quality of life of persons generally. Moral action to save species from extinction would then aim at the common good.[4]

Other instances reflect a utopianism which contradicts the notion of a *practical* morality, one that is literally practicable. In the claim that 'nature shall be respected and its essential processes shall not be impaired', first, there is a vagueness as to what the essential processes are; second, an implied changelessness in nature which is false; and third, a failure to understand or to accept that man's activity in interaction with nature cannot proceed without adding to change. Similarly the claim that 'nature shall be secured against degradation caused by warfare or other hostile activities' is patently impossible. In neither of these cases is there a moral orientation: neither has a claim to be incorporated into an environmental ethic, if the expression is used responsibly.[5]

There is another class of statements which are autobiographical expressions of thoughts and emotions. By their nature these have no necessary concern for others' interests or for the common good, and no other clear moral relevance, though they are apt to be used persuasively by advocates of an environmental ethic. Kant's classification of some things in nature as sublime (tall oaks, shades in consecrated groves and night-time), other things as beautiful (day, beds of flowers, low hedges), is related plainly enough to his personal impressions.[6] Mill recorded the impact of Wordsworth's poetry on him: it aroused the strongest of his 'pleasurable susceptibilities, the love of rural objects and natural scenery' (*Autobiography*, p. 147).[7] But it is important to note the context of this acknowledgement. Mill was describing a state of depression at the time, one which Byron's poetry had failed to relieve since Byron's state of mind was too much like his own (p. 146). He could then say that Wordsworth's poems were 'a medicine for my state of mind', and in that state 'they seemed to be the very culture of the feelings, which I was in quest of', something indeed, 'which could be shared in by all human beings' (p. 148). It is doubtful if Mill could fairly claim generalizability, for he was still referring to the need for something to lift his spirits: 'I needed to be made to feel that there was a real, permanent happiness in tranquil contemplation' (p. 148). Whether tranquil contemplation of natural beauty is a universal source of happiness is a matter for empirical enquiry: the present point is that generalizable inferences do not follow from subjective experiences of this kind, all the more so since Mill was at pains to explain the special circumstances of his thoughts and feelings. Mill did have more to say on the benefits of solitude when he considered the prospect of a more densely populated earth. This we shall discuss in context in Chapter 4. Appeals to authority in order to support an argument for an environmental ethic are not uncommon – especially to a philosopher – for if ethics is a branch of philosophy an *apparent* support of an environmental ethic by a philosopher provides a deceptive air of confirmation. But to avoid the *fallacy from authority* what a philosopher says must be shown to be relevant to the subject, as well as within his competence, for philosophers talk of many things outside of philosophy.

Arguments attenuated from Wordsworth's undoubted reverence for nature as his guardian, and his love of solitude,[8] as well as from other views which relate to broad social values such as those pertaining to a Romantic period in English literature, do not themselves support any claim that man needs nature for his well-being, or that contact with wilderness or 'wild nature' adds generally to the quality of his life.

By contrast, there are matters of environmental concern which *are* unquestionably moral matters. For example, the argument that the entire ecosystem of the world is a common pasture where self-interest motivates each person to increase his herd until the pasture is ruined for everyone, is clearly a moral view.[9] The *common good* is in mind, as against the destructiveness of individual greed. Those who draw attention to the degradation of the land, leading in some cases to desertification, are also taking a moral point of view when they refer not only to the interests of impoverished present inhabitants, but also to the likely interests of succeeding generations. In a wide sense they may be considering the common good of all persons, their very future on earth. A more specific instance of moral concern is for vandalism in national parks, reserves or recreation areas, for then wanton acts of destruction of plant and animal life may clearly affect the particular interests of others.

It has been stressed that many of the concerns, interests and values people have are of a non-moral kind: they are no less strongly felt for that reason. Many of the environmental concerns experienced are supportable with empirical evidence, as well as rationally. There are economic concerns and scientific concerns for instance. But what are not supportable are attempts to turn all environmental concerns into some kind of *new ethic*, aware that they may ill fit any of the major philosophical views on the nature of morality, and therefore call for a deviant inventiveness. For those who defy agreed principles in moral philosophy in this way, no rational justification is needed, for the end-product is self-justifying and circular. This is not a defence of any one moral philosophy: indeed there are many, and there is a strong case to be made for everyone to make his own morality, as long as it does not defy 'logic and the facts', in Hare's expression.[10] But a rational justification would be needed (not yet provided by anyone) for any variation of the agreed principles as stated. A rational approach to all the different kinds of environmental concern is to classify them initially into their appropriate knowledge categories (scientific, economic, moral and so forth), and to consider them according to their respective natures.

Some of the sources of confusion in the attempt to establish a new environmental ethic which expresses, among other things, respect or reverence for nature and bases a supposed environmental morality on it, are these: first, there are fallacies of inference, and a failure to distinguish between logical and empirical questions; second, there is a confusion of moral philosophies' agreed principles with religious viewpoints, where reverencing a supernatural creator is transferred to reverencing nature, the object of creation; third, there are confusions due to a metaphorical use of language, especially in the personification of natural objects; fourth, there are distortions of moral concepts such as interests and rights; fifth, there is an overready acceptance of a stewardship tradition without a frank appraisal of its moral implications.

Some fallacies of inference have already been explained: in arguing, for instance, that close contact with nature is of psychological benefit to some, therefore it is of benefit to all. This is also a failure to distinguish between a logical and an empirical question: if contact with nature is good for all, or is part of a common good, then to promote it with others' interests in mind would be a moral act. But whether it is or is not is an empirical question as yet unresolved. A personal reverencing of nature has led to a diversity of inferential fallacies.[11] One of the earliest conservation enthusiasts in this century was Aldo Leopold, who in *Sand County Almanac* (pp. 223–4),[12] stated that 'love, respect, and admiration for land' are conditions for a land ethic, and that 'a thing is right when it tends to preserve the integrity, stability, and beauty of the biotic community' and 'wrong when it tends otherwise'. He proposed 'a distinctly environmental ethic – founded perhaps upon love and respect, upon an expanded moral sentiment'. These assertions are similar to the subjective expressions of love of nature to be found in the poetry of all nations. It is easy to expose the fallacies of his reasoning (pp. 203 ff) as he attempts to draw an inference that moral boundaries ought to include all objects of nature constituting the totality of 'the land' (even soils), from the premiss that the individual belongs to a community of interdependent parts. But those writing in environmental ethics who are influenced by his fervour into making similar personal declarations of love of nature do him an injustice in failing to understand that he was not writing as a moral philosopher, or as one who understood clearly the nature of moral thinking, and that therefore his espousal of a 'land ethic' cannot be taken as a rational–moral justification for an environmental ethic which embraces the natural world.

An instance of the confusion of literal with metaphorical meanings in environmental ethics is in references to man having more than his share of nature's resources, and even to his *cheating* other things in this respect. The very notion of a literal allocation of shares of resources to each of the myriad forms of animal and plant life on earth is clearly an absurdity. There are circumstances in which we can speak sensibly of cheating animals: a farmer may entice some of his animals away from one field with rich grazing, for instance, to another field with poorer grazing, wishing to reserve the first for purposes of fattening other stock. But nothing can be cheated which does not have desires or interests of any kind: objects such as trees, for instance, whose species may be threatened by forest-clearing.

Standard moral concepts distorted in some environmental ethics include the concept of interests. It is sometimes pleaded that all living things, including plants, have an interest in survival, or an interest in being alive. While we do ascribe both interests and rights to some human beings (such as infants and those who are comatose) who are incapable of awareness of interests and rights, the ascription is both legal and humanitarian for their protection. They do not *have* interests, in the moral sense of not merely being aware of them, but of also being able to adduce reasons in their support and to give them a normative inclination towards others' interests. The ascription is a figurative one. When we speak of the interests of sentient animals, as we shall see in the last section of this chapter, the one minimum condition of interests which we keep is that such animals have one distinctive interest – their capacity to suffer. Higher animals go much further than this minimum in their awareness of enjoyable emotional states as well. Unlike sentient animals, plants have no awareness and no moral interests.

Conditions for holding moral *rights* are even more restrictive than for holding moral interests. One prominent conceptual confusion occurs in attempting to force a connection between legal rights and moral rights. At times the two may coincide, legal rights like moral rights being oriented towards human beings. But moral rights have the particular conditions noted in Chapter 1: ability to understand the rights claimed, and to claim them, assert them, waive or relinquish them at will. Legal rights are primarily to protect individuals from interference by other persons in the enjoyment of the rights. It is easy to extend this legal perspective on rights to claim that non-conscious forms of life such as trees have 'enjoyment of life', just as persons do, and so have a right to live and to be allowed to live. A more specific slide from legal to moral interpretations is in giving trees moral standing. It has been argued that in law, abstractions such as corporations are given *legal standing*, and individuals are able to plead on their behalf.[13] From this position some take the step to *moral standing*, avoiding the usual rights conditions and allocating moral standing on the basis of a general concern for all natural objects, especially for living things such as trees, expressing non-moral attitudes and values. Others argue that trees and other natural objects have an *intrinsic* value, taking an objective view of value. But if we value natural objects, it is we who do the valuing. The dispute between instrumental value and intrinsic value has little significance in a practical morality. Moral standing is not established by confusing subject and object, or by attributing to every concern one has for natural objects a moral status. For instance, a person may be repelled by the intention of a local authority to destroy an avenue of trees standing in the way of a thoroughfare, but it would be odd if he gave as his reasons that the trees have moral standing, an intrinsic value or a right to live, or to develop their full potential. More honestly he would refer to his own preferences. There are, of course, many situations where destruction of trees might be a moral offence, but that is because the interests of persons are involved or – as we shall see shortly – the interests of sentient animals, not because trees have moral standing.

When the stewardship tradition is used in environmental ethics to support the notion of objects of nature having intrinsic value it becomes a dispositional standpoint, with particular beliefs embedded in the attitudes and values held. When the rational combines more clearly with the dispositional in our moral thinking, we may reflect on human credentials for stewardship, as others have done, perhaps taking into account what some have seen as the unnecessary exploitation of nature in our more recent history. On the other hand, if we take a moral and an educational standpoint, we may weigh the possibilities for improvement, for if any beings have the power to act as custodians of life on earth it is ourselves by virtue of our intelligence and knowledge. To view ourselves from as detached a moral stance as possible we may wonder more about our potential for *dispositional* change, on the scale needed for such a vast responsibility, than about our potential for either reason or adequate knowledge.

# DISTRIBUTIVE JUSTICE AND CONSERVATION

On the assumption that contact with nature is capable of improving quality of life generally, according to individual interests, and that the cultural heritage similarly has universal benefit to those who actively share in it, again according to individual interests, it is a matter of distributive justice that opportunities for participation in each should be shared equally, and not be the good fortune of a privileged few. (In the state of our present evidence, the assumption needs to be kept in mind.) These opportunities may be restricted for many reasons such as contingencies of ill-health, but in fairness to all they should not be restricted for economic reasons, or for reasons of race, colour, sex or social class, or the kind of formal education undertaken, or because the person is unavoidably unemployed and not a contributor to the economy. One of the *prima facie* principles of social or distributive justice is that *all persons have an equal right to social goods according to need.* (In this there is an assumption of a fair social contribution by everyone.)

Before there can be an equal sharing of those features of nature or the culture offering a potential contribution to individual well-being, or to improvement in the quality of life, the important precondition is *equal access.* Because of differences in individual interests, attitudes, values and capacities, there can be no actual equality of benefits received. The equal sharing can refer to no more than *equal opportunities* to share, and that invokes a second *prima facie* principle of social or distributive justice (or one that may be regarded as a corollary to the first): *all persons have an equal right to both educational provisions and to educational opportunities according to need.* This too is significant to equal access inasmuch as the equal opportunity to share may be dependent on improvement in educational opportunity, leading to improved capacity for adding to quality of life.

Distributive justice does not imply that there is invariably a cutting up of a social good and the apportionment of equal shares in a material or physical sense. Conservation in the sense of preservation implies exactly the opposite: that some social goods such as natural features or objects in national parks, as well as objects of the cultural heritage which we shall consider shortly, are to be preserved intact for everyone's potential enjoyment, and not apportioned to anyone at all. What are distributed in this sense of distributive justice are benefits or opportunities to benefit. (Justice is in no way diminished if some have the opportunities to benefit but do not avail themselves of them through indolence or priorities of values.) Stated formally, a third *prima facie* principle of distributive justice is that *each person has an equal right of access to both the natural and the cultural heritage.* (This too may be viewed as a corollary to the first.)

What are most in contention in matters relating to the principle of equal access to natural features are first, the exclusiveness of private property; and second, the dependence of accessibility on individual economic circumstances. In each of these respects conservation has strong connections with practical morality through its relation to justice as non-discriminatory. It is sometimes asserted that conservation is for the affluent, both for individuals who can afford to enjoy its benefits, and for nations in a similarly favoured economic situation. But another factor is the institution of private property in land. Has any private owner with a stand of trees on his property, or a natural lake or river, or protection for wildlife which affords pleasure or satisfaction to some persons, a right to reserve these for his own enjoyment? Can he claim a right to destroy or damage natural features on his property for economic gain, when the benefits of these in terms of enjoyment might be more widely distributed? In such questions a conflict is evident with free enterprise views that in some circumstances nature itself is a challenge to competitive individuals to carve out a place for themselves in the world, to succeed by industry, initiative and determination regardless of the needs and interests of others – including posterity – and regardless of the cost to nature.

## Philosophical and Legal Perspectives on Property Rights

The notion that the earth is everyone's possession, and that private ownership of land is a usurpation of this common birthright, has recurred in Western thought, but out of it has emerged the further notion that private ownership is necessary for social harmony. To the Greeks the wilderness outside their city-states was simply a common resource of food, water and firewood. It was much the same in Elizabethan England outside the towns and villages. In the seventeenth and eighteenth centuries there was little need for thoughts of conservation, for there was still so much unused land, so much designated 'wasteland' because it was not turned to economic advantage. This was the standpoint of Locke, for example, who in 1690 observed that ' . . . there are still great tracts of ground to be found which . . . lie waste, and are more than the people who dwell on it do or can make use of, and still lie in common' (*Second Treatise of Government*, ch. V, 45, p. 364).[14] Though 'God gave the world to men in common' it was to be used for their benefit, and so private ownership in the hands of the 'industrious and rational' was God's intention, as he saw it, but not for those who were merely covetous, quarrelsome or contentious (34, p. 357). Hobbes had been concerned earlier with government's protection of all the contentments of life 'which every man by lawfull Industry . . . shall acquire to himself' (*Leviathan*, Part II, ch. XXX, p. 376).[15] In the eighteenth century Hume expressed similar views: 'Art, labour and industry' are needed to give man enjoyment, and 'ideas of property become necessary in all civil societies'. Few enjoyments come man's way simply 'from the open and liberal hand of nature' (*An Enquiry Concerning the Principles of Morals*, Sect. III, part I, 149, p. 188).[16] But the nineteenth and twentieth centuries have seen more questioning of institutional land rights, especially as natural resources are more clearly perceived as limited. Tolstoy argued that there was not the least justification for private ownership of land, for it is 'an indispensable condition of every man's life', he asserted, 'like water, air, or the rays of the sun' (*On Land and Slavery*, p. 25).[17] Mill argued, like Locke, that land 'is the original inheritance of the whole species'. Its appropriation he saw as a question of 'general expediency', justifiable when it causes hardship to no one. But it *is* a hardship, he perceived, 'to be born into the world and to find all nature's gifts previously engrossed, and no place left for the new-comer'. Posterity stood clearly in his sympathies; so too did the situation of the landless. Therefore, though he conceded an exclusive right to land for purposes of cultivation, this did not imply, he believed, 'an exclusive right to it for purposes of access' (*Principles of Political Economy*, p. 288).[18] No such right ought to be recognized, he went on, as long as the landowner's right to protection against damage to produce and his right to 'privacy against invasion' are respected. But if land is not cultivated, with the owner making no use of it, that is, 'he ought to know that he holds it by sufferance of the community' (p. 290).

Legal perspectives on private property in England either dismissed moral considerations as irrelevant, or tended to identify legal rights with moral rights. 'He possesses a right to property to whom the law of the land assigns it', asserted one nineteenth-century moralist.[19] To Bentham, positive law had a clear message: 'Property and law are born and must die together. Before the laws, there was no property: take away the laws, all property ceases.'[20] This positivistic approach had been given clear precedent in the previous century by Sir William Blackstone, in his *Commentaries on the Laws of England*.[21] Philosophically he was in the Hobbes–Locke tradition of jealous defence of property: it was seen as the trust and responsibility of the law to protect personal possessions. Indeed legislators' self-interest in property was justified, it seemed, with the exclusion from the franchise of those without property. These Blackstone described as of 'so mean a situation that they are esteemed to have no will of their own' (Book I, ch. 2, p. 170). Quoting from Genesis, i, 28, he declared that 'the earth . . . and all things therein, are the general property of all mankind, exclusive of other beings, from the immediate gift of the Creator' (Book II, ch. 1, p. 2). But this 'state of primeval simplicity' was changed by man's craft and ambition, and by increases in his numbers. It was these that led to private ownership, thereby preventing 'innumerable tumults' (p. 4). So 'necessity begat property', and with civil society came the necessity for government and laws (p. 7). The waste or common land was vested in the sovereign, again for the sake of peace and security, or else in his representatives – usually the lords of the manors. His summing up of the laws governing property was at once a defence of the law and arguably a misconception of its moral inadequacies from the standpoint of distributive justice.

Philosophical and legal perspectives on property rights in England have illustrated several situations to which we shall return in succeeding chapters: first, the distinction between moral thinking and political thinking; second, the possibility of conflict between administration of the law and practical morality; third, the possibility of legislators serving their own interests in relation to land ownership. Following Mill's lead we may ask, from the standpoint of practical morality, whether all land held privately ought not to be held under sufferance of the people; whether land rights ought not to be given a *prima facie* status only, defeasible and not absolute, so that the interests of others might be considered, with the liberty to enjoy natural objects or features according to their respective interests, but precluding any liberty to destroy or to impair.[22] This matter will be raised again in the concluding chapter.

National parks, recreation areas and similar areas set aside for public use contrast with absolute rights in private property, but only with respect to the purposes for which they are established. Though for community sharing, there is no community ownership which gives the community the right to delegate use for private purposes. They do satisfy principles of distributive justice inasmuch as they are open to all the community, but are in tension with these principles inasmuch as many do not have the means to satisfy the equal access condition.

While our main concern will continue to be with conservation of nature and natural resources, the cultural heritage merits attention too since it also falls under the third *prima facie* principle of distributive justice. But the cultural heritage is a matter for subjective determination according to interests and values. To some, historical monuments take on a world heritage significance: the Pyramids of Memphis, for instance, the former Palace of Versailles, the site of the first Norse settlement in northern Newfoundland.[23] To others, the cultural heritage lies in creative works, including literature and art; to them visits to monuments,[24] even to the birthplace of Shakespeare or Dante or Geothe, have only a secondary value. The principle of access as part of distributive justice is relevant to either interpretation. *Opportunities* for access, through education and economic circumstances, are the central problem.

A consideration of a world cultural heritage has implications for a global morality to which we now turn: there are some things which may have the capacity to unite persons wherever they may live. The site of the first atomic explosion at Hiroshima may deserve moral inclusion in a World Heritage listing as much as the Acropolis (even though the shattered city has been rebuilt).

## A GLOBAL MORALITY AND CONSERVATION

In the fundamental notion of morality and the *prima facie* moral principles formulated from it, political organization into nations is irrelevant. In its most comprehensive sense, morality is universal for human beings, and the universalizability of moral judgements crosses all geographical and political boundaries. Even to think within parochial boundaries as we look outwardly and internationally is to infuse our thinking with some degree of politicization. Practical morality must be seen as aesthetic in its exclusion of all irrelevancies as persons work out a relationship with other persons, and as non-discriminatory in its equal consideration of the interests of all persons wherever they may live. In our moral concern for the interests of seriously underprivileged persons, such as many in Ethiopia and Bangladesh, there are no grounds for blurring the perception of these as individuals with basic desires, interests and life-goals. We give to them as we give to the needy in our own cities, through relief organizations, without seeing the recipients in most cases, content in our perceptions of them as persons in need of help from other persons.

When moral thinking and political thinking are forced into an unnatural conjunction, the integrity of the moral viewpoint *is* blurred. Sometimes it is blurred by paternalism, as when powerful nations assume that they know best what is good for weaker nations which receive their financial aid, denying them the right of self-determination, and acting in their own interests rather than considering the interests of the recipients from *their* standpoints.[25]

In practical morality the common interest and the *common good* are without political, cultural or economic boundaries. From the tiny Greek city-state to the development of modern nations, the orientation of political-philosophical thought has been generally state-centred. The historical survey of political philosophy in the first chapter showed the extent to which thoughts of the internal common interest were catalysed by a threat to security. In the second half of this century the situation is similar, but the threat is of global rather than of national proportions: it is the threat of total nuclear destruction. In this there is a moral connection with the interests of sentient animals, which will be considered shortly.

International law demonstrates other areas where moral concern for the interests of others extends beyond national boundaries. Not only are signatory states bound by covenants not to cause damage to the environment of other states (such as through chemical emissions from factory chimneys); they are also bound to notify neighbouring states if any of their activities are *likely* to affect people of other states.[26]

Another perspective on a global morality is in the widening of concern by present generations for the likely needs and interests of future generations. It is to this question that we now turn, noting that a global morality is not a unique species of practical morality, but one which conforms entirely with the moral principles already stated. There is no implication that solutions to its problems are easy on that account: as in all practical morality there are situations of moral dilemmas when it is not; and in it too it is not always easy to separate morality from prudence. But generally the *prima facie* moral principles, including those of distributive justice, provide clear moral bearings.

## POSTERITY AND CONSERVATION

Practical morality requires no occupational or interest specification such as legal, medical, administrative, educational; and no specification as a 'conservation morality' or an 'environmental ethic'. If our moral thinking and activities happen to be in areas of conservation, they are judged by standard moral criteria. Invalid conclusions have already been illustrated in the implicit reasoning of some statements made in the literature of environmental ethics. In these fallacies the interests of posterity are sometimes mentioned. In so far as a form of reasoning is educible at all in some of these statements, it may be expressed in this way:

Nature is an object of love and reverence
Therefore we ought to conserve it unspoilt as much as possible for the enjoyment of future generations as well as of present ones.

The premiss we have found to be a non-generalizable subjective statement, an expression of a personal attitude and value. The conclusion uses an 'ought', and it appears to be a moral ought inasmuch as it includes the interests of others – those of future generations. But it is not a valid inference. The premiss is irrelevant to it, and what appears to be a conclusion is left simply to stand as an assertion in its own right. A contrary value position might be asserted with equal facility, with a contrary conclusion, by replacing the love and reverence value with one of awe and dread:

Nature is cruel in its enormous powers of destruction
Therefore it is wasteful to conserve natural resources for future generations.

Clearly, again, there is no valid inference to be drawn from the premiss. The connection with the premiss is an equivocation. A more justifiable argument than either of these assertions of a value position might be stated informally in some way such as this:

> The limited natural resources of the earth need to be protected and conserved
> We ought to consider the interests of all inhabitants of the earth
> Therefore we ought to protect and conserve natural resources partly for the sake of posterity.

In this form there are still some unresolved questions. Since our morality is based on the notion of personhood, have we a right to include the unborn, who are no more persons than are infants or the comatose – even less so inasmuch as they don't exist and we cannot be certain that they will? For that reason there is an uneasy slide from the second premiss to the conclusion. Another unresolved question set in this context of uncertainty is whether we ought not to give *priority* in our consideration of interests to *present* inhabitants of the earth, to existing persons. We can scarcely engage in moral thinking of the kind that compels us to give equal consideration to the interests of persons, for we are here bringing together persons and merely potential persons, on the principle of the future being like the present.

To give the argument greater strength, and to increase our confidence in the justifiability of considering future generations at all, we clearly need to establish a strong conceptual link between present and future generations. This will never suffice to satisfy entirely the principle of equal consideration of persons, but it may reduce the scepticism concerning the similarity of present and future needs and interests, and thereby give sufficient grounds for some consideration of posterity. One way to do this is by means of a kinship argument. The form now proposed is a linear extension of the notion of personhood from the persons we do know. It is a projection into the future on the basis of demonstrable extensions from the present to the past, with one significant difference: while the persons of the past have been known to exist, those of the future are merely anticipated. In connecting the present with the past it is possible to establish a continuity of known persons: A knowing B, B knowing C for instance (but without A knowing C or vice versa) which may extend backward in time even to the French Revolution. A may have known a grandparent B for instance, who may have known a grandparent C for a comparable period who was born as long ago as 1789. In this way A may be able to establish a kinship link of almost two centuries. In a similar way there may be established a kinship link into the future, with A knowing B, B knowing C who is not yet born, but again A never personally knowing C (the case of A knowing a grandchild B who in time comes to know his own grandchild C). Thus family continuity through personal knowledge may extend forward for a similar period, given good fortune and a degree of longevity. The three persons involved, or to be involved, in linking the present and the future; and equally those who are involved or who at one time were involved, in linking the present with the past, rely on awareness of the central things which make them all persons – abilities and capacities, attitudes and values, desires and emotions, and so forth. It is not difficult in our personal family lives to perceive an historical continuity from past to present to future. Though in each of the two instances, between A and C and vice versa, there may be a remoteness in some respects, there are usually personal recollections, homes, relics and so forth which leave a nostalgic impression of a positive kinship connection as well as an undeniable perception of personhood. Beyond that period of two centuries or so the perception of personhood in more distant relatives may be dimmer, though always capable of being enlivened by literature and history for those with sufficient reflective capacity and a suitable education.

It is for the very reason of the linear projection of personhood that there is at the same time a *relaying* into the future of duties and obligations, the kinds of duties we claim for our children, which we are justified in claiming as *special* duties with respect to them because of the immediate dependency relationship. Others in the future take over from us. It is enough for our argument to claim normal moral duties to others in the future through the on-going perception of personhood (although in some cultures, such as the peasant culture of China, with grandparents and sometimes great-grandparents living in the same family home, three or four generations may be in daily personal contact, and special duties may be recognized more extensively). It is the continuity of personal knowledge which is central to this kinship argument. The kinship thread of personal acquaintance is not normally broken in the future: there will always be someone to know personally someone at present not even dreamed of. Families, like history, have a continuity. (There are exceptions, of course: some families die out, and some individuals leave no children.)

The kinship argument has a *prima facie* narrowness which can be satisfactorily answered. Each of us thinks of the future mainly from a single family viewpoint: on the face of it such a perspective is self-interested and lacks the impartiality and benevolence required of practical morality: it is a limited morality which restricts the consideration of others' interests to those of our own respective kins. But with respect to the future rather than the present, when no such exclusiveness would be contemplated, it provides a way of justifying a consideration of the interests of future generations, specifically in relation to conservation. In this future orientation to our practical morality, we propose what is practicable. We have no way, normally, of perceiving the personhood of those belonging to other families in the future: we must leave that to members of each of the families outside our own. Thus we expect of them a similar kind of kinship projection through personal knowledge as we have shown to be demonstrable in our own family. In this way we are not legislating morally for our own kin alone: we legislate for others to the extent of imposing on them the same obligations to assume a kinship projection as we ourselves have assumed. The interests of posterity are thus safeguarded not by a unitary kinship effort, but by as many kinship efforts as there are families in the community. In this way, everyone in future generations is taken care of. Moral responsibility to posterity cannot afford to be left entirely on a generalized basis of considering the interests of the future of *humanity*. It needs to be direct, personal, in contact with living persons. With this orientation, the present generation is able to cooperate in making decisions on matters of policy such as the proportion of natural resources which ought to be conserved for use by succeeding generations, returning us to the question of priorities raised earlier. At this point it may fairly be claimed that the kinship approach has answered some of the objections to a moral consideration of posterity, specifically that to contemplate future people violates the notion of personhood, and that we are not justified in viewing the future in the light of the past. It is the kinship connection which challenges any extreme scepticism about the future being so unlike the present as to nullify any of our plans for posterity: on the contrary, despite differences in externals such as dress, modes of transport, styles of housing and so forth, kinship gives us confidence that fundamental personal needs and conative urges, together with interests and values associated with them, will not be markedly different from those of present generations; nor will differences in intellectual abilities and in dispositional tendencies such as sociability or yearning for solitude. The kinship approach to the future moves us closer to acknowledging also that the generation into which one is born is fortuitous, and that, from a detached benevolent spectator standpoint on morality, those of each generation ought to be considered with equal concern. All that we may do for past generations is to make moral judgements as impartially as we can, but for those of the future it is possible for us to make both material and cultural provisions, ensuring first that they have sufficient of the necessities of life so as not to be denied a quality of life we would wish for our own kin who come after us, and doing what we can to maintain and if possible to add to the culture they will inherit as well. Conservation is concerned with each of these provisions for the future.

But it is necessary to sharpen the focus. Ample generalizations such as these leave questions of priority open and unresolved. *How much* of present resources in restricted supply should we keep in reserve for those coming after us? Because we may expect many more persons in future generations than in the present, ought we to make sacrifices on their behalf? One of the greatest difficulties is that forecasters of the future disagree on what future needs will be. Some are apt to let the future take care of itself, in the expectation that human ingenuity and technological advances will show future generations that they do not need our non-renewable resources, such as in coal, oil and gas, or even in uranium. Such apparent rationalizations could easily amount to convenient negligence. But what *is* the evidence for future material needs? Optimism suggests that future generations may be better off than we are, and that we ought not to make sacrifices for them. Others extrapolate from discernible present trends and conclude that at the beginning of the next century, and into the foreseeable future, 'the world's people will be poorer in many ways than they are today', with more crowding, more pollution, more ecological instability and social disruption, and that in general, short of revolutionary advances in technology, life will be more precarious.[27]

Whether we ought to make sacrifices at all cannot be decided without a basis in better empirical information than we have, and if the best judgement is that some sacrifices ought to be made, the extent of each can be determined only by relating present and future needs. On a global scale this is an enormous task, especially in view of the critical situation of many millions of people at present in

Third World countries. At least a beginning is to take careful stock of the evidence that *is* available on the accelerating rate of consumption of non-renewable resources, especially among industrialized countries, and the rapid rate of impairment of the environment, especially in developing countries. Serious stresses on the world environment and on resources are now scientifically documented.[28] Against a background of uncertainty of what the future will be like; disagreement on who should make sacrifices if any should (developing countries understandably resent the very suggestion of sacrifices in the light of their relative impoverishment); rapidly changing technology; environmental deterioration; advocacy of political change or of social reform, or of alternative lifestyles generally much less demanding of resources; solutions to the problem of safeguarding the interests of posterity appear to justify prior attention to the crucial social problems of the present. Practical morality requires that any moral judgements relating the present to the future should take account of the facts of both in so far as these are ascertainable, while not neglecting the interests of present generations on the basis of what is empirically confirmed or confirmable.

The question of what moral principles we should invoke regarding obligations to posterity, once an empirical basis of evidence has become sufficiently clear to avoid unfounded speculation, returns us to *prima facie* principles of social or distributive justice. This is clearly a case of the present generation being fair in its treatment of future generations, a one-way process of obligation since we in the present are in a position to act morally in favour of those of the future, whereas they, unborn, are not in a position to make claims on us, or to evaluate the quality of our morality, or the extent to which we consider *their* interests as well as our own. When their generation in turn becomes the present, and as persons grow to intellectual maturity, they will then be in a position to judge what we shall have done on their behalf, and with the advantage of better knowledge than we had ourselves. For they will not only know much as we know of *our* interests and needs, but will also know much better than we do by our projections into the future what *their* interests and needs are. If they are fair to us they will take into account the extent of our unavoidable ignorance of their situation. Such a continuing intergenerational evaluation may serve to increase moral sensitivity in the present to a perpetuating concern for future generations, a situation that has recently become much more practicable through improvements in education, technological aids in gathering and interpreting information, and sophisticated projection techniques. It is no practical help at all, because impracticable, to imagine what totally rational and totally disinterested persons, possessed of all the information they needed about the future as well as the present, *would* decide about protecting and preserving natural and cultural resources in the interests of posterity. But the ideal of rational and moral perfection, which Plato, Rousseau and Rawls have all expressed, is a useful notion against which to measure the unavoidable imperfections of the present generation as they consider the interests of future generations. We have postulated a new form of generational egoism, where practical morality succeeds only to the extent that those of the present are able to relax some of their egoism, and to move closer to the rational perspective of the disinterested and benevolent spectator. Thus the demands of practical morality grow both more complex and more difficult when we consider an intergenerational morality, oriented usually from the present to the future, but making evaluations of past moral endeavours as well.

It needs to be emphasized that a practical morality requires practicability, not visionary dreams or unrealizable ideals. It would seem that an intergenerational morality has certain limitations for reasons already intimated, particularly in the dearth of relevant information about the future, and in the very large area of unsatisfied interests in the present which demand moral attention. Is it beyond our moral reach, therefore, to contemplate an intergenerational *common good*? In principle there is no reason to doubt that it is. As we have seen, through our personal kinship connections with generations of the past and of the present, we recognize unchallengeable common interests of a very basic kind which affect the *quality of life* of persons regardless of the contingency of time of birth. These include basic survival necessities, adequate recreational facilities to relieve the tedium of regular work, access to natural features which may provide enjoyment according to interests, values and capacities, and access to the cultural heritage. In these respects (others might be added and separately justified), there is an intergenerational common good to which present generations are in a position to contribute especially through their forbearance and moderation, preserving conditions that will enable future generations to fend for themselves. A large-scale nuclear war instigated by the folly of political leaders would destroy an intergenerational common good indefinitely, if not for all time, both materially and culturally. For the first time in the history of mankind the present generation has the capacity to make any effort at conservation totally futile. The transmission of the culture intergenerationally now includes the intellectual resources and knowledge to destroy it. Moral education must therefore include an education in responsibility to our future kin within all the human families that exist, for without moral knowledge and dispositions, and above all without rational control, the very notion of an intergenerational common good is reduced to an ironic absurdity.

There is no formula by which to quantify the moral demands placed on us in considering the interests of those in the present as compared with those in the future. The question of priority is to be made as a practical judgement by those best qualified to judge, following the most thorough research, consultation and public participation. This is the common procedural principle in determining the common good. It is very doubtful if in the foreseeable future the best judges available would conclude in favour of present sacrifices in lowering any *average* quality of life on a global scale, if such a thing itself could be determined, but some sacrifices may be justified from the impartial moral and rational perspective that we would expect of such judges. For instance, recreational interests might be curtailed by protecting waterways and the wildlife inhabiting them; some forests might be saved from destruction by making further grants of aid to impoverished developing countries, obviating the necessity for agricultural expansion in some areas; the insatiability of industrialists for expansion might be disciplined and the level of pollution thereby reduced, and so forth. Again, it is fundamentally man's dispositions, his moral attitudes and values, including his benevolent concern for others' interests, which are the central problem. By appropriate education every person of normal abilities is able to assume a perspective on kin in future generations and to ask, If I were in their position, and knowing my own generation's capacity to provide for others as well as for itself, what is it reasonable to expect of my generation as a contribution to the future? Sufficient fuel resources? Wilderness areas left intact? Forests and pleasant recreational areas relatively close to cities? Documented knowledge in the humanities, science and technologies? Maintenance and enhancement of the arts? A controlled population level to prevent the use of natural resources beyond what is sustainable? With sufficient knowledge of the present, the reliable predictions of at least some future interests, rational and moral decision-makers would be in a position to reach firm conclusions on these matters, without claiming infallibility. Further, if they were rational and not carried away by dispositional fervour, it is most unlikely that any sacrifices would be expected of the present generation which would incur personal suffering, except perhaps for the temporary anguish of some who may have to curtail extravagance and excessive wealth, or surrender ambitions for large families, or give up thoughts of unnecessary agricultural or industrial expansion into natural areas. Questions of savings, sacrifices or priorities are all to be judged under a fourth principle of distributive justice which may be stated in this form: *Present generations have a moral obligation to pass on to future generations, in a fair accommodation of present capacities to future needs, the means to enjoyment of an adequate quality of life, both materially and culturally.* In less question-begging form the negative principle is this: no present generation should so use, impair or destroy its natural or cultural resources as to inhibit the prospects of future generations to an adequate quality of life. In either form, the contribution we make is on the understanding that quality of life will be equitably distributed through fair opportunities for all.

## CONSERVATION AND A MORALITY OF ANIMAL INTERESTS

We now introduce another shift from the literal terms of the moral principles which we have used as our constant touchstone: we extend our reference to consider the interests of sentient animals as part of our moral sphere. It is a shift to the extent that it is we who perceive their interests and can give reasons for them. The animals themselves have variable sentience characteristic of their biological development, but by definition all can experience pain. As we have indicated in other contexts, some may suffer anguish when separated from others, especially their young; some may enjoy play; some may even enjoy combat for dominance of a herd; in short, in their higher forms they do have an emotional life, and they do have mental functions such as memory. But they do not experience interests in the sense of being aware of having interests and having the capacity to give reasons in their support. In this sense their interests are custodial, held by us in trust for them. We do the same for infants, severely retarded persons and others, as we have noted, who are also totally unaware of having interests.

As we extend our sympathy and benevolence to unborn kin of future generations, with others taking over from us as sympathy and benevolence are relayed still further along the line of kinship, so we extend our sympathy to all sentient animals at least on the single dimension which we share with all of them, that of a capacity to suffer. They are not *persons*, mainly for the lack of a rational and imaginative nature which would allow them to formulate aspirations as we do, make choices, plan the means to attain their various goals. The capacity for suffering which all sentient animals have is the base-line for our moral concern for them. This is the *interest* which all have but cannot articulate or give reasons for. (Claims that sentient animals have an interest in survival, or in simply living, will be deferred for later discussion.)

As we consider a morality of concern for animal interests, it is important that we should not stretch the basic conceptual fabric of morality to breaking-point. We have already given it a certain elasticity in considering the interests of unborn generations, but have demonstrated that they do have interests, or more strictly that it is we who anticipate some of the interests of our kin in the future and are prepared to act now on their behalf. We become moral custodians for them, on the basis of our knowledge of human interests, but not of all *their* interests, for they may have some which we are unable to predict – quite unlike any we have ourselves. Now we are proposing something very similar for sentient animals. From the lowest of these to the highest, from crustaceans perhaps to the higher apes, the lowest common denominator is a capacity for suffering, for experiencing pain of some kind.[29] The detached moral spectator, endowed with benevolence and sympathy, must consider this particular interest in sentient animal life. Other interests which higher non-human animals have, such as a capacity for pleasure in free movement, we must also consider from a moral standpoint. Only morally insensitive spectators could confine their concern to the interests of other *persons*, totally ignoring animal suffering, and in some cases animal joy in living in their own way according to higher capacities which some possess.

Yet with few exceptions insensitiveness to animal suffering has been characteristic of human relations with animals throughout history. In the Elizabethan social context it is not surprising that Shakespeare should have described the mortal groans of a wounded stag without any reference to human feelings, such as the hunter's apparent indifference (*As You Like It*, Act II, sc.1, 36–8). A similar situation is reflected in the law pertaining to animals in many countries, where the interests of wild animals receive only scant attention if they receive any at all. In his *Autobiography* Charles Darwin argued that with respect to wild animals any species would discontinue propagating its kind if it were to suffer habitually to an extreme degree, and that by natural selection most or all sentient animals have been so developed that 'pleasurable sensations serve as their habitual guides' (pp. 146–7).[30] From this he inferred that most sentient animals experience an excess of pleasure over pain, though there is still a great deal of suffering, far greater in quantity than that of human beings because of the vastly superior numbers of non-human sentient animals (p. 147). In the *Politics* Aristotle justified man's dominance over animals in his explanation of the rule of 'mind and the rational element over the passionate' (Book I, ch. 4, 1254[b]).[31] For if the converse were to occur, it would be a case of the inferior part ruling the superior, and from this only harm would ensue. All inferiors have to be ruled by a master; that is exactly the case, he held, with animals in relation to man. From a similar anthropocentric standpoint, Hebrew and Greek belief influenced the Christian tradition of man's dominion over every other animal species on earth: fish, fowl, cattle and 'every creeping thing' (*Genesis,* i, 26). God delivered to Noah and his sons every living thing that moved on the face of the earth, inspiring in all of these creatures a 'fear' and a 'dread' (9, 3).

Any presumed lordship of man over animals, or any dominion view by which in man's relations with animals it is his *own* interests which invariably take priority over the interests of sentient animals, fits uneasily with the primary moral principle that we ought to consider the interests of others as well as our own. From a *moral* standpoint, the earth and all it contains is not merely for human use or manipulation: in some instances the interests of sentient animals may have stronger rational grounds for support, from an impartial moral perspective, than have instrumental human interests. For instance, the interests of wildlife using a valley for grazing and its slopes for shelter might be argued to have stronger moral claims than the interests of persons wishing to use it as a recreational rifle range, where animals would be frequently at risk as they wandered into the line of fire, all the more so since they would be offering themselves as moving targets to test the marksmanship of the riflemen. There can be no moral and rational defence for shooting animals for sport, when probable suffering is involved. The sportsman's attitude is the dominion view without responsibility. A responsible dominion view would take animal interests fully into account,[32] but the tradition of dominionship is now foreign to strictly *moral* attitudes and values towards sentient animals. A sympathetic and benevolent custodial protection of animal interests casts off much of the stigma of past values, when men lived in less sensitive relationship with wildlife, often depended on animals for food, and felt morally supported by religious beliefs.

When the dispositional side of our moral thinking is stronger than the rational, as it may be in our sympathetic attitudes towards sentient animals, there is a danger that the moral fabric to which we have referred will be subjected to further unnecessary strains. This is the case when some refer to animal *rights*. There are two objections to this use of rights: first, it is in breach of our standard notions of moral rights; second, it is unnecessary, for a moral case for considering animal well-being is sufficiently safeguarded by attention to animal *interests*. By accepting a custodial trust for sentient animals, we can speak for them, give reasons for the interests we assign to them, whenever their interests are misunderstood. We may need to do this, for instance, in discussions or negotiations with groups of farmers who object to wildlife competing with stock for food, or with recreational hunters. We would be on much less secure ground if we were to argue with such groups that sentient animals have *rights*, rights to satisfy their needs according to their respective natures, for instance, or rights to invade farmer's grazing property in search of food. For the notion of rights clearly requires a stronger rational statement than does the statement of interests from a custodial standpoint. This is partly through the influence of legal rights on moral rights, and traditional conservative overtones of the inviolability of the law. To have a moral right is to have the ability to make a claim against some person or persons, and this involves understanding what the right is about. It is a claim to something, such as to be able to speak freely, against a person or persons who might be obstructing the exercise of the right that is claimed. Hobbes called it 'a liberty to do, or to forbeare' (*Leviathan*, Part I,ch. XIV, p. 189).[33] The morality of considering the interests of sentient animals fully protects them without any forced attribution of rights to them, as the primary moral principle of a consideration of others' interests similarly protects certain human beings who are in a necessary custodial relationship with us. Consciousness and sentience are not enough for rights holding.

It is common among some who attempt to defend an environmental ethic as a special kind of morality to attribute to animals, as indeed to plant life as well at times, a right to life. This we have already observed as a dispositional expression, an assertion of an attitude–value position based on the kind of reverence for all life which Albert Schweitzer called 'the basic principle of ethics'.[34] We may admire the sentiment in this case, or recoil with distaste at the sentiment implied in the following: 'Hunting today is done only when animals are in good condition and can stand the strain. The hunters stay away in winter, when animals must conserve their energy; and in the nursing season.'[35] But it is not possible to draw a generalizable inference on whether animals have rights from either of these contrasting value positions. If it were, the first would be a right to live, and the second a right to choose when to die. The value of a reverence for life leads some into anthropocentricity, when animals are given characteristics of self-identity, intelligence, capacity for reciprocating human feelings and so forth, especially animals such as dolphins which communicate with their kind. Animals may not be accorded rights because in some respects they appear to come close to human behaviour. It is the *differences* between animals and humans that provide criteria for rights – reason, moral understanding and the capacity to act as moral agents through awareness of others' interests. Another source of confusion about animal rights lies in the differences that exist in their own category. Some live by killing other animals, others do not. How can a right to live apply to all animals when some are a necessary food for others – the carnivors?[36] If the nature of moral thinking is recognized as both dispositional and rational, and tendencies to leap from value positions to inferences are avoided; if confusions through personifications of animals in anthropomorphic tendencies are resisted; and if contradictions within species are prevented by a clear appreciation of animal differences; moral rights will be seen as most clearly relevant to humans, not to sentient animals.

Our obligation to sentient animals is to give them the same kind of equal consideration of interests as we give to persons. That is, it should make no difference to us in our consideration of an animal's suffering what its species is, what kind of relations we have with it (whether hostile or amicable), who owns it or what our relations are with its owner, whether it is old or young, in good health or diseased, in appearance appealing or otherwise. Sentient animals are not capable of reciprocating the benevolence and sympathy which we extend to them in their suffering, or which we show to others in releasing them from confinement for the joy of free movement. The *moral* relationship is strictly a one-way relationship of obligation to them. Sympathy is more than the constant affection of a family dog: it involves an insight into the interests of the animal recipient in comparison with one's human interest.[37]

It is sometimes argued that sentient animals have an interest in survival, presumably an interest which is distinct from avoidance of suffering. From Darwin's standpoint this is the very basis of the continuation of species. It is obvious from empirical evidence that pain avoidance and the struggle to survive are instinctual in all sentient animal life: struggle and stubborn defence have been the story of the evolution of successful life forms. There is no need to postulate a kind of consciousness which makes this a purposeful process rather than an instinctual reaction when under threat. Yet if survival is defended as a separate, sentient animal interest, then the killing of any of their species would be morally unjustified, unless there are good reasons for it such as providing a necessary source of food or equally *necessary* subjects for medical research.[38] Then it would become a moral rule not to kill sentient animals, from the principle that the interests of sentient animals are to be considered.

But there are serious difficulties in accepting a survival interest for sentient animals, because of the large differences among them in anything that might be conceived of as awareness. At the lowest limits of sentience, pain avoidance is much more intelligible to us than their survival interest, even though free-moving creatures, such as shrimps, appear to take escape action which suggests a survival response. The main difficulty is in generalizing for all sentient animals any awareness other than an awareness of suffering. The survival interest is more convincing in some of the higher sentient animals, such as those which are hunted for recreation, especially when the animal successfully evades the hunter and suffers no physical pain. But we know so little of any awareness other than of suffering among the lower sentient animals, that we shall not generalize the survival interest to include all sentient animals. In any case it is enough for a practical morality to acknowledge their common capacity to suffer.

## SUMMARY

Conservation is a moral question in many different circumstances, especially when it relates in some way to a practical consideration of the interests of others, including those of posterity.

It is an empirical question whether contact with nature adds *generally* to human quality of life, or to the common good. At this stage the matter must be taken as unresolved. Invalid inferences in support of a positive claim have been made by unfortunate selective references to Wordsworth and Mill. In so far as lack of interest in nature is due to educational deficiencies, it is probable that appropriate educational programmes might increase the numbers who *do* obtain satisfaction from nature in some way, and that such programmes might increase the range of the satisfactions which an individual might derive from contact with nature.

Sentient animals are included in the moral sphere because they have interests. Their instrumental value in providing satisfactions to some persons is not in itself a sufficient reason for this inclusion, otherwise trees and other plant life would also be included, as well as an endless number of other objects in nature. We have obligations to sentient animals because of their capacity for suffering, and in some cases for pleasurable emotional experiences. Sentient animals have moral interests, but not moral *rights*.

We do not know what the interests of future generations may be, and can only make inferences such as from common intergenerational interests of our kin, and from differences which may arise from increasing populations. A theory of intergenerational kinship has been proposed to justify a moral consideration of some of their probable interests, with relevance to conservation in all of the senses outlined.

The question of equal access to the natural and cultural heritage is related to the moral principles of distributive justice. Equal access does not imply that the potential satisfactions of people are the same. The relevant principle of distributive justice relates to *equality of opportunity* to enjoy the natural and cultural heritage according to capacities and values, but this in turn is related to a prior principle of *equality of educational opportunity* which is not identical with provision of schooling for all. Mill demonstrated a liberal attitude to land ownership against a background of determined support by interested parties for private ownership – a tradition equally evident in countries colonized by England. The possibility of land reform with relevance to the principle of equal access is deferred to the final chapter.

There is no need for an environmental ethic as a special branch of moral philosophy. All practical considerations, including those of conservation, fall under the standard moral principles outlined in the first chapter. Attempts to formulate a separate environmental ethic have failed in a number of respects, chiefly in the quality of reasoning and in conceptual confusions. The only objects in the moral sphere are human beings and sentient animals. Natural objects such as trees, the oceans, soil and so forth may have chance connections, as when they relate in some way to the interests of human beings and sentient animals; but the same may be said of any conceivable object under the sun. If one person seizes part of another man's land, that does not bring land itself into the moral sphere; that is, as a moral object in its own right.

In a logical sense the concept of a global morality is redundant, since an authentic moral agent will consider the interests of persons wherever they may live. But it is convenient for extra-national moral considerations.

On the assumption that conservation may be shown by research to be contributory to the common good, the next large question to be faced is, Who is to make the judgement of what the common good is? This will be the focus of much of the next chapter.

# 3 Conservation, Administration and the Common Good

From this point the main theoretical focus shifts from a justification of *prima facie* moral principles, including principles of social or distributive justice, and a basic understanding of conservation and of the common good, to a practical morality involved more closely with on-going problems of conservation. This chapter concentrates on the administration of conservation from a moral standpoint, though still concerned largely with theoretical questions in their application to practical problems. The next chapter is more concerned with the complexities in practice which obstruct moral solutions to conservation problems. Together, the two chapters serve to show both how wide the gap is between moral principles and the practice of conservation, and how difficult it is in practice to have a single-minded moral perspective on conservation which contributes to the common good.

We shall now measure imperfect practice against an *ideal* of conservation morality. As soon as we contemplate morality in action we can expect imperfection rather than perfection, as in any other area of human activity. The *ideal common good* is expressed in the form of principles to guide practice. No one can presume to know what an ideal solution is to the common good as soon as it is applied to a practical problem such as conservation. So the assumption we make in proposing a model of an ideal common good is that such a perception is within reach of no human being: it represents a view which first is perfectly impartial, second perfectly rational, third perfectly benevolent, and fourth perfectly understanding of all the relevant circumstances, or in possession of all knowledge relevant to the situation. It is the perspective which a perfect human being *would* have, one who is completely disinterested as he makes a practical judgement in the interests of everyone (and of those of future generations), his own interests not considered except in so far as he is a member of the community. This model is rather different from Rawls' original position inasmuch as parties to the social contract in his formulation, though rational and mutually disinterested (in the sense of not taking an interest in one another's interests) would operate behind a veil of ignorance – each literally not knowing his place in society, his class or social status, his good fortune or bad with respect to intelligence, strength and other natural abilities and capacities.[1] In the viewpoint now presented, the perfectly rational and moral person would also be completely knowledgeable. The differences between the two models arise from differences of purpose. The primary purpose of proposing a model of an ideal common good is to provide a reference against which *actual* human plans, policies and performances, which claim to be in the common interest with respect to conservation, may be judged. A secondary purpose is to stress that perfection is unattainable, but that at the same time some policies or acts relating to conservation are so far short of perfection that they deserve to be exposed, at least so that their potential influence on others may be reduced.

## UNDERLYING PRINCIPLES

The ideal person – perfectly rational and perfectly moral – would not require principles to guide him. A perfect practical judgement would lead him to right policies and right acts towards realization of the common good. But to guide actual persons in their situation of imperfection, there are certain principles deducible from the ideal model. First, *imperfectly moral* individuals require an understanding of themselves and of others as *persons*. In self-understanding, they need to be aware of powerful natural impulses towards self-interest, and of temptations in that direction. In understanding of others, they need to be aware that others are fundamentally self-interested too, and that some may be organized in pressure groups to assert and win sectional goals that may not be in the common interest or serve the common good. Imperfectly benevolent, they need to be aware too that in practical morality, benevolence – like a consideration of others' interests – may not come readily, and may frequently require moral determination and effort. For the perfectly rational and moral being, and for him alone, practical morality comes easily, and nothing obstructs a view of the common good.

Second, *imperfectly rational* individuals cannot entirely trust the practical judgements they make. Therefore it is necessary to test these judgements in discussion with others.[2] This is especially important because of the dispositional influences on reason which at any time may be either supportive or unsupportive of it. The imperfectly rational person who is conscientiously striving towards the common good must *share* his views then with others. This means that if he is in a position of leadership he must invite *public participation*, measuring his judgement against those of others. He needs modestly to acknowledge that others' judgements – individual and not merely majority – may be stronger rationally than his own. The perfectly rational being is not dependent on anyone else's judgement for confirmation or modification: his judgement is incorrigible by definition.

Third, *imperfectly knowledgeable* individuals cannot rely on their knowledge in making practical judgements affecting the lives of many others. Their rationality too requires to be sharpened to a realisation that they must ascertain the facts by whatever means are available to them. Again this calls for wide public participation, and in particular consultation with experts in various relevant fields. It may involve extensive and thorough research by those skilled in the appropriate methodologies and techniques. As part of the factual information they need which relates to the common good, imperfectly knowledgeable individuals must find out what others' *interests* are, avoiding convenient rationalizations in their own favour. The perfectly knowledgeable person seizes at once on whatever information is relevant to a perception of the common good, and combined with his perfect morality and rationality, sees the common good as Plato's ideal rulers in the *Republic* glimpsed the Form of the good.[3] Plato's conception culminated exactly in a vision of the common good: his philosopher–rulers could glimpse the higher reality in a world above the world of particulars which ordinary mortals knew, and the very few who could be trusted to rule the state *wisely* required this hard-won higher knowledge. For many centuries this has been a source of reflection on governments and administrators the world over, and a reminder to all of the perfection beyond our reach, the vast limitations on our knowledge when we come to consider the common good; therefore the demands for modesty, cooperation, participation and for an acknowledgement that only the perfect ruler unites morality, rationality and knowledge in one perception of wisdom such as Plato attributed to his rulers.

From this three-cornered model there are other subordinate

principles which follow. The most important of these are principles
of distributive justice. The ideal common good means literally that
the interests of every separate person have been given equal
consideration; that is, that whether it is conservation or some other
objective, its benefits are equitably distributed so that the fundamental notion of justice is satisfied, which is fairness in the
treatment of everyone, each regarded as a person, in total disregard
of irrelevances which might bias that treatment. In this sense civil
liberties of freedom of speech and assembly would be respected, so
that there would be no impediments whatever to voluntary
participation in arriving at the common good. While it is true that
perfect rulers would require no public assistance in perceiving this
common good, their moral perfection would compel them to invite
participation out of respect for the individual persons whose good is
being determined. Similarly, though moral and rational perfection,
including perfection of knowledge, would mean that the infallible
perception of the common good would not require that it be given
public consideration for confirmation before the implementation of
policies, moral perfection would again place a duty on the rulers to
publicize their decisions before implementation to show that
personhood is being respected, that decisions are not being imposed
on persons from above as though their opinions on what is the
common good, *their* good, is a matter of no consequence to them.
Together with the duty to publicize their decisions, there is a moral
duty, which perfectly moral rulers would at once acknowledge, to
give *reasons* for their decisions on the common good. For the
common good is made up of a number of individual interests, and
the persons who have these individual interests are necessarily
rational beings. To publicize decisions on the common good without
giving reasons would again be an affront to personhood. (In English
law public participation is a right, but there is no legal right of
citizens to review government decisions before executive action is
taken.[4] A similar legal right exists in the USA and some other
countries with respect to participation.)

In the imperfect world as we know it, public participation on
all matters likely to affect the common good, such as conservation,
may require more than civil liberties of freedom of speech and
assembly. Before distributive justice is satisfied there must be *equal
opportunities* to participate. The equal right to public participation
is not enough. Prior to that two conditions need to be satisfied:
first, actual equality of educational opportunity; second, a degree

of equity in social conditions which gives to each person a fair basis for participation. Stated negatively, the second condition is that in matters concerning the common good, extremes of social disadvantage commonly destroy the incentive to participate with others. The second condition implies that equal educational provisions do not offer equality of educational opportunity.[5] Some social circumstances destroy the will to an acceptance of educational opportunities, preventing free participation in an approximate matching of basic knowledge and communication skills, as well as in socially-oriented attitudes and values. The principles of distributive justice which affect public participation are dependent on a variety of social and political circumstances which may either promote or frustrate them.

The effects on public participation of resentment at social injustice are deep and far-reaching. Indeed any act of discrimination against individuals which violates the fundamental moral principles of equality of consideration of persons' interests normally turns them inwardly rather than outwardly, in a cooperative appraisal of what the common good is. While justice comes to us usually as a matter of course, neither surprising nor elating us unless we live under harshly repressive regimes, anything cuts deep which indicates to us that we have not been treated by the same rules or standards as others have been treated in identical circumstances. Wide public participation is freely promoted when social justice is the norm. Then conservation, or any other matter under consideration as connected with the common good, is seen as equally beneficial to every individual. Yet it is in the imperfect world of imperfect moral agents and imperfect governments and administrators that public participation is most needed, for while perfect rulers encourage participation out of respect for persons, imperfect rulers need to consider others' views, and to weigh others' interests, before they arrive at an estimate of the common good.

'A multitude is a better judge of many things than any individual', asserted Aristotle. For one thing, he explained, 'the many are more incorruptible than the few'; for another, an individual's judgement can be impaired by 'anger or some other passion', but the many are unlikely to 'get into a passion and go wrong at the same moment' (*Politics*, 1286ᵃ).[6] Aristotle acknowledged that in any process where political and moral thinking are combined, judgements can become more rational by the influences of many minds. His was an overstatement, of course, because what is important too is the *quality* of the other minds, their rational and moral capacity and their knowledge. The influence of many minds can itself be detrimental to rational–moral judgements, as some majority decisions have shown.

While public participation is clearly needed on policies and plans which affect the common good, such as matters relating to conservation, there are many administrative decisions to be made by individuals because of the impracticability of universal public participation in decision-making. In the many applications of administrative rules, for instance, judgements are frequently called for, but the benefits of 'many minds' are both impracticable and unnecessary. In such circumstances a clear understanding of the rules is assumed, but beyond that are two significant principles of administration: first, the interpretation needs to be appropriate to the situation; second, in all similar situations the interpretation needs to be consistent, so that at this executive level of applying rules or principles, as determined by others in consultation, a fundamental *predictability* is demonstrated. Unpredictability is a moral affront to other persons on whose behalf the administrator is making his decisions. A distinctly different kind of affront to other persons is the case of secrecy or devious procedures to attain an end believed to be consistent with the common good. It is another fundamental principle of administration relevant to situations where public participation is considered unnecessary or impracticable, that the *means* to the end should be as morally justifiable as the end itself.[7]

A universal moral and political principle is that the common good is the proper aim of every government. This was obvious to both Aristotle and Kant, because each saw political science as the highest of all activities, inasmuch as it led from individual good to the good of the many: that is, the good of the state. In the *Nicomachean Ethics*, Aristotle explained that politics 'uses the rest of the sciences', its end includes those of the others, and 'must be the good for man'. Although, he thought, 'it is worth while to attain the end merely for one man, it is finer and more godlike to attain it for a nation or for city-states' (1094[b]).[8] Kant expressed a similar view in *The Natural Principle of the Political Order*.[9] With clear traces of an influence from Rousseau as well as from Aristotle, Kant saw politics as practical morality, uniting all human wills in the one social life, with each individual a morally free agent, and a civil society as necessary for the development of man's moral nature. He likened a political constitution to 'a hidden plan of Nature', for it is 'the only state in which all the capabilities implanted by her in Mankind can be fully developed' (Eighth proposition,p.21). In *Principles of Political Right*[10] the unity of morality and politics is unequivocal from his standpoint. The civil state is 'regulated by laws of right', and founded on rational principles, including a principle of liberty (p. 35). For everyone 'needs to be convinced by reason in things relating to universal human duty' (p. 60).

In these principles of Aristotle and Kant the contrast is evident between the ideal common good and what is more clearly attainable in the world of imperfectly rational and imperfectly moral persons. Our judgements on others in their efforts to achieve a common good as they see it is fair-minded only when the contrast is kept constantly in mind. For this reason 'the common good' is used from this point in one of three senses, each of which is separately designated. The first is the *ideal common good* as already explained. It is 'fixed and immutable', to use a common expression in moral idealism, following the rationalist emphases of Plato and Aristotle on 'higher truths'. It is only the *idea* of this that can be grasped, its *form*. In the world of particulars, which is the world we experience, it is an ultimate of perfection, and therefore beyond attainment. The second is what is now called the *practical common good*. This is the common good which is within our reach. It is also the best estimate of the common good that can be made by those most suitable to make it, guided by moral and rational principles, and with as complete a store of relevant knowledge as they can command. It is not fixed and immutable, but adjustable. In terms of achievement, it is a level of common good which we may be able to improve upon, as we may be able to improve in our moral and rational propensities, and in our knowledge. Therefore we need to consider a third level, which is a variant of the practical common good, and which we shall designate the *potential common good*. That is the common good which has regard for human potential, for an upward stretch from any preceding practical common good. The fundamental means to lifting the practical common good to another achievable level with fresh objectives, is *education*. This will be discussed in Chapter 5.

We are now in a position to differentiate between the main practical directions in this and the next chapter. The remainder of this chapter is concerned, as it began, largely with a general approach to the practical common good, to theoretical considerations and policies rather than to particulars of executive action or moral shortcomings. Then in Chapter 4 the focus is brought much closer to actual practice, as obstacles to moral solutions of conservation problems are discussed within a context of human limitations. That provides a suitable base for the culmination of our thoughts on conservation and the common good in the final chapter, with its emphasis on the educational challenge to raise the threshold of the practical common good, both in its conception and its pursuit, rather closer to the *ideal common good* through envisaging a continual potential for improvement. The plan is now to build on underlying principles by considering in turn the nature of political thinking, with special application to decision-making and conservation, and to the question of who is best fitted to make decisions for the common good; relationships between the law, morality and conservation; and finally, the particular significance of international law in relation to a global morality and conservation.

## POLITICIANS AND POLITICAL THINKING IN A PARTY POLITICAL SYSTEM

Lest the capacity of political leaders in power to perceive a practical common good should be seen as universally inhibited by ineptitude, pretence or deception, it is important to recognize the exceptional cases in which some have made a distinctive contribution to conservation and the practical common good as they have perceived it to be, and as others have judged it to be in retrospect. Some have had visions of enlarged systems of national parks *for the people*. The visions of others have been frustrated only by national emergencies.[11] Legislation in a number of developed countries has aimed at improving the quality of life of people generally by means of conservation measures. Sometimes even an intergenerational common good is in mind, related to a variety of possible interests of future generations.[12] Some legislation has been aimed at pollution likely to have harmful environmental effects, or to endanger or seriously to disadvantage the general public, or even to inconvenience it.[13]

There is no cause then for a total denigration of political leaders for failing to heed the practical common good as they see it with respect to conservation. But deferring particulars to the next chapter, several questions need to be asked about the political system. First, does the party system of government have a structure and purpose appropriate to a pursuit of the common good? Second, does the system produce politicians with the moral and rational capacity required for a clear perception of the practical common good, as well as the knowledge for necessary evaluative judgements, and a dedication to the pursuit of the common good as they may see it? With common human imperfections conceded, there are justified misgivings on each of these questions.

The party political system has inherent weaknesses which commonly bend attitudes and values away from the pursuit of the common good. Politicians perceive only too clearly that their maintenance of power and their very retention of office are dependent on the will of the electors. With insecurity of tenure which is derived from the political party system, the first priority is to retain power. Therefore they must not only consider very carefully policies and plans which will be electorally pleasing, or at least not electorally provocative or damaging, but they must also continually manoeuvre and manipulate individuals and factions constituting pressure groups which themselves are fundamentally contradictory in purpose to the very idea of a practical common good. The pragmatic lessons of power, compromise and survival need to be learned by all out of self-interest. In this situation pressures on politicians are complex, with conflicting loyalties to family and career, the electorate and the public interest as some may perceive it at times. If it is true that most imperfect human beings, thrown into this kind of political maelstrom, would behave similarly, serious doubts must be raised about the political system itself.

The persistent moral concern in this situation is that both the perception of the practical common good, and its pursuit, depend on the utmost integrity. No one who is unable to assume the impartial and benevolent spectator stance would be in an appropriate position to perceive it. For a politician to discipline himself into perceiving it, and further to discipline himself into a single-minded pursuit of it, there would be required a high-minded unconcern for his own political future, a rejection of pressure groups with sectional interests, a willingness to resist pressures from the electorate which voted him to office, a steady refusal to support any policy or practice that is not open and straightforward, and a disregard of the intrigues of the major opposing party – itself waiting anxiously to assume power as soon as the government is seen to falter. This would be a contradictory denial of political character. Even if the party were to delegate to an advisory committee the task of arriving at the practical common good, it would have to make decisions on implementation of recommendations, so that the best judgement on the practical common good would have to fit into the political context of an already complex assortment of considerations oriented towards retention of power and political survival. It is unthinkable, because it is totally unworkable, that priorities should be reshuffled, with the common good taking precedence over all others, or that pragmatic party goals should all be subordinated to goals that directly relate to the common good – at least as politicians might perceive it.

Some of these inconsistencies are removed in a one-party system of government, others persist: there is still power rivalry and manoeuvring for support, the propagation of policies in the party interest but not necessarily in the common interest. Whatever Plato's intentions may have been in the *Republic*, with a background of wrangling in the tiny Athenian democracy he knew, is it any wonder that he proposed government by the very best minds that could be rigorously prepared for the task, those who both could, and *would*, keep the ideal common good constantly in mind? To Aristotle, those governments which are dominated by the self-interest of the rulers are all defective, while those 'which have a regard to the common interest are constituted in accordance with strict principles of justice, and are therefore true forms . . .' (*Politics*,1279$^a$). For an understanding of the high moral demands of government, and the disparity between principles of the common good and political practice of all times, it is important not to lose sight of this Greek ideal. Aristotle had begun the *Politics* with the explanation that the state or political community 'aims at good in a higher degree than any other, and at the highest good' (1252$^a$). The good of political science 'is justice, or the common interest' (1282$^b$), which is self-evidently the ultimate good.

In considering the party-political system, the one significant element we have omitted is the voting public. For like members of government, they are imperfect, with motives and goals of their own, fundamentally self-interested, sometimes organizing in pressure groups to achieve sectional ends, and exerting influence on elected representatives to act in their favour, regardless of the interests of others in the community. Therefore a significant improvement in the moral quality of politicians may be dependent on a prior improvement in the moral understanding and values of the public, together with an understanding of the complexities of current political processes.

Thus political thinking at all levels, whether among politicians in government or among the electors, tends to be contra-moral inasmuch as it is centred fundamentally on self-interest rather than on a practical consideration of the interests of others, which from a rational–moral perspective leads to the practical common good. We have referred to political thinking as like moral thinking in so far as each is constituted of interacting reason and dispositions. But it is the dispositional component which differs radically in each, comprising all those influences on reason which predispose a person towards a certain judgement or action. In any system of government there are opposing political attitudes and values whose very existence is seen as a threat, making the defence of either set all the more stubborn.

It is dangerous to condone political thinking as of a different moral order from that which counts as *moral* thinking, with the implication that politicians do the best that might be reasonably expected of them given the quasi-moral system in which they operate. Hume referred to a widespread belief '*that there is a system of morals calculated for princes, much more free than that which ought to govern private persons*' (*A Treatise of Human Nature*, Book III, part II, sect. xi, p. 568).[14] He was thinking of agreements made between and among rulers of different states, and conceded that this morality of princes or rulers 'has not the same *force* as that of private persons, and may lawfully be transgress'd from a more trivial motive' (ibid.). Hume argued that agreements among states are not so necessary or advantageous as is promise-keeping among individuals, which is necessary for social continuity. Therefore 'we must necessarily give a greater indulgence to a prince or minister, who deceives another; than to a private gentleman, who breaks his word of honour' (p. 569). That view is now outmoded: we realise that tolerance of political deception, and surrender of almost total power to rulers unsuited to exercising it with respect to matters of the practical common good, are contradictory.

Yet that awareness has been apparent for centuries among those sufficiently literate, from the observation that 'the wit of the fox is everywhere on foot',[15] to Machiavellian traditions of the ruthlessness of rulers in gaining their own ends.[16] In historical context it is little wonder that in England and elsewhere a strong tradition of limiting the power of rulers developed in political philosophy, from Locke to the nineteenth-century liberalism of Mill with his declaration that 'there is a circle around every individual human being, which no government, be it that of one, or of a few, or of the many, ought to be permitted to overstep . . . ' (*Principles of Political Economy*, Book V, ch. XI, p. 563).[17] Mill's stance was from principles of liberty, but it also marked a recoiling from alleged government responsibility for the practical common good. No English political philosopher from the time of Hobbes had recommended more rather than less power to governments.

It is the conflict between morality and pragmatism which rules politicians out of contention as guardians of the common good. There are some questions – the largest questions of all facing governments – which require single-minded practical judgements by minds disciplined to consider the common good above all else: matters which are related to conservation, for instance, such as declarations of nature reserves, world protection of wildlife, aid to impoverished countries where the earth is being degraded, military expenditure and the amassing of nuclear weapons – all affecting the practical common good for both present and future generations. There are also priority decisions to be made in the context of limited resources, in political hands traditional opportunities for setting aside the public interest for short-term electoral gain. The judgement that political leaders are not suitable for determining and pursuing the common good is fundamental to the argument that follows. It is the first step in deciding who ought to be given responsibility for protecting and pursuing the common good.

## POLITICAL THINKING, DECISION-MAKING AND CONSERVATION

We shall give support to this judgement by sharpening the focus on political decision-making, considering, first, a model of decision-making; second, the limits of political decision-making, including the propensity to compromise, or to favour a balance between contending forces, and the nature and influence of pressure groups; third, the likely consequences of political decision-making for large conservation questions, leading to first thoughts on who should make the decisions.

**Decision-making: a Moral Standpoint**

A decision-making model to use as a standard by which imperfect administrative practices may be evaluated is necessarily both *moral* and *rational*. It takes account of the nature of all practical deliberations which lead to conclusions, judgements or decisions and then on to action, but while all of these deliberations are both rational and dispositional, it is the dispositional element which may not be inclined towards morality.

Moral decision-makers are open, impartial, perceptive of others' interests and sensitive to them, mindful of all others as persons, as leaders able to share decision-making with others, to be completely undistracted by personal status or reputation, to pursue morally compatible objectives with skill and determination, to seek consultation from those better informed than they. In each respect there is a reflection of a person in command of his own powers but modestly perceptive of others' capacities. Guided fundamentally by moral principles, his concern is for the interests of persons rather than for purely institutional ends.[18] As a contrasting model of administrative inadequacy stands the leader who is unable to trust others, has little concern for their interests, fails to communicate objectives, rules, criteria, relating to the activities which affect all members of the organization, in the face of opposition is uncertain of his position, succumbs readily to flattery and in return to nepotism, is subject to hasty decisions based on insufficient information. The antithetical model is of one who is without clear and constant moral values, and without rational self-mastery. Certainly he has an unfortunate combination of disabilities, but the point of the contrast between the two models is that in the first, assuming normal rational powers and an absence of any abnormal temperamental excesses, the person who is consistently loyal to clearly-held moral principles has a self-confidence and a directness in his decision-making, is predictable in his procedures and in his relations with others and, other things being equal, generates a confidence in others, a cooperativeness among them in willingly sharing goals, contributing to plans, working to the best of their abilities. The unifying and directive force in such a situation is *moral attitudes and values*.

**Pressure-group Influence and Compromise**

If clarity of objectives, firmness of resolve and directness in pursuing objectives were all that mattered in decision-making, and were all separated from the qualities which attract widespread cooperation, the Machiavellian model of the ruthless self-interested ruler would suffice for quick results, brought about largely by fear. It is when the moral base is on shifting sands, as it frequently is in political decision-making, that decisions are often delayed, ambiguous and withheld from all except a trusted few until the last minute. For on matters crucial to political survival, decision-making is often a question of balancing a large number of conflicting interests both within and outside the political party in government, without any particular regard for others as persons. This is evident in concessions to the interests of powerful lobbies in the electorate, which may have been influential in the government's accession to office, seen rather as power groups than as separate persons, and as such not to be alienated, for reasons of political survival.

This picture characterizes some but not all political decision-making, for obviously some is of such immediate concern to all parties and to the public at large that the route to it is speedy, moral in outlook and unequivocal, as in cases of national and international disaster. It is overdrawn for some other situations. Its special application is to those situations where there is a fundamental *self-interest* in government decision-making; that is, an absence of a moral intention, or of a practical consideration of the interests of the people as separate persons, and above all, of any clear perception of the practical common good, whether it relates to conservation or to something else.

In the absence of any unifying force on decision-making other than principles derived from moral attitudes and values (there are other possible unifying forces in times of national emergency, for instance, such as a common threat to security), political decision-making invites public participation on some issues, but because representations to it are usually too numerous for individual hearings, representatives of groups are most commonly heard, the groups constituting those of similar interests. Further, the government is usually obliged to hear *opposing* interests, each of which is a pressure group whose function is to influence government decision-making towards the interests which it represents. In most circumstances this access to government decision-making is considered sufficient for the purposes of the respective pressure groups.[19] But the very process of sitting in judgement on opposing points of view, and the acceptance in principle that government members are open to persuasion, rational and moral or otherwise, tends to divert attention from moral perspectives. Indeed the very acceptance by governments of a *self-interest* representation is in principle an acceptance of an a-moral position. Pressure groups are as political in purpose as are political parties themselves, beginning with similar a-moral premises. They function too with similar political deception when they each purport to be acting in the 'public interest' or the 'national interest', when it is clearly their own interest which they have in mind, not the practical common good. As might be expected of someone who saw civil society as a means to man's moral development, with a moral 'general will' directed towards the common good, Rousseau condemned all political sub-groups in the state, all 'sectional associations', holding that 'every citizen should make up his own mind for himself'. Only in this way could the general will be expressed (*The Social Contract*, Book II, ch. 3, pp.72–3).[20] But politicians are often in a vulnerable position because of their urgent need of information on pressing issues: when insufficiently knowledgeable themselves, they need to be in a position to impress themselves on public confidence with an authoritative command of relevant knowledge. In some circumstances, therefore, political decision-making may be moulded by pressure groups on whom it is dependent for information.

**Who is to Make the Decisions?**

Questions of conservation fall under social issues which are seldom classifiable on any unitary principle of morality, economics or politics. They are more usually all of these in their various facets. Our concern is to show that any decision-making on large conservation questions of the kind to be illustrated needs to begin with a steady *moral* perspective, one that is not necessarily assumed by economists or by political leaders. This will be explained by considering several of the major conservation issues of our time: those of the preservation of tropical rainforests, establishment of wildernesses and national parks, and the threat of nuclear war.

Tropical rainforests attract the attention of conservationists for the great density and diversity of life-forms, an environment whose general characteristics are stabilized by high humidity and ample rainfall. For millions of years opportunities have been provided for living things to adapt themselves to specialized conditions in the jungle, new forms of life are continually being discovered, undoubtedly many more await discovery. In some countries the tropical rainforests continue to be cleared for agriculture. There are problems emerging in the depletion of forests the world over: their progressive destruction might eventually affect the quality of the air we breathe, though no conclusive evidence is yet available on this question. This is clearly a problem with various dimensions. As we have observed, political thinking has a tendency to seek compromise, balancing as best it can, and to its own advantage if possible, the various competing claims. A short-term solution would be to permit *some* agricultural expansion, but not as much as agriculturalists are demanding. This would provide employment, improve the economic situation, satisfy some of the government's critics. From a rational–moral standpoint, the question to be asked is, What is the solution which best serves the practical common good? This is a question of far-reaching ramifications, requiring the most competent scientific evidence available of the life-forms inhabiting tropical rainforests, a consideration of problems of access to them, likely developments in future generations which might facilitate this access, the likely increase in demand for access through appropriate education, the question of economic alternatives to making further inroads on the forests for agriculture, including the need for external aid in some circumstances, the ecological damage already caused by agriculture, the practicability of reafforestation and so forth. The solution would be one for present generations and one for future generations, and one for the people of the world. But it is not, by its nature, a problem for political decision-making.

Similar considerations apply to wilderness areas. These are primitive areas of land, usually with clearly identifiable natural boundaries and of substantial size in which the ecological systems remain relatively undisturbed by man. They are as close as we are able to get to natural plant and animal life before human civilization and occupation, without reminders of any of man's works in roads or tracks, buildings or commercial enterprises. They provide for some an opportunity to enjoy solitude. Scientists are interested in observing plant and animal life in them. Laymen go there to observe and to learn (some claim to learn as much about themselves as about other living things). They are seen by some as places of quiet recreation in the literal sense, as opposed to the noisy recreation of competitive sports and motorized vehicles, places where adjustments may be made by quiet reflection. But there are many questions to be asked. How many of the community wish to use such places according to the principles on which they are established? If they have too many users, they will soon lose their wilderness character. Will they be accessible to all, or only to the affluent? Are future generations likely to need them more than we do, in view of a continuing technological revolution, population increases and a possible increase in leisure? Have they economic potential? What is their scientific value? If there is no obvious self-interest to a political party in such questions, politicians might seek public opinion and be guided largely by it. Once again, though, public opinion surveys might yield a misleading impression of the common interest, one which is a distortion of the common good, yet one which politicians are ill-equipped to evaluate or to overrule when necessary. If minerals happened to be discovered in wildernesses, there is always a possibility that political opportunism would seize on possibilities for economic exploitation, pressing for construction of roads, and foreseeing an easing of an unemployment burden which might have short-term appeal to a short-sighted group of the public. Similarly, if politicians wish to expand the country's industrial capacity, opportunities might be all too apparent for power generation by hydroelectric works, involving the damming of a wilderness river. All opportunistic short-term perspectives on wildernesses are conceived from the traditional stance of unused land being *waste* as Locke saw it: in political and economic terms, the wilderness may be a potential for industrial growth and increasing national strength, currently left idle. The protection and preservation of wildernesses is too large a question to be left dependably to political leaders.

Assessments by economists of the value of wildernesses are also apt to be one-sided. For instance, they might conduct surveys on which to base a cost-benefit analysis of wildernesses and similar natural resources; or they might resort to Optimum Control Theory or a more sophisticated technique, despite the problem of an unpredictable degree of technological progress in the future, the difficulty of predicting what future individuals' interests and values might be, and therefore the distinct likelihood that the optimum benefit may change, leaving uncertain which of two or more courses of action is preferable.[21] If economists base their judgement on the fact that wildernesses have a 'low-density recreation value'.

assuming that the value of such places depends on the *intensity* of use, politicians acting on their findings may very well choose one of various incompatible options, each of which has irreversible consequences when implemented. The question may be of such delicacy and complexity that the best decision might be that *no* action be taken, until such time as clearer evidence becomes available. From a moral standpoint which considers the interests of others as *persons*, the appropriateness of quantification techniques based on questions of relative degree of use are of little assistance in reaching the best possible decisions on the practical common good. The benefits to some of opportunities for solitude, for quiet reflection and observation, are unquantifiable, as are all utilitarian estimates of satisfaction if conceived as quantifiable. Above all, a political decision to open a wilderness area to commercial exploitation would be irreversible: wildernesses are not for patching up, once serious blunders have been committed.

National parks are like wildernesses in some respects: they are of substantial size, are held in reserve because of their natural features and the natural resources of vegetation and wildlife which they contain. In some countries roads and tracks have been made through them to provide easier access to particular points of interest, and in general their use by the public is encouraged as part of management policy. They differ from wildernesses too in that sometimes mineral exploration and mining are permitted in them, though this has been a contentious issue. Some countries have established separate nature reserves whose aim is specifically to retain for present and future generations certain characteristic and representative ecological systems. They are therefore intended usually for more restricted use than are national parks, by those of the public wishing to observe, from a scientific or an educational standpoint, the various interrelationships of soil, climate, vegetation and wildlife. This is a moral consideration of the interests of others, for without regulation the interests of those wishing to learn by direct observation would be impaired. The Second World Conference on National Parks recommended that governments should 'ensure that adequate and representative samples of natural biomes and ecosystems throughout the world are conserved in a co-ordinated system of national parks and related protected areas . . . ' (p. 442).[22] Ironically in the light of these far-reaching recommendations, there was reference to an urgent need to evaluate the contributions of national parks to the well-being of the community in social, environmental and economic terms, recognizing that the needs of all the people of the country are to be taken into account (p. 447). This kind of research needs to be directed also towards individual quality of life, so that comprehensive evidence is weighed on the question of a relationship between national parks, or other nature reserves, and the practical common good. If their benefits are established, but found not to be widely distributed, then we are justified in asking questions of distributive justice. This will be deferred to the particular practical considerations of the next chapter. It is to be observed again that the social complexity of the total problem is not one for undependable political determination.

The third of the selected major conservation issues for discussion is the threat of nuclear war. This is a moral issue too inasmuch as it concerns the interests of every living person and of sentient animals as well,[23] with far-reaching consequences for the future as well as the present. Conservation of tropical rainforests, wildernesses, national parks and other nature reserves – indeed all human efforts at the preservation and protection of plant and animal species – would be nullified in a full-scale nuclear war.

One of the main sources of difficulty in persuading the public of the abuse of power by some political leaders in their continuing drives to increase their destructive nuclear capacity is that weapon systems themselves tend to be clouded in technicalities and secrecy. Massive education campaigns are needed using some of the compendiums recently available, with ample information on military expenditure compared with social welfare expenditure, details of nuclear warheads already produced and their total destructive power compared with that of the Hiroshima bomb, details of radiation fall-out, current speculation by scientists of a nuclear winter and its devastating effects in killing many species of plant and animal life, especially in the tropics.[24] The critical danger of the present situation, where 'all peoples inhabiting the earth are dependent on one highly fragile policy of the two superpowers',[25] has to be handled rationally and morally by those who have their own interests in survival and quality of life to protect, but who are also benevolently concerned for the similar interests of all others. Morality and conservation have both become hostages of the increasing number of nuclear powers in the world, though predominantly of the superpowers.[26] Decision-making on life and death is clearly not for elected representatives in government: people the world over need to be better advised of the powers they have surrendered to their elected representatives. (The nuclear problem will be considered further in the next chapter.)

The seriousness of some of the greatest social issues of our time, especially the gravity of the last of the conservation issues, has left many people uneasy about the suitability of their political leaders to decide certain kinds of problems. Pending a further consideration of political reform in the final chapter, and chiefly in the meantime to underline the unsuitability of present governments to make some of the decisions they are empowered to make, a proposal is now made that a relatively few of the outstanding social problems, such as those of conservation, should be handled by the very best persons available in the community, who as a group we shall designate a *Commission*.

In some respects its members would be distinguished. Fundamentally they would be disinterested, able to consider all present and future interests from the *moral* standpoint of impartial and benevolent spectators. They would be Plato's rulers inasmuch as they would be highly selected persons from the community, but still with their feet firmly in the world of particulars, of imperfection. Being themselves imperfect they would have their own attitudes and values on conservation, as on other practical questions, but being rational too they would, by mutual vigilance, do their utmost to check any distorting dispositional influences on reason and the common good from within their own ranks. They would not be influenced by the strength of popular expressions either in support of nature reserves or against them, but on all such matters would seek the widest possible information, understanding others' interests and values, making allowances for prejudices and all sectional biases, however influential. With respect to nature reserves, for instance, they would appreciate that people's interests are varied, that there may be benefits to some in healthy recreational walks, to some others in intellectual curiosity and scientific observation, to others again in the aesthetic appeal of an environment removed from interpersonal conflict and industrial pollution, while others may find emotional experiences of a simpler kind such as peace and release from the burden of competitive pressures. But only research would ascertain the relevant facts, and the Commissioners would make their judgements on what they find to be the case.

# THE LAW, MORALITY AND CONSERVATION

Since the courts have the responsibility for impartial judgements as they interpret the law of the time, we are justified in enquiring into their capacity for relating morality and conservation, again leaving to the following chapter any *particular* moral problems which emerge in the administration of the law.

We shall consider, first, the relationship between law,[27] morality and the common good, with special reference to the functions and limitations of the courts in supporting the common good; second, land use, the law and the common good.

## Law, Morality and the Common Good

The distinction between legal rights and moral rights has already been intimated in the attempt to assign legal rights or standing to trees and to other natural objects, such as by arguing that trees might be represented before the courts by legal guardians, just as collective abstractions such as corporations and municipalities in fact are. These are as incapable of asserting claims themselves as are trees, creeks, mountains and so forth, but each may require legal representation, so it is held, by having someone speak for them.[28] Infants and others need our moral protection too, but there is no need to assign moral rights to them to justify our moral obligations. Moral rights require, as we have seen, sufficient rational understanding of what the rights are and the capacity to claim them against other persons who may be threatening or infringing them.

Other connections already observed between law and morality refer to statutes of various legislatures and political intention, which may be no more than a rationalization of a moral purpose, or even an attempt at public deception, though in some cases statutes have been clearly oriented towards morality in the genuine concern of governments to improve the quality of life of the people.

There has been a widespread fear among jurists that considerations of morality might confuse and complicate purely legal considerations, especially following the efforts of Natural Law theorists to bring law into conformity with a morality of particular religious teachings. The reaction of positivists such as Jeremy Bentham and John Austin was to declare that the law is law, good or bad: in fact, as Austin said, jurisprudence is concerned with positive laws regardless of their 'goodness or badness'.[29] The stand of the legal positivists was that there is no necessary connection between law and morality, while acknowledging that much legislation, such as that emanating from Bentham's reforming impulse, had a moral direction and purpose. Other jurists have taken the view that the primary function of the law is to promote community cohesiveness or solidarity, or specifically to reduce friction by ensuring a high degree of justice in the distribution of social goods.[30] But conflict avoidance and cohesion are pragmatic in purpose rather than moral, unless it is shown that each genuinely adds to the quality of life: that is, is without any underlying immoral intention, for order and stability may suit the long-term purposes of an autocrat who intends eventually to deprive the people of their fundamental liberties.

Other jurists have seen in the traditions of common law a powerful moral influence on social attitudes and values, referring especially to the scholarship of judges, their experience in viewing contentious matters impartially, their capacity for exercising reason and their awareness of human complexities.[31] With this legal and moral tradition, some have viewed with concern newer forms of law such as *environment law*,[32] lest the same rigorous and scholarly traditions should become atrophied: if ready access to courts were granted, cases might multiply to the point where such traditions might be lost altogether under pressure of numbers and popular misunderstandings. Yet it is in the courts themselves, rather than in the opinions of jurists, that the clearest relationships between law, morality and the common good become evident.

For purposes of contrast, and for applications in the next chapter, it is again helpful to state what the administration of law by the courts would be like if both the law and the courts were perfect. In ideal form the law would be unambiguous, so clear and direct in the rules it establishes that it would be open to one interpretation only, and therefore would be completely predictable. So too would be the judges, perfectly moral and rational in their concern for elemental justice, or fairness in the treatment of persons. In this elemental justice (sometimes referred to unnecessarily as 'natural justice', since it refers simply to the fundamental idea of justice), all court hearings would be free of bias and open to all interested persons. In the constancy of fair determinations, and the directness and clarity of rules of law, there would be a stability and public confidence in the law's administration, and a respect for its consistency.

If the rules of law were also *moral* in intent, clearly directed towards a consideration of the interests of persons in the community, the respect for law would be strengthened. But as we have seen, some theory of law is strongly supportive of a separation of law and morality, not only from positivist perspectives but also from the emphasis on the social function of the law in conflict-reduction and stability. Positive law is seen generally as a body of juridical rules traditionally derived from community custom (customary law), cases decided in courts or other tribunals creating precedents for other cases (case-law) and legislatures (statutes). A perfect administration of a perfect system of rules, functioning, that is, in a completely *formal* sense, would ensure that two principles are satisfied: first, the principle of the equitable (*aequum*), second the principle of the good (*bonum*). In this formal sense, the principle of the equitable presents no difficulty in establishing a link between the law and morality, provided that the system of rules is itself moral and not immoral. According to the principle of the equitable, every person and every case coming within its terms would be judged strictly according to the rules, with no exceptions, favours or biases. But in this there is no indication that the rules themselves are necessarily moral in their orientation towards an equal consideration of interests, regardless of who the persons are.[33] Similarly the principle of the good (*bonum*) takes no account of whether the good is a moral good or not. It is no more than the good, or the *purpose*, of the law-maker, and this in a formal sense has no moral significance. On the assumption that the rules are perfectly clear, the courts simply apply them to cases accordingly. But it is for the very reason that the rules are sometimes unclear, or ambiguous, that the judges are empowered and required to give their interpretations of the rules. In bringing together the equitable and the good (with the good in a formal sense morally neutral), judges may be free to interpret statutes on moral principles of a consideration of others' interests and of justice as fairness in the treatment of persons. Their greatest moral contribution though, and certainly their clearest moral opportunities, have been with respect to common law,[34] to which the courts have contributed, tending to decide cases in ways consistent with the moral values pertaining in the community, especially those relating to equity. On the other hand it is statutes which have most relevance to *conservation*: here the courts have an opportunity to contribute to the common good whenever the law is vague, leaving room for interpretative direction towards moral considerations of others' interests, especially in terms of quality of life. It is the gap between ideal law and imperfect law which, as we shall see in the next chapter, may give the courts a strong moral responsibility in relating aspects of conservation to the common good, at least as they perceive it to be.

Judges are not themselves equipped to act in lieu of the Commission on large questions of conservation and the common good, though some judges may be suitable for membership of the Commission. To consider a question such as whether a dam should be built in a wilderness, for instance, in order to provide hydroelectric power to a state, or whether unused land should be appropriated for a national park or a special nature reserve, their talents and experiences would need to be augmented from other sources. Their personal moral influence in some cases has been conspicuous, especially with respect to common law. A judge who comments that an employing authority ought always to give *reasons* for rejection of some applicants is asserting a moral principle of respecting others as *persons*. In cases of brutality towards animals, a judge may contribute to social values in his remarks on animal suffering. In these respects their influence on moral and social values is contributory only, as is that of other prominent public figures whose judgements receive wide publicity.

Even more public, in some countries, is the influence of *constitutional law*, or that derived from constitutions, though not all countries have committed their constitutions to a single document,[35] and except with newer socialist states, constitutions tend to become outmoded and to require more frequent amendments than they receive in order to keep pace with changing social values. Socialist countries use their constitutions extensively in ideological instruction and reform. In China for instance, Article 9 of the constitution has become a ready reference in cases of wilful damage to natural resources or wrongful appropriation of land, proclaiming that 'mineral resources, waters, forests, mountains, grassland, unreclaimed land, beaches and other natural resources are owned by the state, that is, by the whole people . . . 'Article 12 reinforces this by asserting that 'socialist public property is sacred and inviolable', and that its appropriation or damage by whatever means is prohibited.[36] It is an empirical question as to whether the people actually *experience* a common ownership of the land and of all natural resources, and another as to whether this understanding, if it is experienced, provides a moral incentive towards protection and preservation of natural resources by taking the interests of all others into account. It is only the formal structure of such a moral incentive that is offered by the constitution. A third empirical question is whether the young who are indoctrinated in the schools in these measures of their constitution do themselves learn moral attitudes and values from them. Morality and conservation have thus no more than a *prima facie* unity by means of the constitution.

Constitutional law in free enterprise societies is generally less obvious publicly in relating morality and conservation, but there are exceptions. The constitution of Italy is clearly oriented in some of its articles towards the potential quality of life of its citizens, referring to the safeguarding of health as a fundamental right of the individual, protecting the natural resources of the countryside, as well as the cultural heritage of the nation in its historical and artistic aspects. Though its architects clearly had the common good in mind, there remain doubts again as to the efficacy of this constitution in influencing moral attitudes and values relating to conservation. Some of the separate state constitutions of the USA refer specifically to conservation, without any obvious moral connection. For instance, Florida's constitution (as revised in 1968) asserts 'the policy of the State to conserve and protect its natural resources and scenic beauty'.[37] The Italian constitution states that economic enterprise is not to be pursued in any way that endangers public safety or impairs human dignity. This too has paved the way for statutes to put into effect the concern of the government for the common good as its members understand it.

Since a number of national constitutions were drafted before conservation became the social problem it now is, and because amendments have not been made to include conservation matters, the constitutions have often been by-passed by statutes. Throughout most of the free enterprise societies a wide variety of conservation statutes have been enacted, some of which are clearly directed towards a moral purpose. In the Federal Republic of Germany, for instance, one of the declared aims of government is 'to give man the kind of environment he needs for health and life in human dignity',[38] and anti-pollution legislation is one of the means towards this end.

Traditionally national constitutions have been declarations of liberties or assertions of citizens' fundamental rights. Historical circumstances have led to a diminution of their significance generally as focuses for popular rallies, but on some of the largest conservation questions of all, such as nuclear armaments, a new need has developed for bringing the older constitutions up to date, incorporating reforms of political systems so that crucial decisions are made by those in the community most competent to make them.

**Land Use, the Law and the Common Good**

Questions of land use and the common good have been raised in connection with government legislation to establish wildernesses, national parks or nature reserves. It is proposed now to extend these considerations to establish a broader perspective on land use, and to demonstrate once again the need for a body such as a Commission, rather than an elected government, to consider problems that fall within it.

A rational–moral land-use policy would be based on an entirely impartial appraisal of individual interests in the community, set against the comprehensive common good to which individual interests lead. Since the perspective would be moral as well, it would concentrate on the interests of those now living and the likely interests of those in the future, on a principle of justice to all, which is fair treatment to everyone as a person without discrimination. This would be a benevolent perspective as well as a detached one: no one with an interest in land would be making the decisions. It is probable that it would follow Mill's rational principle of recognizing the community (the nation) as the owner of the land, with rights to use in a variety of different ways – some used commercially, some set aside for public use in parks, recreation areas and so forth. But in this rational view, any persons using the land for profit would be accountable to the people for the way the land is used. Therefore access to the courts would be open to any citizen or group of citizens able to present a case against a land-user for damaging the land in a manner which affects the interests of persons in the present, or with suitable argument and evidence, predictively those of the future. Rights to use would also incur obligations to grant open access, with particular reference to land in the countryside, always with appropriate safeguards to protect the interests of lawful users. The dual rights of right to sue, and right of access, would destroy merely historic support for land tenure under common law, with something like a fee simple in English law conferring ownership to a person 'and to his heirs forever'. A rational and moral perspective would acknowledge that social circumstances change, and that if it were ever true that private ownership is required for social cohesion and stability, as Blackstone had claimed in the eighteenth century, it is not necessarily true today. It would not be possible to make rational judgements on land use without thorough research into people's interests and the capacity of the land to satisfy those interests. The second point is as important as the first. In some countries the extent of arable land is limited and of variable value, as is land suitable for cropping or grazing. It is general knowledge that the land itself can be very seriously damaged by erosion if it is used improperly, especially in drought when farmers are under stress for economic return or for basic food supplies. On the basis of the best knowledge available from research, a rational–moral appraisal of national land use would classify land according to recreational, educational or scientific, or economic use, including in an appropriate category an allocation of nature reserves for the potential enjoyment of present and future generations.

One classification which is challengeable under a morality of distributive justice is an allocation of nature reserves to a particular section of the community such as indigenous people. The situation of the Australian aborigine in claims for land rights is relevant in the present context only with respect to restitution settlements from parts of national parks or from areas likely to be conserved for public use. There is no challenge to what can easily be established: first, that Australian aborigines were both wrongly and brutally treated in historical circumstances of two centuries ago when land was taken from them in the original occupation, as well as by pastoralists subsequently;[39] second, that at present aborigines are a disadvantaged group. But to use conservation politically by legislating to give them areas of public land in attempts to wipe the moral slate clean of historical injustices, is to confuse the historical situation with the present one, and to use the second as a false justification for present action to remedy the first. There are clearly opportunities for political gain by appealing to popular emotions, but there are not rational–moral grounds for using conservation as a tool for political ends in this way.[40] It is in such situations that the law governing land use conflicts with the common good as it might be perceived by an impartial, dispassionate and benevolent Commission, giving equal consideration to the interests of all.

# INTERNATIONAL LAW, A GLOBAL MORALITY AND CONSERVATION

If we follow Mill's principle that 'no man made the land', that it is everyone's 'original inheritance' and that therefore 'its appropriation is wholly a question of general expediency',[41] it is clear that a global perspective is needed on land use everywhere. In these circumstances it would be improper to consider conservation of resources solely within national boundaries: impartial and benevolent national Commissions would not confine themselves to national concerns; some of their judgements would necessarily be related to the interests of people of other countries, from the consistently rational–moral perspective each would assume. That consistency is not to be expected of governments in present political systems.

Plato's ideal theory in the *Republic* is not applicable to world government, or even to international cooperation. In the context of his times it is understandable that neither of these prospects occurred to him. Indeed when he eventually wrote the *Laws* his utopian society was to be established on Crete, and was to be cut off almost entirely from contact with all other states. It is because of the vastly different circumstances of today's world that in relatively recent times concepts of international cooperation for the well-being of people everywhere have emerged almost as a matter of necessity. The common good of mankind has been glimpsed by some from moral perspectives, but by others often from a perspective of prudence, such as in international cooperation for mutual security and health.

Commissions of the kind proposed would be capable of an altruistic practical morality, even though they would be preoccupied at times with national concerns. Since each national Commission would be similarly constituted of highly selected persons, using identical criteria, conferences among them would be sufficient to consider those relatively few, but large, matters of the common good properly taken from the control of politicians for the reasons given. It is believed that mutual enthusiasm for matters affecting the whole of mankind, such as nuclear disarmament, would draw the national Commissioners together in such conferences; that recommendations made by them would be a-national in character, with every Commissioner sensitive to any signs of political partiality in others.

The kind of problems facing conferences of national Commissioners would appear to overlap with some of the wide and effective work undertaken by United Nations agencies,[42] but the Commissioners would be concerned fundamentally with world problems affecting the common good of mankind in present and foreseeable future generations. It would be a world voice on *moral* questions, making judgements on the quality of life of human beings, and on preventable suffering of sentient animals. The Commissioners would find themselves devoting more of their time than does the United Nations to problems of posterity, and the moral demands on present generations. Prominent among these questions relating to the reorientation of self-interest of present generations towards a practical consideration of the probable interests of future generations are, first, the world population problem in conjunction with poverty and the degradation of the earth, including widespread desertification; second, international aid on a much larger scale than at present to improve the quality of life in impoverished countries, thereby safeguarding as well the inheritance of a productive earth by future generations; third, preservation and protection of world heritage, both natural and cultural, in the interests of future generations as well as those of the present. In each of these areas the research and activity of United Nations agencies have been invaluable but, as we shall explain in the final chapter, procedural techniques would be developed by Commissioners, with constitutional powers, to make their recommendations mandatory upon governments, as well as to involve the peoples of the world in conjunction with extensive educational programmes. Then their recommendations would be appreciated as being directed towards an improved quality of life generally for mankind.

In some respects the specifically moral thrust of the Commissions would build on international cooperation already achieved for protecting and preserving buildings of world heritage value such as the Acropolis and Borobudur,[43] seen as a prospective contribution to quality of life for those with adequate education to appreciate their cultural significance. The contribution of international law to a global morality will now be considered.

International law is made up of a large number of treaties which are technically known as *conventions*. Unlike the statutes enacted by legislatures it has no enforcement authority to refer to, no police force drawn from signatory states. Although there is an International Court of Justice as one of the United Nations agencies, it decides cases only with the consent of the disputing countries and has no powers of enforcement. International law puts heavy demands on *moral values* and the influence of international opinion; for that reason conservation and morality have prospects of a close relationship, exerting pressures on governments to legislate on relevant matters.

The character of contemporary international law is derived partly from the nature and purpose of the United Nations organization itself, which is not aimed primarily at a form of world government with enforceable powers (despite one or two provisions suggesting this in the UN charter) but rather at promoting a system of attitudes and values stemming from a perception of mutual interests and advantages. The moral influence of the United Nations has become apparent in the increased willingness of nations to cooperate, and to take notice of any world opinion against them. A large number of treaties have been successfully promoted by the United Nations, contributing substantially to international law in our time.[44] Although lacking any enforceability measures, a moral obligation is on signatory states to keep faith, and in a large number of cases they do. (International law defends failure to comply with provisions of treaties in cases where there are significant changes in circumstances after the treaties were originally signed.)[45] Its rules of general application, dependent on the consent of states, lack the binding quality of statutes, and statutes which follow up these rules do much to strengthen the legal effectiveness of international law by means of enforceable support; but *morally* international law stands firmly on its own feet, and is widely respected for it. Like the United Nations and its agencies, trust and responsibility are the main values underlying international law: in this respect there is evident a moral quality of respect for persons. In an imperfect world moral lapses are no more surprising in international law than in any other and scepticism directed at its lack of enforceability is unwarranted.

The Stockholm Conference in 1972 demonstrated that international agreements sometimes extend beyond protection of states' self-interest to an understanding of a wider global morality in which there is a clear consideration of the interests of others. Principle 21 refers to the responsibility of states 'to ensure that activities within their jurisdiction or control do not cause damage to the environment of other states or of areas beyond the limits of national jurisdiction'. The Draft Declaration at the Stockholm Conference referred to the duty of states to notify and inform other states about any of their activities which could have harmful effects on those other states.[46] In 1976 the Barcelona Convention for the Protection of the

Mediterranean Sea Against Pollution again conveyed a distinctly moral purpose, namely, 'to preserve this common heritage for the benefit and enjoyment of present and future generations'. One of the most difficult of all human achievements has been to consider the interests of persons in other states. 'Human Nature appears nowhere less amiable', observed Kant, 'than in the relations of whole nations to each other.' Yet in some provisions of international law we have now come to accept a moral law as transcending state law, adopting Kant's 'principle of Right as determining what the relations between men and States ought to be'.[47] Whether born of prudence and necessity or not, international law is drawing attention to the wide opportunities in our times to consider the interests of persons everywhere, regardless of state, such as in the pollution of the atmosphere and of the oceans.

There is little difference between some of these provisions of international law where the direction is unequivocally moral, and the practical judgements envisaged in conferences of national Commissioners where the stance would be both moral and rational, and as impartial as humanly possible. The stigma from which United Nations agreements may suffer, at times, is related to the Charter, to which reference is sometimes made in international law, and specifically to the political flavour of some of the agreements. (The Charter was itself drafted largely by politicians and expresses ambiguities which still raise questions of interpretation.) By contrast with the occasional lapse into moral exhortation in United Nations conventions, Commissioners would make no paternalistic presumptions: armed with the best knowledge research could give them, they would state their viewpoint openly and directly, without any implied admonition, explaining why states ought to consider the interests of others. The World Charter for Nature might have become a significant policy statement on conservation based on moral principles, but instead is confused on moral questions. It asserts its conviction that 'man must be guided by a moral code of action' from its value assumption that 'every form of life is unique, warranting respect regardless of its worth to man'. This is similar to the false value inferences already observed in some environmental ethics. When it goes on to assert that 'man can alter nature and exhaust natural resources by his action' and therefore must conserve natural resources as a matter of urgency, all semblance of morality is lost: man is now forthrightly pragmatic, considering his own interests. Its tone is mandatory: its principles as set forth 'shall be reflected in the law and practice of each state, as well as at the international level' (Article 14). In contrast, some of the treaties relating to specific aspects of conservation, guided largely by technical experts in the respective fields rather than by political representatives, have a more cooperative and unassuming tone, even if the moral connection is still almost universally lacking.

Yet in a morality encompassing the earth there are many situations where conservation has moral aspects. There are no moral aspects more significant than ascertaining the relevant facts and being in a position to say what does and what does not affect the interests of others, or what fails to consider others as persons. An illustration of some of these will be given in the next chapter.

# SUMMARY

Decision-making has emerged as the most relevant theoretical aspect of administration relating to conservation. The principles of rational–dispositional thinking apply here as they do to all practical judgements.

Political thinking in a party system of government faces complex pressures and the compromising of moral principles. In this situation perceptions of the common good are apt to become distorted by pragmatism. In one-party systems of government again, self-interest and party interest may become dominant over the common good.

The moral demands on politicians are higher than they are able to accommodate within their political systems, even if they were all to have moral intentions on first taking office. Politicians reflect the norms of the community: some realise that it would not be in their interests to govern strictly according to moral principles, subjecting everyone to an equal consideration of interests and regarding each as a separate person.

There are large issues of conservation which may affect the interests of posterity as well as of present generations. Decisions may be best made in these matters on the assumption that they *do*, because with respect to tropical rainforests and the life-forms in them, the protection of nature reserves including wildernesses, national parks and special ecological areas, decisions made on contrary assumptions may be *irreversible*. To wait for complete evidence may be imprudent, for if it could be established that the undoubted interests of some in conservation are generalizable to all people through appropriate education, the common good would not be served by present destruction or neglect of natural and cultural resources. In this situation prudence and practical morality are indistinguishable.

In the relationship between law, morality and conservation, it is judges in the courts who have the greatest power to influence attitudes favourable to conservation in its assumed relationship with quality of life, since they still 'make law' in their interpretations of statutes, and still influence social values at times from the judgements they deliver and from the publicity they receive. In most countries statutes are necessary to give strength to constitutional articles that may relate to conservation. The older state constitutions, drafted before conservation became an issue for quality of life, have not always been amended to bring them into conformity with current social values and purposes.

Mill's liberal views on land ownership and land-use policy are taken as a model for possible land reforms. The right to sue, and the right of access, are both needed for our time.

In the making of international law, states have combined voluntarily, in the main to protect their own interests rather than with a moral perspective on the unity of all people on earth. The various conventions under United Nations sponsorship sometimes do suggest a moral purpose but have little impact on conservation in practice, partly because of the relatively ineffectual relationships between that organization and national governments, influenced partly perhaps in some cases by the style of the conventions as they are communicated to governments.

On large issues of conservation, including the stockpiling of nuclear warheads and preparations for their use at short notice, decision-making needs to be taken out of the hands of politicians and entrusted to the very best persons selected from the community for their capacity to make practical judgements from moral standpoints, their depth of knowledge, experience in rigorous reasoning, confidence, self-mastery and commitment to the common good of the people. It is suggested that each nation needs a Commission of such persons. This raises many administrative and constitutional questions. Some of these are deferred to the final chapter, particularly the question of relationships with elected governments. But having decided now who are unsuitable both to perceive the common good, and to make practical judgements on it and who alone *are* suitable in each respect, we shall return in the next chapter to the notion of *quality of life* as it might be served by practical conservation measures.

# 4 Conservation and the Quality of Life: Practical Problems and Obstacles to Moral Solutions

When 'quality of life' is applied generally to all members of a national or world community it may refer vaguely to the *common good*. In this description it does not refer to any objective standard, but rather to one which is subjectively determined in particular historical circumstances and within a pattern of particular social conditions and values. What is acceptable as a quality of life in one society, or at one period of history, may not be acceptable in another. If there is anything in common to all of these judgements of quality of life it is an adequacy of the basic necessities of life. But 'quality of life' is more than a descriptive expression: it is also normative or prescriptive. It conveys the notion that the enjoyments or satisfactions to which it refers are those everyone *ought* to have as a person – a judgement which conveys an appreciation of a *potential* common good. Further, it is normative in its insistence that some persons in every country, such as those living at bare subsistence level, ought to have a higher standard of living, one which enables them to enjoy a basic quality of life enjoyed by others.

When quality of life refers to natural or cultural objects which are claimed to have the potential for contributing to it, it becomes falsely objectified. There is no necessary connection between any object such as a river, lake, mountain, historical monument or work of art, and a quality of life. The determination is to be made at the other end, in an empirical enquiry into individuals' interests, values and capacities.

A natural feature such as a tropical rainforest or the Great Barrier Reef could be established as contributory to the general quality of life, or the common good, only by showing that *all* individuals (the population would of course be sampled), or potentially all, given that a minority could be brought to appreciate it by education, find that it adds to quality of life. The great difficulty and complexity of ascertaining the kind of information needed for sound judgements on this question would be challenging to a Commission of the kind proposed, but in some circumstances it might reach a decision, as we have explained, without complete research evidence, in order to prevent irreversible action that might turn out later, according to the tenor of evidence that *is* available, to be contrary to the common good.

The ideal theory presented in the previous chapter will now be brought forward to this, with the model of rational–moral decision-making in particular, and perfect law and administration contrasted with imperfections in practice. But as we move closer to practical or concrete situations, the gap between perfection and imperfection will be seen to be wider than that already foreshadowed. This will be shown to have two main sources: first, the complexities of conservation problems, with various economic, political and social pressures confronting any attempt to reach any single-minded moral solutions; second, human limitations – referring both to moral and rational imperfections, and to imperfections in command of relevant knowledge and in administrative skills as well. The plan is to consider first, moral and rational fallibility in decision-making; second, unequal economic and social conditions between developing and developed countries; third, industrialization and technology, leading especially to industrial pollution of the atmosphere, effects on soils of agricultural pollution, and urbanization problems; fourth, world population and a sustainable level of demands on natural resources; fifth, conflicting political systems, international rivalry and the nuclear threat; sixth, the complexity of the total conservation problem, as an inference from preceding considerations.

## MORAL AND RATIONAL FALLIBILITY IN DECISION-MAKING

Occasional mistakes in practical judgements are to be expected, even from Commissioners. But on questions of conservation, politicians and administrative agencies who currently make the judgements have demonstrated bias and a yielding to influential pressure groups of more than incidental occurrence; deception, reluctance to act or, conversely, acting clumsily and hastily without seeking expert advice or failing to give due weight to it if it has been received. Patterns of this kind leave no doubt that some administrative misjudgements concerning conservation are deliberate, while others stem from insufficient relevant information or from administrative ineptitude. Together they constitute one of the major impediments to rational–moral decision-making on conservation. In the instances that follow, the contrast between decisions actually made (by politicians or their agencies) and those likely to be made by Commissioners with the qualities attributed to them, needs to be kept constantly in mind. They would be operating as close as is humanly possible to the ideal of decision-making as outlined in the previous chapter.

### Political Bias and Deception

Political bias and deception reflect improper intentions on conservation by governments and their agencies. In the USA for instance, air pollution control legislation has given industry substantial representation on commissions or boards for carrying out legislation – representation to the very industries, on some occasions, against which pollution complaints have been made.[1] Air pollution control legislation has frequently protected industry. Loopholes in legislation have enabled industry to continue with a level of pollution which has been opposed by public health interests, making convenient use of provisions such as 'allowance to be made for economic feasibility'. In cases of water pollution, legislation has again been industry-protective by an over-narrow specification of wastes likely to cause pollution.[2] Because of their responsiveness to pressure groups representing special interests, there has developed a distrust of administrative agencies established to protect the common good in matters of conservation.[3] Degradation of the earth has occurred on a large scale through activities of industries such as mining, supported by governments, and without any widespread distribution of benefits. The extent to which administrative decision-making bends the interests of the many for the sake of the influential few is at times extraordinary: in one extreme case, sportsmen persuaded authorities to poison reservoirs established as public water supplies in order to destroy certain species of fish and to have them replaced with other species preferred by the sportsmen.[4]

It has been suggested that some of the conservation questions affecting the common good are too large to be resolved by governments. The situation is aggravated, however, when the task of defining the *common good* (more commonly the less thoroughly investigated 'public interest') is delegated to agencies whose members lack the very demanding qualifications for the task which would be required of Commissioners. Federal agencies in the USA have used 'public interest' deceptively to represent and to achieve what are fundamentally their own interests. When they purport to be expert and professional managers, some are able to deceive the public and Congress too into believing that policies they pursue are authentically in the public interest at least, even if thoughts of the common good are beyond their capacities.[5]

Some of the commonest instances of deception in decision-making on conservation matters occur in those countries which call for Environmental Impact Statements (abbreviated conventionally to EISs), ostensibly to weigh the claims of development against those of conservation. While some of these statements have served a useful purpose of breaking down the secrecy that has often surrounded negotiations between developers and administrators, especially when decisions have been challenged by citizens in the courts (in the USA in particular), there have been other instances of deception by administrators who have made agreements with developers, and concealed them from the public until irreparable damage has occurred. Regardless of the EISs, development projects usually proceed.[6] As in all acts of deliberate deception, decision-makers who act in secrecy and make only a token acknowledgement of public interests in conservation, are guilty of moral offences against the standard principles of equal consideration of interests and respect for all as persons: no persons are to be held in contempt or undervalued, or treated as immature, or merely as lay persons as opposed to professionals, or in any other way considered as unworthy of serious attention for the views they hold.

Professional administrators who wish to trifle with public opinion, interests and values by means of EISs, may find opportunities for evasion and deception in some of the inherent weaknesses of the EIS system. The chief of these is that in many circumstances any reliable judgement as to whether a development ought to proceed can be made only with much greater resources than administrators have at their disposal (or than developers are prepared to expend if the responsibility is theirs). Pursued thoroughly, the complex EIS might take years to produce in some particular cases, after the collection of all relevant scientific and social evidence. If developers are instructed to prepare an EIS they may engage consultants who, once in their paid employment, are seldom prepared to oppose their plans and policies. Weaknesses of administrative guidelines are exploited at will. In the end the EIS usually presents partial, selective and superficial information based largely on subjective impressions. This is the kind of information which sometimes suits administrators and developers in attempts to reach time-saving compromises.[7]

## Ineptitude and Compromise

Government leaders and their administrative agencies may act in other ways which disregard the moral requirement of a practical consideration of others' interests: they may assume more power than is warranted in matters affecting the common good, and may act too slowly or too hastily, in each case holding in contempt the interests and values of others. In Australia as in other countries, it has not been unusual for a minister to defy public opinion on a conservation issue, with very controversial consequences. Where the common good is concerned, government power may be exercised improperly.[8] National governments may act too slowly on questions of moral import, knowingly organizing their priorities and their budgets to favour more publicly appealing courses of action. Nowhere is this more evident than in questions of international morality which relate to conservation questions as well. In the Sudano-Sahelian region the immensity of the world problem of desertification, drought and famine has not been recognized in moral proportion by national political leaders. The Executive Director of the United Nations Environment Programme reported the year 1983 as 'a steady forward grind against indifference, ignorance and miserliness'. He saw ample evidence of a lack of moral commitment by political leaders, prepared on the one hand to sit down and discuss how best to protect and improve the environment, on the other hand using much of their financial, technological and human resources on defence. He detected a lack of political will and determination to give practical consideration to the interests of others in desperate circumstances in other countries. He regarded actual assistance as far below what was needed. In this situation the rapid increase in poverty was seen to be paralleled by an intensification of land degradation.[9] The global common good is clearly at issue, though either unperceived or ignored by governments, largely in their own interests. Rational–moral decision-making requires that we ascertain the relevant facts and act on them. Political leaders who are given these facts by scientists are sometimes slow to act, if they act at all, whenever the costs to industry or to the economy of the nation are appreciable. The management of the nation is usually in pursuit of short-term economic objectives. Considerable medical research has been conducted into polluting chemicals that are harmful to health; some are harmful to plant and animal life in nature reserves and elsewhere. Yet sometimes action decisions on such matters are delayed to serve sectional interests.[10]

In some instances relating to both morality and conservation a decision *not* to act may be the more justifiable. Certainly it is preferable to acting hastily on evidence that is ill-researched or emotionally-biased, as it is when farmers are given approval to use desperate remedies against insect pests. Indiscriminate use of DDT has caused incalculable suffering to sentient animals which may have been avoided in every case by using alternative control procedures before the pest invasions presented a dramatic threat to livelihood.[11]

The political propensity to compromise is expressed sometimes as *balance*, which is apt to be used conveniently and euphemistically for economic priority. The concept is so imprecise as to invite self-interested political rationalization, or a capitulation to the strongest pressure group. A government land-use policy which presumes to judge what is the common good by invariably seeing two opposing forces – conservation of natural resources and economic utilization – begs the question on what the best rational–moral solution is to a particular land-use problem.

Human fallibility is not to be confused with moral fault. The above instances illustrate the importance of motive or intention in practical morality: if the end of government is the *common good*, and if political leaders or their agents act intentionally in ways which are clearly contrary to the common good, or even potentially and remotely opposed to it, to that extent they are acting immorally. Administrative ineptitude may be due to inadequate education or training, or to inexperience: in each of these cases it is morally neutral, all other things equal. But administrative action which is lazy-minded or apathetic in the sense of the agent not bothering to ascertain information that might be relevant, though his training has made him aware of relevant possibilities, is morally negligent. In the administration of matters pertaining to conservation, such cases are not infrequent. Protected species of birds have been overlooked when a government authority, responsible for regulating the flow of waters in certain rivers and wetlands, has cut off the supply to a large breeding area midway through the breeding season, causing many thousands of birds to perish.[12]

## Fallibility of the Law

The fallibility of the law, including the judges and the courts, offers further obstacles to moral solutions of conservation problems. Some of the inadequacies have no obvious or consistent moral connection, such as a vagueness of the statutes themselves, a disjunction of legislation and its enforcement, the traditional conservatism of the law and the practical difficulties of the courts. Other instances *do* have obvious moral connections, such as laws against pollution or vandalism, and especially a failure to ensure a complete independence of the judiciary from the influence of elected governments, or resistance in some states to granting citizens standing to sue, by which they might defend what they see as the common good against the force of influential developers. The first category will be given brief mention only before turning to the more morally relevant second category with clear moral connections.

There have been instances in most countries of statutes so incomplete and unclear that they may be turned to serve interests unsympathetic to conservation, and even contrary to practical morality. Inadequacies of legislation may be due to nothing more than the unsuitability of governments for the task. In the latter part of the sixteenth century Montaigne described French law as 'a true testimony of human imbecility, so full it is of contradiction and error'.[13] Three centuries later, Mill found English law little better, especially property law which had 'extreme uncertainty' and was encumbered with a 'maze of technicalities, which make it impossible for any one . . . to possess a title to land which he can positively know to be unassailable'.[14] The law according to Montaigne was simply a product of unclear minds, but to Mill the lack of clarity had a hidden purpose: the Commons, still influenced in part by landowners, resisted amendments to the law in order to protect their own individual titles. It is by no means certain, then, that the vagueness of statutes is unintentional. Not only vagueness, but conservatism in the law as well may serve the interests of those in power, and in some instances these are strongly inclined towards economic return rather than towards conservation.[15]

One of the recurring criticisms of law as it relates to conservation is of a disjunction of legislation and its enforcement. One jurist has commented on some of the ways in which a congruence of the two may be destroyed, including inaccessibility of the law, as well as 'bribery, prejudice, indifference, stupidity, and the drive toward personal power'. From a rational–moral standpoint no person can be expected to obey a law that is unintelligible, or is contradicted by another relevant rule, or is so changeable that few know what the law is at any particular time.[16] A number of countries have reported a weakness in enforcing both common law and statutes, such as in the pollution of rivers and estuaries in England and Wales.[17]

Apart from the obvious difficulty faced by judges in interpreting unclear statutes, another significant practical difficulty is that the courts are frequently too hard-pressed to give the time needed to consider wide questions of conservation and the common good. While they have been tolerant and impartial on some questions relating to Environmental Impact Statements, in some instances insisting that alternatives to the development plans proposed be more fully explored, it is not their practicable task to give proper attention to matters of the *common good*, with wide-sweeping implications for both present and future generations. The judiciary no less than the legislature needs therefore to leave this largest of all political and moral questions to an appropriate Commission.

It is because a Commission would necessarily consider opinions of individuals on what the common good is, that the interpretative opinions of judges on the question would never be dismissed as unimportant. But every citizen is in principle in the same situation. As a person he is to be respected for whatever views he has on the common good, and a Commission would be attentive to every viewpoint within the limits of practicability. This raises at once an important moral question of the attitude of the law and the courts to the right of a citizen to sue in court to protect what he perceives as a threat to the public interest, which he tends to identify vaguely with the common good. Legally the issue is one of 'standing to sue', or *locus standi*, which in most countries is resisted by the courts whenever claims are made by private persons that they are acting for the public good with respect to protection and preservation of the environment. The conflict between the law and morality is apparent. Every citizen has a moral right to contest a conservation issue which he believes, and can support with suitable evidence and argument, to be a threat to the public interest, even though it is unlikely that he will comprehend fully what the common good is. The courts are to some extent justified in their reluctance to grant access to private plaintiffs allegedly supporting a public issue, and a suitable regulatory control would always be needed to prevent a flood of cases which are ill-prepared, emotional rather than rational, prejudiced and even asserting a private interest in the guise of a public one. The most conspicuous achievements in granting standing to sue in conservation questions have been in the USA. Described as 'the single most important development in recent administrative law', the courts have been opened up to citizens and citizen groups, both at hearing and at appellate stages.[18] Most suits are directed towards *protecting standards* in conservation rather than towards enforcement, standards relating to pollution of drinking water for instance, to waste controls and air pollution. In these matters it has not been unusual for courts to uphold the non-quantifiable social values of health, safety and comfort against the readily quantifiable financial costs to industry of pollution control.[19] Standing to sue therefore may contribute to safeguarding the common good. Its impediments are practical, not moral.

The civil law of some European countries has recognized various associations similar to public interest groups in the USA which oppose continuing pollution, and there is a slowly increasing acknowledgement in case law of a right to sue. Sometimes suits are rejected on the grounds that appellants do not have a specific legal interest.[20] Other countries such as Australia are still reluctant to recognize standing to sue on questions of conservation,[21] following principles adopted in England and other common law countries. Even in the USA, access to courts has been granted mainly by judges' interpretations of statutes: common law there too, as in England, Australia and elsewhere, is inadequate to offer standing to sue; it is concerned with matters of conservation mainly when they are related in some way to ownership or legal occupation of land. These shortcomings of the law are an indication of the need for statutory reform to recognize the moral and rational justification for standing to sue, for assuming that groups have strong reasons to support claims to be acting in the public interest they have a moral right as persons to be given a fair hearing, regardless of what a more thoroughgoing Commission would determine as the common good. In so far as they might stimulate public interest in large conservation matters which are raised before the courts, their contribution to the work of Commissions in their efforts for the common good might in some cases be significant.

There have been ample indications generally that social values are not clear on some conservation issues. To that extent conflicting public opinion is usually of little support to the courts in reaching their decisions. That in turn justifies further 'judge-made law' through the interpretations which the judges make. While in some instances that has been beneficial, as in opening the courts (especially in the USA) to greater citizen access, in other instances it has left the way open for an expression of judges' personal values which may or may not serve the common good. The worst aspect of this situation is that it ignores the ideal of a judiciary independent of the legislature.[22] Another possible consequence is that on questions of conservation the conservatism and relative predictability of the law are surrendered for decisions that become a matter of particular judges' tastes and preferences. (That was the general situation, as Hume expressed it in the eighteenth century, when 'the preference given by the judge is often founded more on taste and imagination than on any solid argument'.[23])

The obvious moral connections between the law and conservation with respect to pollution and vandalism require little explanation. Each presents a further scope for fallibility in decision-making. Pollution will receive further attention in the area of industrialization and technology. When it is clearly related to quality of life through presenting risks to the environment (as well as to health), and at the same time is tolerated long after it has been brought to the notice of governments or their agencies, it may be another case of moral negligence, in which event the interests of others are not given the concerned consideration which practical morality requires; or it may be an instance of political deception, where those with power give way to the interests of industry which are concerned predominantly with economic return, resisting any pressures which might add to their production costs – as regulatory pollution measures generally do, at least initially.

Vandalism is so widespread that it is almost a universal problem in the administration of national parks and other nature reserves the world over. By definition the vandal is a destroyer of valued property (which may be something belonging to the natural or cultural heritage) who acts either wilfully or ignorantly. Therefore law enforcement frequently faces a problem of determining guilt. From a deterministic stance, courts might take the view that the accused is not responsible for his acts. (There have been some judges who have universalized this principle to embrace all offenders and all types of offence.) But in the law of England, and of those countries which have inherited, with their own modifications, the English comon law system, there is a strong influence of the notion of *mens rea* applying to criminal law. That is, there is an understanding that the onus is on the courts to establish that the accused had an intention to commit the offence, or a knowledge of the wrongfulness of the act. In the case of vandalism the *mens rea* is often difficult to establish. Fundamentally the problem may be seen as an educational one, of modifying existing attitudes and values relating to public property. If there were strong psychological evidence of anti-social aggression, with an impulse to punish society retributively for the accused's limited prospects for employment or future life-satisfaction, the courts might well wonder whether the vandal is clearly responsible for his action, or whether the moral responsibility lies with society itself. This perplexing situation may be aggravated by national parks' management policy, which is often oriented towards public cooperation rather than law enforcement that might aggravate an already sensitive public relations problem. There are probably many instances where law enforcement is weak, and where vandals are taking advantage of the situation and at the same time harming the interests of others who use national parks. In this sense it is not only the vandal who raises moral questions in acting sometimes with intent to cause damage to public property, and also with full knowledge of the law and of the harm he is causing to others with different interests, attitudes and values; in some cases it may also be managers of national parks, who in their concessions to vandals may be giving too little consideration to the interests of others in the community. As with many social problems, the solution is complex and probably long term: re-education of attitudes and values may need to be preceded by a reform of social conditions, as we shall consider further in the next chapter, with a more equitable distribution of social goods, including opportunities for education.

# DEVELOPING AND DEVELOPED COUNTRIES

We now move from national concerns of morality and conservation, with their roots sometimes in fallibility in decision-making, to the wider sphere of global morality in so far as both morality and conservation are again related to it. We shall consider first the moral situation with respect to the developing countries, then the conservation situation which is often inextricably involved with it.

When Aristotle saw the common good as the end of government, his perspective was national, rather than international. There was not then, and never has been since, any world government. As we have seen, in both the *Republic* and the *Laws* Plato also saw politics and morality as a matter for the state. The present world situation is a broad reflection of the separate state situation: as in each nation there are rich and poor, some acutely poor, so there are some nations in the same predicament of imbalance in relation to other nations. From a moral standpoint of a practical consideration of others' interests, within any one nation of extremes of wealth and poverty it is obvious that the quality of life which some enjoy ought to be distributed so that, at the very least, and as a start to a more comprehensive moral solution, the extremes of poverty are removed. From the same moral standpoint, but looking outwardly from any one nation to the world of nations, exactly the same imperative follows: all are persons, all people of the earth, and all deserve an equality of consideration of interests, beginning with the removal of extremes of poverty wherever they might occur. It is very unlikely, for reasons given, that political leaders preoccupied with their respective national concerns, would be in a position to give adequate attention to such a far-reaching demand. Rather it is a task for national Commissions, specially prepared intellectually and morally, and with a demonstrated propensity for rational–moral thinking rather than for political thinking. For the stance of benevolent impartiality towards people everywhere is of such unique challenge, with heavy demands for an accurate knowledge of the world situation, that only a select few from each nation might be expected to have the required capacity. Some members of United Nations agencies have already demonstrated a capacity for this work, and so have some judges and leaders of humanitarian organizations, so that composition of national Commissions, given an expectation of a degree of fallibility even with the best of moral intentions, is by no means beyond realization.

From the purely moral perspective the judgement of human need in desperate situations of impoverishment is similarly not difficult to achieve. At this point the national Commissions' recommendations would be such as could be made by anyone from a moral stance. Complexities arise when practicable priorities are to be organized, for every developed nation has a problem of some acute poverty within the boundaries of its immediate political concerns. Further complexities arise as soon as the most acutely impoverished receive proper attention, for no nation in human history, however affluent, has had sufficient resources to cope with all the demands placed on it internally. This situation of limited resources everywhere, which Hume considered to be a fundamental moral premiss, makes the impartial task of national Commissions so much more complex, heavily dependent as their recommendations must be on their broad acceptance within the nations of the world before implementation could be assured.

The high level of serious poverty in the world is undisputed. Reliable estimates indicate that the problem is worsening. By the year 2000, it seems likely that 850 million people may be living in what is described as 'absolute poverty'. Over 17 per cent of all people in the world may be affected.[24] Nearly half of the rural population of developing countries are living below the poverty line as determined by the Food and Agriculture Organization.[25] Although poverty lines may vary slightly according to the economic and social criteria used, those falling below them are generally prone to malnutrition and disease, and forced to live in substandard settlements. Quality of life in these circumstances falls below any minimum demanded by the moral notion of persons.[26] Most governments of the world resist diverting substantial resources to the removal of substandard human settlements: to them these constitute one of the 'unproductive' social problems, yielding no obvious political or economic return.[27] The international problem of poverty is far too serious to be resolved internally by the respective governments: the demands of morality are above political concerns. When three-fifths of those living in developing countries do not have ready access to safe drinking water, and three-quarters of them have no sanitary facilities of any kind, it is evident that people of developed countries have a *moral* obligation to help those in situations where quality of life is at such a precarious level.[28] The problem of poverty is not being seen in isolation: it is related to conservation, as we shall explain.

Moral questions are raised even in granting aid to the developing countries. Just as doing nothing shows no practical consideration of the interests of other persons, so in some circumstances doing something may be deceptively self-regarding and equally contrary to practical morality. While scientists and economists may help substantially as advisers, the moral thrust comes more clearly when aid is of such proportions that impoverished people of developing nations are helped to develop self-respect in managing their own affairs, without paternalistic gestures of any kind from affluent countries, and particularly when they are not obliged to accept humiliating political conditions. The national Commissions would, in their benevolence and impartiality, rise above such political restrictions on aid. Well-meaning economic advisers too have been morally insensitive enough to make recommendations for developing countries from the standpoint of developed countries, without making the moral effort to see the developing countries from *their own* standpoint, struggling to achieve subsistence living for many of their people.[29]

Nothing has offended the self-esteem of developing countries more than have recommendations from developed countries for worldwide strategies on *conservation* which would include some sacrifice from developing countries, those least in a position to make them. From *their* standpoint, the greatest harm to the environment generally has been caused by developed countries. Some suspect that developed countries wish to restrict development elsewhere for their own advantage. Almost all the developing countries are insistent that they need help first of all to develop sufficiently to provide basic necessities of life for their people.[30] They are aware of having an unequal share of the earth's resources; any constraint on their development would simply compound their relative disadvantage. They have no wish to remain economically underdeveloped, or socially deprived of a quality of life which they see others enjoying. As social goods need to be more equitably distributed throughout the world, so do social burdens, including the responsibility for conservation measures to restore the damage to the environment incurred largely by developed countries.[31] This is the tenor of reaction from some of the developing countries to suggestions for cooperation to protect and preserve the natural resources of the earth: it is 'a rich man's problem'.[32] It is also a measure of the insensitivity of some in developed countries to the global moral situation: the obligations of the developed to help the developing, especially those struggling to live as persons. When impoverished countries are asked to cooperate in setting the global conservation house in order, they are apt to conclude that developed countries are by-passing the prior moral problem.[33] Since the community of persons is worldwide, our moral obligations have the same dimensions.

This connection between morality and conservation in relations between developing and developed countries is immensely more significant when the direct effects of impoverishment on conservation are considered. A basis of factual evidence is again needed before practical moral judgements may be made. In the last few decades poverty in Africa and Asia has led to overstocking and overgrazing. When vegetation has been eaten out, erosion has followed. Soil degradation leads frequently to desertification, which now affects the livelihoods of 700 million people in the world.[34] It is no overstatement that 'poverty is by far the most important cause of environmental destruction'.[35] Because of the intense demand for firewood, wide areas have been denuded of trees.[36] At present desertification threatens more than one-third of the land surface of the earth; one in five of the world's population are affected.[37] Social and economic reforms are needed, achievable only with substantial aid from developed countries. The impoverished themselves are unable to stem the continuing tide of desertification, as in the case of the southward extension of the Sahara. They do not have the resources for the obvious work of restoration, using techniques of known effectiveness. The earth is ours as much as theirs, ours as it is the inheritance of future generations of our kin. This entails a common responsibility not to use it beyond sustainable levels, as well as a common moral obligation to help the acutely impoverished who are often contributing greatly, though unwittingly and unavoidably, to the destruction of natural resources. But from their standpoint, as equal sharers of the earth, there are questions to be raised of the developed countries on morality and conservation which in the long term may be of even greater magnitude.

# THE DEVELOPED COUNTRIES: INDUSTRIALIZATION AND TECHNOLOGY

It is both the industrial and the technological revolutions which have led to some countries being designated 'developed'. In our time such countries are relatively prosperous economically, chiefly because of their capacity to adapt to new technologies and to produce a large range of goods for the competitive markets of the world. In this aggressive competition for markets, successful industries tend to feed on themselves, generating a seemingly never-ending cycle of increasing demand for goods, extending production and extending markets, with seldom a thought for struggling industries in the developing world. These characteristics of growth economies may be seen as a reflection of individual man's insatiable desire. In Aristotle's rueful comment, at one time 'two obols was pay enough'; now men want more and more (*Politics*, 1267$^b$). The fundamental weakness of this consistent pattern has been a failure of distributive justice: the undoubted social benefits of development to some have not been well distributed. From the standpoint of a global morality, instead of a sharing of the earth's resources, competition has brought conflict, and in the process *conservation* has been at risk in ways which relate to the interests of present and future generations.

While on the one hand it is industrial development which has led to impressive improvements in communications, transport and amenities of many kinds, including the establishment of national parks and other nature reserves, there is an adverse side to development which is expressed in relations between morality and conservation. This will be considered particularly in connection with pollution of the atmosphere, and pollution of soil and water. Each of these constitutes a moral threat to quality of life inasmuch as both industry and governments, in their concentration on economic strength, may give inadequate attention to the interests of the community generally.

## Pollution of Atmosphere

If a global morality considers the interests of persons everywhere on earth, as well as those of sentient animals with respect to preventable suffering, it must be concerned with effects of industrial development on the condition of the life-supporting biosphere (the earth's crust and the mixture of gases in the atmosphere surrounding the earth). Impairment of the biosphere may affect the quality of life on the earth; even if it is the quality of life of future generations only that is likely to be affected because of long-term effects of present industrial practices, there may be a present moral problem. Judgements as to whether a moral problem exists can be made only by reference to empirical evidence. The first evidence is on carbon dioxide in the atmosphere, the second on sulphur dioxide and nitrogen oxides in the atmosphere.

The source of increased quantities of carbon dioxide in the atmosphere is largely the chimney stacks of industries. The burning of fossil fuels – coal, oil and gas – releases carbon dioxide into the atmosphere, and because of the great expansion of industrial activity in developed countries in the last few decades, it has been suggested by some scientists that if the burning of fossil fuels continues at the present rate the amount of carbon dioxide in the atmosphere will increase to such an extent that it will block the normal escape of some of the earth's heat into space, resulting in a general rise in the earth's temperature. At this point there is considerable speculation on the climatic changes that might occur, and in what ways these would be likely to affect human habitations. If global temperatures were to rise by as much as 5°C, it has been suggested that in a few decades the melting of the West Antarctic icesheet would raise sea levels by as much as five metres. Cities such as London and New York, and others relatively close to sea level, would be flooded. In the southern hemisphere too some of the consequences would be severe. Parts of northern Australia would probably be flooded by greatly increased monsoonal rains. In some areas droughts would become more frequent. Since warming would be greatest at the Poles, the temperature differences between these regions and the equator would be lessened, affecting the entire atmospheric circulation of the globe, and altering climate in many different ways.[38]

Scientists invariably caution that much is yet to be learned about the probable climatic effects of rises in the carbon dioxide level. What is clear is that the level has already increased by about 10 per cent. Further, substantial scientific opinion holds that a doubling of the carbon dioxide level could occur in fifty to eighty years unless there is a radical departure from the use of fossil fuels. There is as yet no firm evidence of global warming: some scientists expect this to come as the carbon dioxide level rises progressively higher.[39] On the assumption that within a few decades scientists will understand these relationships sufficiently to be able to predict climatic changes with greater confidence, and that their recommendations point clearly to a move away from coal, oil and gas as energy sources for industry, a decade or two would probably be needed to phase out these fossil fuels. The complexity of the total situation is another instance of the need for a Commission to undertake the decision-making. While scientists provide the evidence, and politicians tend to pursue short-term objectives, a Commission would examine the total situation from a rational–moral standpoint, considering the needs of industry within the framework of the quality of life everywhere on earth. It would relate present needs to future needs, so that proper consideration is given to the interests of posterity. It would appreciate the extent to which the problem is related to conservation as part of a practical morality. Radical climatic changes, with floods or droughts in ecological areas where previously they were not encountered as part of regular climatic patterns, would not be expressions of Heraclitean change to which all things in nature are subject; these would be man-made, or more accurately, made by those with interests in industry (including the industrial interests of socialist states). In radical climatic changes the preservation of many species of plant and animal life would be at risk, even entire nature reserves in some cases. But while these effects of carbon dioxide pollution on conservation and quality of life are at present partly speculative, the effects of other atmospheric pollutants which we shall now consider – sulphur dioxide and nitrogen oxides – are more obvious.

As industrial emissions, sulphur dioxide and oxides of nitrogen are converted to sulphuric acid and nitric acids in the atmosphere, and when blown by winds from the sources of emission may fall as acid rain on countries hundreds of miles away. This again is a problem of global morality, as well as of conservation. If one country's atmospheric pollution drifts into another country, leaving the country of origin relatively free of pollution, clearly political boundaries have no relevance to morality: persons and their environment are being affected somewhere. (There may be a serious effect on health, as when high concentrations of sulphur dioxide in the London smog of 1952 are believed by some to have contributed largely to the deaths of about 4000 people. But again, the relevant facts need to be established before judgements are made.)

The burning of fossil fuels is largely responsible for high levels of sulphur dioxide in some countries, especially the burning of coal and fuel-oil, so the problem is highest in densely-populated industrial cities. People living near fuel-burning factories are especially at risk, as are those who live near smelters. When metals such as copper, lead, zinc and nickel are extracted from their ores by smelting, large quantities of sulphur dioxide are again emitted. Not only may the health of near-by inhabitants suffer, but in some cases that of sentient animals as well. A major moral and conservation problem may occur as the aesthetic aspect of quality of life is impaired by the slow destruction of vegetation. (For a quarter of a century after 1896 the inhabitants of a town in Tasmania witnessed thickly wooded hillsides transformed into desolation. Unburnt sulphur and sulphur dioxide were emitted from the chimneys of smelters, and acid rain fell. For miles around all vegetation was killed: the countryside took on the wasted appearance of a dead planet.[40])

As an atmospheric pollutant sulphur dioxide is not a global threat in the same sense as carbon dioxide is: its effects are much more localized.[41] The main moral and conservation problem relates to the effects of acid rain, and the responsibilities which both governments and industries have for protecting health and natural resources contributing to quality of life. In some industrial cities the local problem has been largely solved by insisting that power stations and factories which burn fossil fuels have tall chimneys. Then people living close to them are not seriously affected, because the ground-level pollution is small. Instead, the sulphur dioxide and nitrogen oxides are emitted high enough into the atmosphere for them to be dispersed.

When dispersed internationally, there is at the same time an international moral and conservation problem. It is believed that quality of life in terms of health and convenience has been impaired already in a number of countries far from the point of pollution origin, that sentient animal life has suffered and been destroyed, and that natural resources related to enjoyment of life have been damaged.[42] Some of the effects of acid rain on forests have been apparent, though because of the beneficial effects of nitrogen on plant growth the extent of damage on balance is uncertain. Where forests are relatively close to large industrial areas, such as the Ruhr in the Federal Republic of Germany, the effects of acid rain are believed to be much more severe, though recent evidence is conflicting. To some the loss of quality of life aesthetically is appreciable.

The rational–moral judgement of a Commission is likely to be both more knowledgeable and more just to all of those who suffer from the effects of acid rain than are political judgements, because of the differences between moral thinking and political thinking observed in the previous chapter. Once again it might insist on an extension of scientific research in all advanced countries on the effects of pollution from sulphur dioxide and nitrogen oxides, as well as on alternative sources of energy, especially since the burning of fossil fuels accounts for most of the pollution.[43] Conferences of national Commissioners might recommend that offending nations compensate those whose quality of life has been demonstrably impaired elsewhere, provided that the sources of pollution are confirmed. Preferably the problem would be solved by the relevant national Commission, holding both industry and government morally responsible for continuing economic activity which seriously affects the interests of some both at home and abroad. Administratively it might recommend that any disjunction of law and enforcement be rectified, or that the law be reformed to control self-interested activities of industry which are not acting in the public interest, but rather creating a public nuisance.[44]

**Soil and Water Pollution**

Acid rain does not affect soils as much as waters, but some soils are more vulnerable than others (especially those with a low lime content). Further sources of industrial pollution of soil and waters will now be considered. Some of these are caused by industries directing waste chemicals into waters, some by mining industries building up tailings and allowing a run-off from them into rivers, streams or lakes. But some of the most serious pollution has been caused by the use of pesticides by farmers or local government agencies, and this pollution will be considered first.

In the heavy use of chemicals such as DDT, farmers may be unaware of the most insidious consequences of their actions. There may be contamination of groundwater, for instance, carried beneath the surface for miles until it emerges at points as springs and is used for drinking by humans or by sentient animals, or even runs off into streams and rivers where again the contamination is unsuspected. It is probable that only a few farmers and others who use DDT for its short-term benefits are aware of the complexity of the soil itself, with its bacteria and other life-forms bringing about a decay of dead plant and animal forms and adding to the nitrogen content of the soil needed for plant growth; and of the food-chain including earthworms – themselves beneficial to the soil – which might lead to the destruction of birdlife through poisoning, with potential consequences for quality of human life.[45]

In the discharge of chemical wastes into rivers or seas the moral connection is clear but the conservation connection not so obvious. One of the most widely-publicized cases is that of Minamata in Japan, where a chemical factory discharged inorganic mercury (converted to methylmercury) into the nearby sea, poisoning fish and unsuspecting humans who partly depended on fish for food. The Rhine and Mississippi rivers have also been polluted by toxic chemicals. Both rivers are used for drinking water by humans and animals.[46] The connection with conservation and morality lies in the threat to sentient animal life, and especially to the quality of life of humans through the pursuit of self-interest by industry. A similar consideration applies to the neglect of tailings from disused mines, where water percolates through the deposits, dissolves heavy metals such as copper, and eventually washes down into waterways. Such pollution destroys life, while conservation aims to preserve and protect it, and practical morality considers the interests of others.

A more obvious connection between conservation and morality is with respect to non-renewable energy resources, such as fossil fuels and uranium. The high rate of consumption of fossil fuels in particular, when measured against known reserves, raises questions about a proper moral concern for future generations. Since we have defended an intergenerational morality, there is no doubt that someone in the present ought to be evaluating present needs and consumption in the light of the likely requirements of future generations. It would be a moral contradiction to consume the earth's resources and to leave them almost depleted for our own kin in the future. Speculation or *ex cathedra* claims on how much of any resource we should keep in reserve would be idle: no fair judgement can be made by anyone without the most thorough, impartial and benevolent enquiry, after the widest possible consultation and public participation. One of the current speculations is that we are using resources excessively and even redundantly, since we are manufacturing some consumer goods which we can well do without. The final judgement on this matter, and on all other relevant matters, would be made by a Commission, under conditions of morality and rationality already explained. But the judgement would not be final in a temporal sense: it would be adjustable as additional evidence came to hand. A Commission's judgement in drawing together present demands on resources and likely future needs would be one of the most difficult human beings could ever be asked to make. If it were to find that with respect to some resources it could not reach a decision on the evidence before it, it is possible that it would give the benefit of the doubt to future generations by curtailing present consumption. Since it is engaging in moral thinking and not political thinking, it would not assume that necessity is the mother of invention, that future generations can always be depended upon to find new technologies which would make some of our non-renewable resources redundant. That would be too high a risk for moral and rational persons to take. It might well take the view that research into alternative sources of energy is an urgent social priority, concluding that fossil fuels are not worth passing on to future generations. (It might take a similar view on uranium, for reasons to be considered soon.) Alternatively it might find, from recent research evidence available to it, that the effects of carbon dioxide and acid rain are not as serious as thought at first, or that the problem of pollution by sulphur dioxide and nitrogen oxides is more complex in the relationship between chemistry and biology than is suggested by simple chemical explanations of acidification.

Atmospheric pollution, soil and water pollution, and the rate of industry's use of non-renewable resources are several of a number of ways in which conservation and morality are related in the *developed* world. In developing countries, the two are related with respect to the quality of urban settlements, but in developed countries too such settlements are inadequate when constructed close to industries. Assuming that there are benefits to quality of life to be derived from wildernesses, national parks and other nature reserves – given a variety of individual interests and values – it is evident that those living huddled close to industrial centres in the developed world are often alienated from them, cut off by economic circumstances, and in some cases by lack of an appropriate education in what they have to offer. This social problem is fundamentally a moral problem of distributive justice. It is aggravated by additional risks to health from industrial pollution. When the developed world enters the developing, establishing its industries in them as at Bhopal, moral questions of a different kind are raised.[47]

## WORLD POPULATION

Since in this chapter the central concern is quality of life in its relation to conservation, and situations which obstruct moral solutions to conservation problems in practice, world population trends must be of concern to us as they were to Mill. In *Principles of Political Economy* (vol. 2) Mill warned against allowing wealth and population to increase to an extent that it would deprive the earth of a 'great portion of its pleasantness', thereby increasing population at a cost to 'happiness' or quality of life. He foresaw a need for the two to be 'stationary, long before necessity compels them to it' (p. 331).[48] Mill pointed out that 'the increase of wealth is not boundless', that at the end of any progressive state lies the stationary state (p. 326). In this view he disagreed with Adam Smith that a progressive state is necessary if the mass of the people are not to be left in a 'pinched and stinted condition': even in a progressive state of capital, Mill argued, restraint on population is indispensable to prevent the condition of the poorest in society from further deterioration. As though anticipating the present contrast between developed and developing countries, he asserted that 'it is only in the backward countries of the world that increased production is still an important object' (p. 330). He believed that even if a crowded population were all well fed and clothed, a crowded world would be a poor place to live in: 'solitude . . . is essential to any depth of meditation or of character; and solitude in the presence of natural beauty and grandeur, is the cradle of thoughts and aspirations which are not only good for the individual, but which society could ill do without' (p. 331). There is no reason to believe that in this eloquence Mill was doing any more than extending the autobiographical impressions noted earlier. It is more pertinent to reflect that in our obligations to posterity we may have been remiss in not keeping a closer eye on population growth in almost fourteen decades since Mill foresaw the advantages of a 'stationary state'. The degradation of parts of the earth that we have noted has been aggravated by rapidly growing populations in the affected countries. The most fundamental question to be asked therefore, if we are to honour our moral obligations to posterity, is this: What are the sustainable levels of population in various parts of the earth which first, will leave it in a fit state for future generations to inherit; and second, will enable the maintenance of an adequate quality of life for all people, both now and in the future?

In the large-scale historical adjustments of populations to their environments there have probably seldom been thoughts of posterity, or any moral thoughts at all. Both migration and conquest have been common outlets for population pressures. In our time, with all our recent technological inventions, we are forced to ask questions about the carrying capacity of the earth we inhabit, but more morally than in the past, putting that question in conjunction with the problem of future generational needs, as well as with the problem of maintaining and distributing an adequate quality of life. False adjustments of populations to new environments occur in the case of increasing urbanization throughout the world, for if populations of rural areas exceed the capacity to support them, and there is no simultaneous economic development in cities to absorb the populations drifting to them, quality of life obviously suffers through unemployment and substandard human settlements. Governments have not acted with moral concern to prevent these effects.

It is the maintenance of quality of life in this complex problem of population growth which defies simple solutions. Moral demands understandably complicate social problems. Mill appeared more generous than Hume in declaring that penalties of overpopulation were caused by 'the niggardliness of nature, not the injustice of society' (*Principles of Political Economy*, Book I, ch. XIII, p. 238), but Hume was probably nearer to the mark than Mill in observing that justice is derived from 'the concurrence of certain qualities of mind with the situation of external objects': the qualities of mind were 'selfishness and limited generosity', as noted in Chapter 1; the situation to which he referred was 'the scanty provision nature has made for his wants' (*A Treatise of Human Nature*, Part II, Book III, pp. 494–5).[49] If nature were more bountiful in matching man's wants, the earth could carry a much larger population: as it is, much of it is desert, still more uncultivable, most of it is ocean. In the sense of global morality Hume's observation is pertinent too. The 'limited generosity' of nations has been largely instrumental in preventing any international balancing of populations in the past from less productive to more productive territories. National sovereignty has itself been a stumbling block to a moral solution of population problems. Mill foresaw the dangers of population outstripping the human capacity to feed itself, leading to a progressive deterioration in quality of life and eventually to famine and death (Book I, ch. XIII, pp. 239–41). He had been impressed by the views of Malthus on the dangers of unrestrained population growth. In his *First Essay on Population* Malthus asserted with conviction that 'the power of population is indefinitely greater than the power in the earth to produce subsistence for man' (p. 13).[50] While subsistence increases only in an arithmetical ratio, population increases, unless kept in check, in a geometrical ratio (p. 14). Therefore a strong and constantly operating check on population growth was necessary, so that all might be free of anxiety about 'providing the means of subsistence for themselves and families' (p. 17). The moral concern of Malthus was evident; the practical relevance of his concern is more apparent today than it was two centuries ago.

There seems little doubt that without a check on the rate of population growth, and without near miracles of science in food production, eventually human life would reach the point of exhausting the earth's life-sustaining resources. But in his moral thinking man is also rational, so that such a total consumption of resources is unthinkable, if not for political leaders everywhere, at least for national Commissions which are becoming more and more a requirement of our times. In the 'tragedy of the commons'[51] the inference to be drawn is that we cannot afford to leave decision-making on large issues such as world population to political leaders.

Population growth is not merely a question of multiplication of births: migration and mortality are also to be considered. Where migration is nil or negligible a nation's population grows from a favourable balance of fertility over mortality. But this balance may be favourable from a population standpoint and distinctly unfavourable from the standpoint of a morality which puts high value on quality of life. Where a disproportionately high mortality is due largely to social conditions, and national governments are powerless to alleviate it, the moral responsibility for improving quality of life rests at least partly on the developed countries.[52]

Population comparisons between developing and developed countries have implications for both morality and conservation. The world population is now over 4.5 billion, three-quarters of which is in developing countries. In developing countries the rate of population growth is more than double that in developed countries. It is in the developing countries where quality of life is lowest, and where there is also, through the association with poverty, the greatest degradation of the earth and loss of natural resources. Conservation receives most attention in developed countries, least attention in developing countries where it is most needed. If present population trends continue, 90 per cent of population increase to the year 2000, when world population is expected to reach 6½ billion or more, will be in developing countries.[53] In some developed countries fertility rates have declined, but so too have mortality rates, so that population continues to rise steadily.

World population, conservation, social and economic conditions and morality are thus complexly interrelated. Any unitary approach to the world population problem, such as by an education of rural and urban communities of developing countries in family planning, is unlikely to be successful, as is any other piecemeal approach. Similarly, inadequately controlled research, the use of inappropriate methodologies and reliance on ill-founded assumptions may lead to simplistic solutions and to the delineation of dramatically false trends.[54] Apart from competent research design and cautious interpretations of findings, another primary requirement is an education of moral attitudes and values so that people of the world come to *care* about quality of life everywhere, and include in their moral caring a concern for the well-being of their own unborn kin in the future.

The outstanding contribution of international conferences on world population has been their focusing on social conditions and the need for social reform. Although delegates to the Mexico City Conference on Population in 1984 used very similar evidence and arguments to those used a decade earlier at the Bucharest Conference, at Mexico City it became much clearer that developing countries were prepared to accept the idea of population control. It was generally recognized that in the intervening period insufficient had been done to reduce the birth-rate, or to cooperate in a better distribution of population.[55] It noted the need for population goals and policies as integral parts of 'a social, economic and human development aim' to improve standards of living and quality of life, recognizing the complexity of the socioeconomic factors involved, and the need for international assistance to developing countries.[56] More controversially from a moral standpoint, it upheld 'the basic human right' for couples and individuals to decide without coercion the number and spacing of their children.

At least two moral questions arise. First, the massive international support needed to achieve objectives relating to population growth, conservation and quality of life in developing countries, must come in some way from the resources of *developed* countries, and that implies a probable reduction in material standard of living in those countries. Given Hume's perception of our fundamental self-interest and 'limited generosity', the moral demands for the sake of ends that are global rather than national fall heavily on developed countries. If this were to involve a general lowering of standard of living in developed countries, establishing a balance between available resources and the demands from the world's people for them, what would be an appropriate sacrifice for the people of the developed world to make? (It is assumed that some sacrifice would be needed, and not merely a readjustment to alternative lifestyles involving lower demands for consumer goods in developed countries.) If world population growth is successfully curbed, and is to be eventually stabilized at approximately three times its present level (some believe that four times might be more realistic), there has to be a corresponding increase in food production, not only to cope with the increased population, but also to give all people of the world an adequate quality of life. The pressure on increased food production becomes clearer still when it is recognized that the greater rise in population is likely to occur in developing countries, which have the greater proportion of soil degradation and desertification. This consideration places a heavier burden still on developed countries. If marginal lands are to be restored to productivity, substantial international aid is needed for this purpose alone.[57] The general effect of these demands for assistance to developing countries can scarcely be anything but a lowering of a material standard of living in developed countries. It is not a question of whether our 'limited generosity' would accept these demands: it has become rather a moral imperative to act, both for the sake of improving the lot of persons in acutely under-privileged social circumstances and for the sake of saving the earth for present generations and for posterity.

On the face of it, the recommendations of the Mexico Conference are made from a rational and moral standpoint, and this is precisely what would be expected of national Commissions. While the Commissions might reach similar conclusions on the need for action, their enquiries would be more thorough and far-reaching on the capacities of the respective developed countries to contribute – materially, scientifically and educationally. Rather than a loose, hortatory and comprehensive statement of international obligations to help (with no specific obligations on particular developed countries), in their international conferences the Commissions would attempt to arrive at a just distribution of the burden on developed countries, as well as a just distribution of the benefits to the developing countries.

The second moral question arising from the Mexico Conference recommendations relates to the supposed right of individuals and couples to plan how many children they will have and what the spacing of these will be. Here there is a conflict of principles. While there may be agreement on the desirability of individuals and couples so to decide, purely out of self-interest, there may be a reinforcement of long-standing cultural values which insist on large families and on a continuation of the happiness deriving from close family bonds. From a global moral standpoint which considers the interests of persons everywhere on earth, such an individual right, if pursued worldwide, would be in conflict with the common good of all people of the earth, whose quality of life can be safeguarded only by population restraint. The situation in China, with its acceptance of the need to control its population growth, is a microcosm of the world population problem.[58] Sacrifices may need to be made by some for the sake of the many: sacrifices for a higher standard of living in developing countries may turn out to be no more than necessary adjustments the world over. In short, the supposed human right of couples or individuals to decide themselves how many children they will have may conflict in some countries with a global common good which justifiably takes precedence over it, and if there are any sacrifices to be made in any country – developed or developing – social justice demands that those burdens be distributed. Similarly global morality must take precedence over national policies or aspirations: national fertility policies may themselves conflict with a fertility policy from a global standpoint. Assertions of the sovereign right of each nation to decide what its population policy shall be carry little moral conviction from a global standpoint – the only perspective from which the moral notion of persons can be fully accommodated with respect to quality of life and its connection with conservation.

## POLITICAL CONFLICT AND THE NUCLEAR THREAT

It is from the same moral principles of an equal consideration of the interests of *persons*, wherever they may be, and of a practical consideration of the interests of others which is directed necessarily towards their well-being or quality of life, that rational–moral thinking is in sharp conflict with any war-making, whether in the use of conventional weapons or of nuclear weapons. No leader of government sends a nation to war (except defensively when all negotiations have failed) from a rational–moral stance. When leaders of each of the opposing forces claim that they are fighting for a just cause, the irony escapes the mass of the people. War-makers are fundamentally immoral for regarding their people not as separate persons, but as expendable pieces in a power game. They become presumptuous and vainglorious in their identification of their own personal attitudes and values with the national interest: personal ambition overrides considerations of others' suffering. They are unmindful too of the total cost in damage to natural resources, and of the probable consequences in deterioration of a quality of life once the war is over.

Conventional warfare is a euphemism for non-nuclear warfare. In fact the powers of destruction by non-nuclear weapons are continually increasing through technological advances. To make war with conventional weapons may be considered by some government leaders to be rational, such as for relatively quick solutions to extreme population pressures: it could never be considered *moral*, for the reasons given. To initiate a nuclear war on the other hand, for whatever reason, would not only be immoral, it would also be totally irrational. A sobering reflection is that it would take only two opposing Hitlers to destroy the habitable earth. That fortuitous circumstance might arise at any time in the future unless select Commissions take over from governments all responsibility for coping with international conflicts, and all responsibility for the size and type of defence forces. The situation is that unless reason and morality are brought together in the governance of human life on earth, the future may be one of unpredictable calamities. This judgement is made with a dispassionate regard for the relevant facts of the situation, some of which must now be stated to justify both this and the further judgements that are to be made.

A general account of the effects of a nuclear blast will be given first, then information on present nuclear capabilities, especially those of the superpowers. On the first there is a base-line of evidence from the devastation caused at Hiroshima by the first atomic explosion in war: beyond that, given the physical ingredients of nuclear weapons, mathematical calculations on destructive power are not difficult to make. The consequences of a limited nuclear war between the superpowers alone would be devastating for the two nations and seriously harmful to others: the almost complete destruction of city buildings as at Hiroshima, the killing of over 100 000 people (estimates vary) and serious injury to as many again, would be repeated many times over, given nuclear warheads of no greater explosive yield than that of the Hiroshima bomb. The world ecological system would be seriously at risk and much of it destroyed. Apart from this vandalistic breaking of life-webs, and contributing to it, many hundreds of thousands of species would become extinct. The crust of the earth would be not only much less diversified in life-forms, but also probably damaged for all living things by a change in solar radiation reaching the earth through changes in the composition of the stratosphere.[59] Radio-active material would persist to affect life on earth, as well as in water and in the air. Apart from the destruction of many species entirely, others would be genetically altered by radiation. There would be an incidence of deformities in human births.

Suffering to humans and to sentient animals from the number of blasts occurring in a nuclear war would be on a scale beyond precise quantification. Little imagination is needed to construct a representation of life without shelter, without warmth once the fires subsided, without access to clothing supplies, or to food or drinking water free of dangerous levels of radiation, without even air to breathe that would be safe against the risks of cancer in the months or years ahead. Medical services from outside the destroyed cities would be able to cope with only a tiny proportion of those needing urgent health care, hospitals and schools would be destroyed, as would libraries, supermarkets, warehouses, food factories – including bakeries. From the decaying corpses of humans and animals, disease would spread rapidly, generated by certain viruses with more resistance to radiation than have higher life-forms. With resistance to disease already weakened, disease would kill many of the survivors of the bombs, missiles and other nuclear devices used. But the greatest killer of all would probably be simple starvation.

Political leaders who knowingly invited such consequences for a nation would not be in a healthy mental condition, but a deterioration in the mental condition of a political leader is not historically novel. Even political manoeuvring for power advantage between the superpowers appears diabolical against such a background. From a standpoint of rational egoism alone (that is, without benevolence), the odds against the continuance of each of the two nations are absurdly high. From a rational–moral standpoint, the situation speaks for itself. In 1961 the UN General Assembly passed a resolution (with a majority of fifty-five to twenty) which declared the use of nuclear weapons illegal. Prudence in national diplomacy persuaded the minority, mainly from the Western or non-communist bloc, to oppose the resolution, simply because at that time their intelligence sources convinced them that the Soviet Union was stronger in conventional forces than they were, so to them it was worth keeping the nuclear alternative alive at least until a balance of power could be achieved. While the Western bloc rationalized by arguing that the use of nuclear weapons is not illegal, the Soviet Union also concealed its motives: it could afford to declare nuclear weapons illegal while it had a superiority in conventional weapons (though it could still use nuclear weapons if necessary), so its primary concern, like that of the Western bloc, was for a superiority in destructive advantage over its main opponent.[60] With this evidence of political duplicity and total absence of moral purpose on either side, international agreements on whether wars should or should not be fought with nuclear weapons could not be given high credibility. Above all, whether wars should be fought at all is the central question to be taken out of the potentially dangerous hands of political leaders.[61] It is ironic that the superpowers can reach agreement on a matter that does not affect power rivalry, notably on *environmental protection*, claiming it to be beneficial to each nation as well as to others.[62] On the one hand, while conservation of natural resources is seen as a mutual interest and value, on the other hand each side threatens the other with nuclear warfare which would nullify such cooperation, for on large areas of the earth's surface there would be little left to conserve. It is ironic too that the only countries that have cooperated to prohibit nuclear weapons are Latin American countries, which are out of contention as rival world powers because of socioeconomic circumstances.[63] In a number of other countries there are widespread aspirations to become nuclear powers, even among developing countries. The declaration of nuclear-free zones in some local regions (such as the Pacific) would provide little protection in a nuclear war.

It is worth emphasizing that it is not necessary that the warfare be nuclear to be destructive of natural resources and, for many people, of quality of life for a generation or more. While a nuclear war would be vastly more devastating, with probable climatic changes and the effects of radiation fall-out over much of the earth, the destructiveness of other weapons is already critical. Preparations have been made over a long period for chemical and biological warfare. The defoliants used in Vietnam have had such a toxic effect on mangrove swamps that it has been estimated that recovery will be longer than if the vegetation had suffered during a nuclear war. Governments are in fact building defence capabilities in both non-nuclear and nuclear weapons. That they are much more concerned about military strength than about quality of life, or conservation of natural resources which may contribute to it, is evident from their budgets. In *developing* countries almost as much is being spent on defence as on education and health combined.[64] Expenditure on conservation of natural resources is negligible.[65]

While defence capability in non-nuclear weapons would itself present a formidable threat to morality and conservation, it is overshadowed by the awesomeness of the nuclear capability. Practical judgements from a rational–moral standpoint, and the arguments leading to them, can be made only by reference to relevant information. It is this kind of information on which Commissions would rely, but which governments of the world regard as of secondary importance to military strength or supremacy.

It would take only a few thousand nuclear weapons to destroy the earth's habitability, each one of which could destroy a city. Yet by the end of 1983 there was already a stockpile of over 50 000 nuclear weapons (produced mainly by the superpowers), which included over 17 500 strategic weapons of the intercontinental type, capable of reaching a target over 9000 kilometres distant. In comparison with the Hiroshima bomb, the total explosive yield now available in nuclear warheads is already *one million times* greater. Again with the Hiroshima bomb as a known reference point, long-range strategic missiles now available (such as the MX in the USA) have twice the range, can travel four times faster, have an accuracy far greater because they are computer-guided and do not rely largely on weather conditions for visibility of targets, and have vastly superior versatility. The MX (whose deployment is currently under review) carries ten nuclear warheads capable of being directed at independent targets, which are together more than 300 times as destructive in explosive yield as the Hiroshima bomb. Versatility is increased in delivery vehicles, with strategic submarines each of which may carry as many as sixteen missiles, as well as strategic bombers.[66] Nuclear warheads vary in quality of accuracy, range and explosive yield, and research is continually in progress to improve their destructiveness.

No Commission would justify huge military expenditures, especially by the USA and USSR, on the rationalization on each side that they are necessary as a deterrent against the other's ambitions. Preventing an attack in this way, even if politically fool-proof, is not a moral procedure because it diverts expenditure away from social welfare programmes aimed at improving the quality of life of the nation. On an economic–social scale applied for six years to the end of 1983, the standing of the USA and USSR has each shown a decline corresponding to increasing military expenditure. From a global perspective the expenditure is even less morally justifiable, because some of it could have been used to increase aid abroad to alleviate the situation of absolute poverty (estimated at one in five in the world) which is often associated with degradation of the environment; to help in establishing industries to ease the unemployment problem (estimated at one in every three in the developing countries); to help improve health standards (with an estimated 450 million people suffering from hunger and malnutrition, and two billion without safe drinking water).[67] The dimensions of moral neglect are as large as those of immoral preparations for destruction and suffering, and conservation is related to each.

The possibility of what has been called a 'nuclear winter' is not so far-fetched as to be lightly dismissed as science fiction. If the sun is ever blanketed by smoke and dust in the stratosphere following a series of nuclear explosions, the consequences are likely to be catastrophic for all life on earth.[68] It would be folly to delay decisions to end nuclear war preparations until there is definitive research on the possibility of a nuclear winter. Finite evidence may be impossible to achieve except by putting nuclear warfare to the test, and then the theoretical benefits of the satanic experiment would be out of all proportion to the cost.

Once nuclear warheads are produced, they remain a constant threat to the world even in storage. The fissionable material (so far isotypes uranium 235 or plutonium 239) cannot be dismantled into safe form once it is manufactured for use, so the world stockpile of nuclear warheads presents a problem either of disposal in a safe place or of reuse in other delivery systems at some time in the future. The second Strategic Arms Limitation Treaty (SALT II) limits each of the superpowers to 1200 intercontinental ballistic missiles, which are more than enough to reduce each country to ruins, including destruction of natural resources. Beneath the ruins, in deep underground storage systems, there may be many dismantled warheads that would be usable in a future conflict if there were sufficient survivors to use them.

Public cynicism of political systems and distrust of political leaders is not enough to prevent a nuclear disaster. The more critical of the people appreciate that politicians feed on popular support, and manipulate the less critical by sustaining public apprehension of an external threat to the nation. At the present state of public education, it is only a few who appreciate that politicians are often without clear moral purpose in their manoeuvrings to exploit treaty loopholes. The Outer Space Treaty of 1967 stated that 'States parties to the Treaty undertake not to place in orbit around the Earth any objects carrying nuclear weapons or any other kinds of weapons of mass destruction, install such weapons on celestial bodies, or station such weapons in outer space in any other manner' (Article IV,1). Because it did not specifically include satellites, both the USA and USSR have begun programmes of space-based laser and particle-beam devices which will enable each to intercept and destroy enemy missiles. Political leaders on each side assert an ironic quasi-moral defence that they are observing the relevant treaty. It is obvious that their manoeuvrings are *morally* lawless, even if they do comply with the letter of international law.

The question of using atomic energy for peaceful purposes is now mentioned briefly in the context of the threat of nuclear warfare, since any nation that has the technology to develop nuclear power has the capacity to produce nuclear weapons. One of the dangers is that fissionable material will fall into the hands of fanatical terrorists who, once armed with a nuclear weapon, could hold an enemy nation to ransom and even threaten the civilized world. Another constant danger is in the toxicity of high-level nuclear waste, and the increasing uncertainty of waste disposal procedures as nuclear energy is used more and more for industry. Nuclear waste comes from a variety of sources: some of it is classified as low-level waste, such as from hospitals or research institutions. Some comes from uranium milling and the build-up of tailings. Other nuclear waste is classified as *high level* in its radioactivity. While it is recognized that it is very toxic when first produced, this high-level waste undergoes a gradual process of decay which may go on for hundreds of years. High toxicity continues throughout the early stages of decay. The greatest danger is from careless disposal which might place future generations at risk.[69] Although the entire question of nuclear energy is controversial, and has become emotional through insufficient knowledge of its benefits as well as its dangers, serious consideration is now given in developed countries to safe waste disposal, such as by isolating canisters in deep, stable geologic structures. Since whatever is done is likely to present some threat in the future, as from earthquakes, and the problem of safe disposal of high-level waste is unlikely to go away completely, a Commission acting from a rational–moral position might be expected to recommend greatly increased research efforts into alternative energy sources. But without all the relevant information which a Commission would have, firm moral judgements are not possible on whether nuclear energy should be used at all for peaceful purposes.[70] The problem of waste disposal remains. Some believe that the only safe repositories for high-level nuclear waste are a few of the world's largest deserts: those which have a record of geological stability of as much as ten million years, which are without groundwater and are not close to large population centres.[71]

## COMPLEXITY OF CONSERVATION PROBLEMS

The need for political reform of a kind which puts decision-making on the large questions of quality of life and habitability of the earth in the hands of the very best persons available, becomes increasingly evident through an appreciation of the complexities of social problems in modern societies and the unsuitability of present political systems to solve them. Well-informed rational–moral decision-making has to take into account economic, scientific, technological and administrative concerns as well as moral ones, but on no occasion would moral considerations be suppressed by the combined weight of the others. The common good as perceived by the few is the proper end of government. Within the complexity of social problems generally, large questions of conservation cannot be isolated and given separate attention.

Industrial development has yielded undoubted benefits to quality of life for many people. It has helped to solve social problems of how to achieve wide employment and an adequacy of basic necessities of life; of the accumulation of sufficient production surpluses to devote to social welfare, and to technological research for a variety of purposes, including defence. Among developed countries the interlocking production–consumption–employment–

defence situation demands constant effort to keep abreast of other industrial nations. A collapse of substantial markets, or a world economic recession, has penetrating effects on quality of life and on community concern for conservation. Industrial nations are so locked into an economic–political–social system that to break out of it with single-minded schemes such as *voluntary simplicity*, experimenting with alternative lifestyles to demonstrate that many consumer commodities are unnecessary, is not practicable on a national scale without courting disaster. In the world industrial system to surrender political independence by any such deviance from world norms, with obvious effects on defence capability, would be imprudent and potentially self-destructive. Even to scale down the momentum of industrial growth would be economically and politically hazardous to an industrial nation, as well as socially harmful, for the capacity to provide employment and a suitable standard of living in health, housing and other welfare provisions, depends on a sound economy. Indeed everything the nation provides, even social services for those who choose alternative lifestyles without contributing to society in return for what they receive, has to be paid for by some of the people. From a present perspective of a global morality and an imagined situation of total international accord, there would probably be good reason to reduce industrial production in all countries except those in the initial stages of industrial development, ceasing production of consumer goods which people can do without, and setting a goal of a cleaner environment, conservation of forests and of representative ecosystems in the world, and a restoration of the earth, as far as practicable, from the most offensive visual effects of industrialization. Such a goal would be placing a high value on the aesthetic value of life, and perhaps also on intellectual and moral development rather than on material progress. But the irony is that until there is a reeducation of attitudes and values the world over, it is very unlikely that people generally would accept a surrender of some of the material goods they now enjoy.[72] Thus practical judgements on the complex social questions of which conservation is a part need themselves to be complex, made by holding together all relevant aspects in the one informed and disciplined perspective.

Failure to appreciate the social complexity of conservation problems in their moral, economic and political aspects continues to produce naive solutions, and sometimes intolerance. While public interest groups may press for urgent legislation to establish clean-air standards, they may do so in ignorance of the costs to industry, the narrow margin of profit that may already exist in particular cases, and the social consequences in unemployment should an industry be compelled to close down. When some conservation interests urge a land-use policy which is based on as little alienation of public land as possible, they may be considering their own interests very largely, or alternatively they may be acting more morally in considering the interests of younger generations of the present and of posterity; but at the same time they may be ignoring economic considerations, perhaps unmindful of the fact that the successful economies of all nations have been based in some way on the use of natural resources. By contrast, *exploitation* of natural resources occurs when they are used unnecessarily for industrial expansion; and political mismanagement occurs when land-use policy is turned to the interests of those in power, or is delegated to agencies of government which by-pass the common good, making judgements on insufficient evidence and with inadequate thought to the long-term consequences of their decisions. There may be some cases where the economy of a nation *needs* hydroelectric power from a natural resource such as a river or waterfall. Similarly, the conservation of large wildernesses has not always been economically and socially feasible: from a thorough economic and social appraisal of alternatives, that is, sometimes the best decision may have been to use at least part of these, giving proper weight to the interests of present generations as well as of future ones. The complexity of practical situations demands that economic and social matters be considered in conjunction with moral questions, not taken independently and supported by one-sided advocates of each. Air pollution legislation may be openly recognized as contributing to the economy by reducing the incidence of pollution-related illnesses; it may also be explained in moral terms as improving quality of life.

Intolerance as part of human imperfection has been evident when the public interest is narrowly conceived, and there is no appreciation of a common good. In federal and state relations, for instance, federal legislation may be thwarted by state rivalries. In the USA the principle of equal state sovereignty has led some states to obstruct early and full-scale development of projects flowing from federal legislation.[73] Conservation may suffer as a result.

The complexity of conservation problems will receive further attention in the concluding chapter, including the nature and significance of practical judgements. A Commission would avoid one-dimensional judgements through a clear perception of the complexity of conservation issues in practice. Its final decision would be a moral and rational one, even if sometimes it favoured development of a natural resource.

# SUMMARY

Quality of life is a normative expression, in the moral sense referring to a universalization of certain basic satisfactions which only some are presently enjoying. Descriptively it is relative to historical circumstances and social conditions. Practical judgements which may influence quality of life need to be lifted above the political plane of short-term, expedient ends. In so far as conservation measures may contribute to quality of life, they frequently interlock with economic and social questions of great complexity.

The obstacles to moral solutions of conservation questions are general human imperfection in decision-making, both moral and rational; political subterfuge and short-sightedness and a preoccupation with short-term ends. In the practical situation it is only highly selected groups, constituting the separate national Commissions, who would be capable of sustaining rational–moral efforts towards the *common good*, both nationally and internationally.

In their legislative capacity, politicians in government have demonstrated both a vagueness in some of their statutes relating to conservation (which in some circumstances may be intentional), and a lack of resolve in ensuring that their laws are carried out. At times there is a conflict between law and morality: legislatures may serve their own interests by circumventing the decisions of courts on conservation; in all countries there is a need to reform the law with respect to *standing to sue* and *right of access*.

Developing countries have incurred the greatest degradation of the earth in recent years, through population pressures and impoverishment, compounded by drought. Massive aid is necessary from developed countries – involving a probable lowering in their own material standard of living – first, to improve quality of life; second, to protect and preserve natural resources, for the sake of both present and future generations.

Developed countries have contributed most to atmospheric, soil and water pollution, constituting a threat to quality of life and also a threat to the preservation and protection of the natural resources which may be related to it. The rate of use of non-renewable energy resources such as fossil fuels and uranium raises moral questions, but since each poses risks to quality of life, alternative sources of energy are desirable to safeguard the interests of both present and future generations.

If quality of life is to be sustained for some and improved for the majority, checks on the population growth rate throughout the world are unavoidable. If the earth is everyone's, so is the moral responsibility to people who are degrading it through conditions of abject poverty, associated often with overpopulation. There is a complex interrelationship of population, conservation, economic factors and the common good. The right of couples and individuals to choose how many children they will have is questioned from the standpoint of the common good, which in this respect is in conflict with principles of individual liberty.

The nuclear threat is both a moral and a conservation problem when grounded firmly in available evidence. In this area, as well as in others examined in this chapter – international aid involving electorally unpopular sacrifices at home, world population growth, the likely interests of posterity – political leaders are unsuitable to make the decisions, as they are also in committing the nation to war. The tenor of argument and evidence to this point leaves no doubt on the moral and rational imperative to have national Commissions, of the best persons available in the community, to take over decision-making on all the large moral issues of our time which influence quality of life. Conservation is one of these issues.

Radical political change is not practicable, though, without a large measure of public acceptance, since ultimately (ruling out revolutionary means as a contradiction to a practical morality based on equal consideration of the interests of persons) it is the people who must become aware of their moral and social predicament. As Mill believed, the possibility of educating them out of widespread apathy appears to be the only prospect for the future of mankind. It is to this question that we turn in the concluding chapter.

# 5 The Potential Common Good: The Challenge to Education

In Chapter 3 the ideal common good was explained as a philosophical concept, an unattainable ideal used as a standard against which imperfection may be measured. The practical common good is a provisional end, not a final one. Once broad objectives formulated under it have been achieved, the time has come for fresh objectives to be formulated which constitute a reordering of the practical common good, in the light of a realised potential for improvement. The *potential common good* is thus a practical judgement of what the common good would be like if human beings were improved in various ways according to their potential for improvement: if they were made more rational, more moral, more knowledgeable, though still within the limits of human imperfection. Intellectually and morally there is normally not one potential only, but ever further potentials ahead once some gains have been made. In this perception there is a generalizing of individual differences among persons: more accurately the potentials are individual, not common potentials for a given population. But in the generalized perception, if it were established that the large majority of human beings the world over are a-moral, or act morally only out of fear of social disapproval or to win social approval; are fundamentally persons of desire or appetite rather than persons of reason; and are vastly ignorant of the world about them beyond the home, the workplace and their recreation locations; uninterested in conservation, apathetic about world political tensions and the possible consequences of war, the practical common good would be a heightening of public awareness in each of these respects. Then with some objectives realized, the practical common good could be adjusted to take account of a perceived potential for still further improvement.

This is in fact no more than an account of a process of *education*, and the perception of a potential for improvement is no more than a standard educational perception. One of the major responsibilities of a national Commission entrusted with setting the community on a course directed towards the common good is to assume such an educational standpoint. This does not imply any pedagogical skill or professional expertise, but simply an appreciation that the common good involves particularly changes *in the minds* of people, not merely their access to material comforts and conveniences, or even to material necessities, and that the *primary means* to such changes is education.

The general purpose of this chapter is to review the preceding perspectives on morality and conservation, to throw further light on some of these through additional explanations, and to bring education into conjunction with them. That will indicate some ways in which conservation problems may be given moral–educational solutions, but it too will be found to have limitations and to call for more radical and comprehensive change in other directions, though always through education. The first step is to understand the notion of education itself.

## THE IDEA OF EDUCATION

Education is fundamentally a *becoming*, as Aristotle understood it to be (*Politics*, Book VIII, ch.1, 1342$^b$).[1] Although there are various learning objectives which an educator may keep in mind for his students, or which a student may set himself, there is no end distinct from these particular learning ends which may be designated as an end of education, though misleadingly educationists may refer to learning objectives as educational objectives. Education does not entail a comprehensive end of any kind. If all the conceivable knowledge objectives were put together, for instance, they would not in this cumulative form constitute an end of education, because education is not an accumulation of all possible knowledge in the world: indeed, the idea of education is not to be identified with simply the acquisition of knowledge (of any kind or magnitude). Another misconception is to speak of an *educated* person. We may use certain criteria by which we may evaluate a person's store of knowledge, or capacity for thinking independently about it, but there is no conceivable way of determining what a person would be like who had reached an *educated* state. There is no such state. As a becoming, education has a different substantive meaning for different persons: each is on his own course of becoming, dependent upon his unique cluster of potentialities. But it is important that the becoming have some direction, and it needs to be a *moral* direction, with an orientation towards the individual's well-being. Otherwise potentialities could be in the process of developing in ways which are heading the individual towards inevitable suffering, both to himself and possibly to those with whom he is in close personal relationship.

To this point we may say that education is a *developing* (and not a development) of individual potentialities. This formulation acknowledges individual differences in potentiality, as well as the fact that the becoming is not towards a finite end. But the fundamental idea of education is incomplete without some idea of direction, otherwise the becoming could be intellectually and morally regressive. The direction in the formal idea of education is always towards *improvement*, with the implication that it is improvement in ways which promote the person's well-being or quality of life, increasing his satisfaction rather than leading him to increased suffering. Education as 'a developing of individual potentialities in improving directions' could still be misconstrued by the inclusion of improvement in trivial activities or immoral activities, and these need to be excluded with a further qualification. In the statement that 'education is a developing of individual potentialities, consistent with social values',[2] there is an implication that civilized societies would not support learning programmes in their educational institutions which ran counter to the basic moral and intellectual values which those societies espoused; and also an implication that in formal schooling at least, there are some moral and intellectual values, broadly accepted by the respective societies, which they wish their young to learn.

The developing of individual potentialities in continually *improving* directions raises the question of judgemental criteria by which improvement may be gauged. In this context improvement is synonymous with the educational process itself, so that in the formal idea of education there is discernible a judgemental aspect. No one could recognize an individual's potentialities in a state of becoming, or developing, who did not assume some kind of detached stance on a progressive span of achievements: acknowledgement of a single achievement, without reference to preceding achievements, would not be enough. Further, since change of any kind, including regressive change, is a developing, a becoming of a sort, specific criteria are needed by which to judge that the developing is indeed in a forward direction, towards the individual's increasing well-being. In some respects this *improvement*, which is central to the notion of an educational progression, is easy to detect: improving skills in communication or in reasoning, for instance. But in other respects, especially in connection with moral attitudes and values, the task is much more difficult, for it is not always easy (except in the case of young children) to determine that a modification of attitudes and values is in the direction of the individual's well-being or quality of life.

In the formal idea of education as a developing of individual potentialities, consistent with social values, education stands distinct from *learning*. Many things are learned which may contribute in no way to education. Drilling by means of repetitive tasks, as in life-boat drill on shipboard, or bayonet drill in infantry training, has no necessary connection with a developing of potentialities, and each of these may be found to be quite unsatisfying in itself, regardless of how long it is practised. By contrast, once selected potentialities have been developed beyond the first effortful learning activities, there is usually individual satisfaction from the experience of one's growing powers. One can see, that is, that the educational process is directional and therefore purposeful, contributing to a well-being or quality of life in which there are increasing satisfactions.

## The Potential Common Good

The fundamental idea of education as a *developing* of potentialities consistent with social values matches the notion of a *potential common good*, and shows at once that education is the means to that good. But the idea that education has an instrumental value, a purpose beyond itself, is distasteful to those who are dedicated to the liberal idea of education as an end in itself: the development of the intellect alone, so that individuals are supposedly taught to think clearly, openly and independently, to set aside prejudices and biases of all kinds and to get straight to the point of a discussion or argument. This liberal idea of the making of minds owes much to Plato and Aristotle: their influence has persisted, conspicuously in the last century,[3] perhaps less so in this. But no matter how rigorous and disciplined the preparation, the clearest minds are still found to be unclear and emotional on some questions, the most impartial still subject to lapses under the influence of preconceptions and prejudicial attitudes. The liberal idea of education as a preparation of the intellect and as an end in itself is not strictly sustainable if it implies any consistent capacity, though in the developing of potentialities few would question that it is the developing of intellectual powers which is the most significant of all; neither moral nor physical potentialities can be developed very far without intellect. It is the social aspect of education which points to its instrumental value for the *potential common good*, contributing to an improvement in quality of life through various kinds of learning: acquisition of pertinent knowledge and understandings, the learning of attitudes and values, of skills such as coordination or computational skills. In these various learnings, some of which may occur informally rather than formally, awarenesses develop which are related to an individual's quality of life: a self-understanding and understanding of others, for instance, including an understanding of the moral aspects of interpersonal relations; an awareness of elemental justice as fairness in the treatment of persons, so that one is aware of one's rights as a person, including one's civil liberties; an awareness of the requirements and benefits of good health and a clean environment, of the satisfactions that may be derived from nature reserves of various kinds, of the satisfactions of security of employment and income, of satisfying working conditions and of occupational suitability, and so forth. In addition to these, wider awarenesses develop which may threaten quality of life in the future: awareness of political and military rivalry between major powers, and awareness of world population trends. In all of these awarenesses an assumption is made that human life is worth sustaining, especially when substantial progress is made towards the realization of a perceived potential common good. It would be contradictory for rational persons to acknowledge that on balance they are enjoying a quality of life, but that human life is not worth living.

In previous chapters the burden already placed on education as instrumental to a realization of a potential common good, including a widely distributed quality of life, has been a heavy one. In the first chapter there were noted the demands on moral education for understanding of interests and rights; in the second, the importance of a conservation education which, in conjunction with moral education, aims at an understanding of present and future resource needs, an understanding of sentient animals in their capacity for suffering, of distributive justice in the matter of equal access to the natural and cultural heritage, and of a global perspective on morality which sees all persons as worthy of equal moral consideration, wherever they may live; in the third, the need for social reform as a prerequisite to wide general education so that there is a willingness to learn and to become socially involved, for political education to develop awareness of the need for institutional reform, for education in critical thinking, and for education in the potential contributions of nature reserves to quality of life; in the fourth, the need for selected and pertinent knowledge of political tensions and of the inadequacies of political systems to solve large social issues; for moral education in world situations of acute need, and in the demands of practical morality on both a global scale and on an intergenerational scale extending into the future. In all of these demands on education as a means to the realization of a potential common good, with an improved general quality of life as part of it, a qualification needs to be made on the limits of what is humanly realizable. As with an individual, so with a community of persons, potentialities can never be *completely* realized: some of them conflict, and in any case there is no time for them all to be realized. Therefore one of the tasks of formal education is to select some for development above others. In principle, when individuals reach intellectual maturity according to their individual capacities, they need to have freedom, as persons, to choose those which they prefer to develop within the pattern of their interests and values – still consistent though with social values, at least in the minimal sense of not running into conflict with them. But education's positive relationship with social values demands attention as well. Indeed, the demand is more pressing in general community education than it is in an individual's education. No Commission would be in a position to pursue what it perceives as a potential common good if individuals were completely free to pursue activities according to their respective interests and values once they reached a variable intellectual maturity. At least until a community became so well-educated morally as to be able to distinguish between self-interest and a common good, it seems likely that a Commission would need to organize a common core curriculum for public education, still leaving scope for the pursuit of individual interests which are not in conflict with it.

With this background into the nature of education and its service to the realization of the potential common good, the plan now is to consider first, the nature and requirements of practical judgements, extending some of the earlier explanations in Chapter 1 on the nature of moral thinking, and in Chapter 3 on decision-making; second, relevant human imperfections; third, the need for political reform; fourth, the need for social and legal reform; and fifth, a set of priorities for a practical programme of action which unites education, morality and conservation in one composite perception directed towards a continuing realization of a potential common good.

## PRACTICAL JUDGEMENTS

Practical judgements are those judgements which are made on what ought to be done when individuals face practical situations in which there are normally two or more courses of action open to them. They may be made by administrators, economists, researchers, politicians, or indeed by any person privately in his daily activities. The *ought* may be an administrative ought, for instance, which is guided by institutional ends of efficiency, or it may be a moral ought, which is guided by moral principles and moral ends. In the context of conservation the ends may be mainly administrative, as in the management of national parks and other kinds of nature reserves, or they may be mainly moral, as in the determination of a policy of land use which puts a moral value on conservation of natural resources; and in some cases they may be both administrative and moral.

We shall consider first the nature of practical judgements as part of moral thinking; second, the significant requirements of sound practical judgements which are both moral and rational, including the kind of knowledge needed with respect to problems of conservation; third, the limitations of an individual's practical judgements on questions which affect the interests of others, and the need therefore for an understanding of formal discussion techniques. Similar considerations and principles apply whether the individuals making the judgements are members of a Commission, or of government, or are private citizens. Differences in the quality of the judgements will reflect differences in the intellectual and moral qualities of the individuals concerned.

**General Nature**

Practical judgements leading to decisions, judgements or conclusions have been explained briefly in Chapter 1 in connection with intuitions, attitudes and values; and reference has been made to them again in Chapter 3 in the contrast between moral thinking and political thinking, and between rational–moral decision-making and political decision-making. Practical morality requires an orientation towards action, not merely good intentions. But pure reason alone will not give this action directiveness.[4] In all our practical deliberations on what we ought to do in a given situation, reason is accompanied by a complex of emotions and desires, motives or intentions, attitudes and values which together, or in some combination of these, *predispose* an individual to decide in one way rather than another. Particularly influential in this predisposing mental complex, as we have explained, are attitudes and values in unison, since they are habitual and tenacious, defended usually with emotion, often closely identified with the self-image. Whatever is valued is highly esteemed, by definition, so a challenge to a value is commonly regarded as a challenge to the self. On the other hand, stubborn and resistant to persuasion as attitudes and values are, as well as to viewpoints in conflict with their central cognitive core of ideas, beliefs or opinions, and indeed to any change or threat of change, they have themselves been learned in some way, and are not so intractable as to be completely unmodifiable by fresh learnings. Potentially they constitute the strongest dispositional force on reason (using 'dispositional' in the predisposing sense). Their influence on reason in a particular deliberation may be favourable or otherwise, or reason may be sufficiently strong to overrule the dispositional influence entirely. But because of their deep-seated *habitual* character, in many situations they may exert an influence without our being aware of it. Unlike reason alone, in their interaction with reason their tendency is towards a practical judgement (decision or conclusion) which leads to action. Therefore while on the one hand their influence on reason may in some circumstances confuse or complicate deliberations, on the other hand they are necessary for action to take place at all. In particular, in the context of practical morality, they are necessary for the fulfilment of moral thoughts or intentions in action. It has been observed that pure reason can justify total egoism, or a life without any practical consideration of the interests of others. In Hume's language, ' 'Tis not contrary to reason to prefer the destruction of the whole world to the scratching of my finger' (*A Treatise of Human Nature*, Part III, Book II, sect. iii, p. 416).

In this naturalistic explanation it is important to note that practical morality is not merely a description of psychological tendencies, a statement of an *is* position without any moral oughts related to them. On the contrary, moral oughts as imperatives for practical morality are individual expressions of moral convictions, as part of our moral attitudes and values. These have direction and directiveness: it is these that exert a necessary influence on reason so that from the interaction there will be moral acts or action and not the inertia of pure reason alone. In Kantian language, when one legislates for oneself one legislates for all others too: the moral values that we hold we universalize as values all others ought to have too. Criticism of naturalism in ethics refers usually to desire or inclination, especially to the desire-satisfactions of those for whom the practical judgements are made.[5]

The habitual nature of our moral attitudes and values does not put them in a separate compartment of our moral thinking, such as is sometimes suggested in Hare's explanation of moral thinking at the two distinct levels of the intuitional and the critical.[6] On the contrary, attitudes and values are to be distinguished from notions of acting out of 'blind habit', or from intuition, for in their learning and in the consolidation of the cognitive core that is characteristic of them, it is to be expected that some reasons are weighed for the value preferences that are made. In the case of moral attitudes alone, before sufficient reasoning powers develop to enable value preferences to be made, there is a danger that the moral habits learned by very young children will continue to be defended uncritically long after the ability to reason independently has developed. It is therefore an educational responsibility to impart an understanding of moral rules as soon as possible, and to keep alive a critical attitude to them so that habit does not exert an unwarranted influence on reason in making practical judgements.

Since all persons at some time are called upon to make practical moral judgements, *moral education* attains a central importance. No person can make practical moral judgements who is hesitant and unsure of the moral position he holds; or recognize the flaws in another's practical judgements unless he is critical of moral rules and conventions. It seems likely that in many of the moral judgements we make we put such faith in our settled convictions of right and wrong that we tend to make categorical judgements, or deontic assertions, rather than deliberating critically on the moral situation confronting us. Detachment, benevolence, sensitivity to the interests of others and a critical attitude to one's own standards as well as to those of others, all contrast with a consistently easy-going dependence on habit. Though our moral attitudes and values may be reflected in strong impulses to act (or not to act) in ways characteristic of them, even in the making of deontic assertions of categorical moral imperatives as Kant did, normally reason and moral values are brought together at some time before action, leading to an understanding of the consequences of our acts. Despite this consequentialist tenor of our moral thinking, it needs to be acknowledged that the distinction between consequentialist and deontic moral conduct is not always clear-cut. In some situations of everyday life – as when we are confronted with some conservation problems – we are both consequentialist and deontic (referring to firm convictions of *duty* which require no reference to consequences of acts). In considering the moral implications of polluting lakes and rivers with toxic industrial waste, for instance, we need to weigh carefully the consequences for the well-being of human life and for sentient animals. But in passing judgement on a situation where an animal is hunted for sport and made to suffer, we may pronounce, as a matter of moral conviction, as well as of moral *duty*, that it is wrong: it is not a question of weighing up the pleasure it affords the hunter and asserting (if that were possible) the greater pleasure to the hunter over the pain caused to the animal. Pain is an evil in our value system, contradicting the notion of well-being and quality of life. Yet even to understand what others' well-being is, in the range of situations we may face, implies a critical approach.

### Rational–Moral Requirement

Apart from a well-exercised critical inclination, sound practical judgements (including the moral) require both a general knowledge relevant to individual and social needs, and a particular knowledge of circumstances relating to a situation. The knowledge requirement has been explained in reference to the decision-making of national Commissions, but since this depends on public participation it is necessary that citizens too be suitably informed in the practical judgements they make on matters which they regard as in the public interest, such as conservation. Perhaps the sharpest contrasts between sound and superficial practical judgements become evident on the criterion of informativeness. But beyond that, in complex situations the merit of sound practical judgements is related most of all to the capacity to *hold together* multidimensional information, giving it shape and proportion, when the mind is not carried away by one-sided enthusiasms such as academic specialities or preferred ideological commitments. In that sense they are a function of the trained mind, disciplined in a manner similar to the liberal ideal, able to take an impartial position in so far as this is humanly possible, and able to keep personal dispositional tendencies firmly in control by reason, again within the limits of human imperfection. The shallow practical judgement may be no more than simply ill-informed; but it may be unbalanced as well to the extent of ignoring relevant information which conflicts with preconceptions; it may confuse value judgements with empirical knowledge; and it may engage in rational–dispositional deliberations in which reason is defeated by the force of motives, attitudes and values. Anyone who makes practical judgements on global conservation for instance, needs, among other things, relevant knowledge of natural science and economics, and not merely a superficial acquaintance with the excesses and social ill-effects of industrial economies in free enterprise societies. Without such knowledge, practical judgements may be simplistic, as in the claim that conservation problems will be solved only by returning to preindustrial lifestyles of close contact with nature. In holding the problem of global conservation steadily in view from all relevant perspectives, both the complexity of the problem, and a clear perception of what is practicable and what is not, would be gradually brought into focus with appropriate knowledge from economics, political science, sociology, practical morality, psychology and natural science. The resulting multi-perspective would develop a widening awareness of a diversity of living things and their potential for contributing to quality of life; of social values including those relating to sentient animals; of social needs and the needs of future generations; of individual differences among persons in desires, motives and aspirations and capacities.

**Discussion Requirement**

Finally, it needs to be acknowledged that practical judgements, as the products of imperfect minds even at their best, need to be regulated and sometimes rectified by exposure to other minds in active discussion situations. It is not the casual sharing of opinions that is in mind, but rather a kind of formal discussion technique that requires to be learned and exercised. If we return to the notion that all practical deliberations involve dispositional–rational thinking, the habitual force of attitudes and values is recalled, with their capacity to distort or bias reason unless we are on guard consistently. Members of a highly select Commission would be subject to such lapses, though less frequently than others: both they and members of the public whose support they would need would require skills of formal discussion. But although all would be bound by mutual obligations to expose individual prejudices or preconceptions which stand in the way of success as they pursue an agreed common goal, perfection would never be realized.

## HUMAN IMPERFECTION

Not even the formal discussion technique, practised within the limits of human imperfection, is able to guarantee that the collective practical judgement, reshaped and polished by such a procedure, is finally in a form that will contribute to the well-being of persons, where the ends sought are moral and not merely institutional. In government, whose end is the practical common good (adjusted to take account of human potential for improvement), errors of practical judgement may have far-reaching consequences.

The imperfections of politicians figured prominently in Chapter 3 as a contrast was drawn between rational–moral decision-making and political decision-making. These imperfections became conspicuous partly through the unrealistic demands of the public, ironically expecting perfection once some of their members are elevated as their representatives, uncritically closing their eyes to their own imperfections as electors. Yet such an observation in no way diminishes politicians' unsuitability for the task of reaching moral and rational solutions to the largest social issues of our time. For this role, exceptional persons are needed, selected in an entirely different way.

The realization of a potential common good implies that human imperfections still leave room for improvement. By contrast, in the static social order of Plato's *Republic*, it was only a few, the very best of men, who were capable of progressively improving their condition, by long and rigorous training in rational thinking. Ultimately they would attain a divine capacity to glimpse that which is (like all the Forms) above the world of imperfections – the Form of the good, which 'must be seen by whosoever would act wisely in public or in private' (Book VII, 517, p. 210).[7] They would thus be made ready for ruling, for they would then be able to see the 'real good' as distinct from imperfect expressions of it, using this Form of the good 'as the pattern for the rest of their life'. Though spending most of their time in philosophy, they would take their turn to 'endure the toil of directing politics and being rulers for the sake of the city' (Book VII, 540, p. 236).

This highly selective system was also narrow in its restriction of general human improvability. The formal idea of education implies that all persons are capable of improvement, and the notion of the potential common good conveys the same understanding, while recognizing individual differences. Beyond limited achievement characteristic of occupational groups, Plato cut off the possibility of further improvement. The largest range of improbability he saw in the *most able* of men, though great and determined effort was still needed by them. But his comments on the least able also have a general relevance to the attainability of a common good. These were the artisans and the money-makers, who were tied as well to occupations suited to their natures, in a state of educational and social immobility. In the tripartite division of the soul, it was they who were dominated by appetite, desire or inclination (not by courage, which characterized the soldiers, or by reason, which characterized the philosopher–rulers). Plato was speaking of dominant tendencies: he was well aware that the rulers were not to be tempted with possessions, and that in their preparation they must be protected against 'meanness and any other ugly thing that they must neither do nor be able to imitate' (Book III, 395, p. 77). Indeed, once the limits of attainability had been reached, no one was to attempt to overreach his natural powers: a craftsman or a money-maker was not to be 'so elated by his wealth, or his numerous supporters, or his bodily strength' to aspire to the warrior class, for instance (Book IV, 434, p. 121). It is this last group which commands our attention now – the people at large who appear to be dominated by desire much more than by reason, by self-interest, by thoughts of personal gain or craving for personal possessions. Is there a sobering thought in the *Republic* which prompts us not to expect too much of a potential common good? In the *Laws* in which Plato directed his attention to the education of the citizens of a new state he stressed the learning of habitual moral dispositions in childhood. When later the citizen learns the laws of the state he will reflect on his learned moral values, Plato says, and find that they are correct (Book II, 653, pp. 85–6).[8] He had limited faith in universal reason: stability was preferable to innovation, and the innovator in education he held to be 'the biggest menace that can ever afflict a state' (Book VII, 797, p. 283). Apart from that, the general craving for money had to be strictly controlled (Book V, 742, p. 211).

Plato was not alone among philosophers in suggesting that we should not set too high an expectation for a potential common good because of evident human limitations in both desire and reason. Having noted – as Hobbes and others had done – the extent to which men are governed by their own interests, Hume commented that 'even when they extend their concern beyond themselves, 'tis not to any great distance . . .' (*A Treatise of Human Nature*, Part II, Book III, sect. vii, p. 534). Though one may have good resolutions with respect to remote situations, say twelve months ahead, when they draw closer 'a new inclination to the present good springs up', making it difficult to adhere to the first purpose and resolution (p. 536). This tendency of human nature to be influenced by present inclination is itself a serious impediment to any collective perception of a common good.

Mill foresaw that 'the labouring people' in nineteenth-century England, long despised as uneducable beyond rudiments of learning, swayed by emotions and without potential for reasoning, must be guided as equal members of the public, and with the advantage of improved education drawn into 'all discussions on matters of general interest'. Indeed 'the prospect of the future', he saw, 'depends on the degree in which they can be made rational beings'. He believed them to have a potential for further 'intelligence' or critical thinking, anticipating that they would become 'even less willing than at present to be led and governed, and directed into the way they should go by the mere authority and *prestige* of superiors' (*Principles of Political Economy*, vol. II, Book IV, ch. VII, pp. 339–40).[9]

Philosophers' misgivings on human limitations in the centuries since Plato are not entirely dispelled, even if imperfections are not clearly tied to social classes or occupational groups, as Plato believed them to be. An improved learning of skills in critical thinking is still fundamentally necessary to any realization of an improved quality of life through individual involvement: that is not practicable without *social reform*. As will be explained in the last section of this chapter, it is necessary to pursue objectives according to clear priorities.

# POLITICAL REFORM

In preceding chapters there has been an emphasis on the inadequacy of present political systems, through their political leaders, to make sound practical judgements on the largest and most complex of social and moral problems, including conservation's relationship with problems of general land use, world population growth, aid to impoverished countries, the interests of future generations and military preparations of disproportionate and dangerous dimensions. The aspects of Commissions which require further explanation are first, the theoretical rational–moral model; second, the practical instrument of government. These will be considered briefly in turn.

**The Commission as Rational and Moral**

In so far as a Commission is a model at all, it is a model of imperfect man at his rational and moral best. It acknowledges all the human imperfections referred to in the preceding section, including the limitations of dispositional–rational deliberations. Its members would have some of the attributes of Plato's rulers: they would have a demonstrated skill in critical thinking acquired through some kind of appropriate preparation; they would have breadth of knowledge, and above all, a demonstrated interest in the people of the state and their common good. They would be among the most selfless persons in the state: in their lives they would have already demonstrated a moral interest in working for the well-being of others. They would not be conspicuously wealthy men, or have any dominant interest in material gain. They would not be value-neutral, since that would be a denial of human nature, but they would not have been prominent in any partisan organization of any kind, and in particular would have had no active background in party politics. They would be chosen rather for impartiality or fairness, and would be so perceived by the people. They would already have been conspicuous for a certain stability and predictability, for industry, foresight and a demonstrated capacity to work cooperatively with others. Above all, they would have Mill's moral stance of detached benevolence.

Plato's philosopher–rulers were to have departed, after service to the state, to 'the islands of the blest' (*Republic*, Book VII, 540 p. 236). The highest satisfaction possible would have come their way in the experience of 'insight and reason', and the knowledge that they had fulfilled their function in the service of others. They would seek no public honour: that is the prospect of the soldier acclaimed by 'victory-lovers'. They would seek no attractive financial reward: that is the prospect of the 'money-maker'. Of the three types of pleasure, theirs is the highest (Book IX, 582–3, p. 283). Therefore their talents, as gifts of nature, call for no special recognition. Even the admiration and respect of the people would not be sought.

Members of a Commission would not assume any individual responsibilities: they would necessarily be making practical judgements which are first, the judgements of the most rational and moral persons who are willing to serve; second, the collective product of interaction among members. All their judgements would be publicized widely as Commission judgements; individual members who were invited to explain conclusions to groups of the public would invariably refer to the Commission's judgement, never to a minority judgement on any matter. There would therefore be no temptation to attract personal reputation in any way. Such a consideration leads to the practical aspects of the Commission as a political instrument. At this point it is sufficient to note the very high demands of integrity, knowledge and practical morality placed on all members, without conceding the sheer impracticability of recruiting suitable persons. (Those who declined to serve would be expressing their unsuitability for the highest position in the state, unless they had adequate personal grounds for declining, such as ill-health.)

## The Commission in Practice

The Commission as a practical instrument of government is much more difficult to formulate, and any administrative suggestions would necessarily be reshaped many times before a final scheme was found to be both practicable and acceptable to the public. The following explanations are intended therefore not to supersede the efforts of political scientists at devising an instrument for political reform, but simply, first, to point to some of the very appreciable practical difficulties that lie in the path of reform; and second, to dismiss any presumption that reform is impracticable. Among procedural principles for the selection of its members there is first the requirement of open eligibility. There would be no barriers to eligibility on irrelevant grounds of sex, age, racial background or previous employment (though in the final selection questions might be asked about both age and occupation in particular cases). In this and in all other respects the standard principles of social justice would prevail to prevent discrimination or any other form of unfairness. There would be both a constitution for the Commission, and an amendment to the national constitution, where relevant, to accommodate it. The constitution of the Commission would stipulate the number of members and their tenure of office. No one would be appointed for life: with the best of intentions and the most careful of selection procedures, mistakes might be expected from time to time, even in the appointment of Commissioners, as they are in the appointment of others such as judges, executive heads of departments, university vice-chancellors and professors, and so forth. The number of exceptional persons suitable for office would not be large, but there would be an opportunity for various individuals to take their turn, as in Plato's system. The national constitutions would need to be amended to establish a clearly workable relationship between the Commission and the legislature. Within the budgetary constraints known to the Commission, the elected government would be obliged to legislate without delay on all Commission recommendations, once they had been given wide publicity and full opportunity for public discussion. It would be the Commission's responsibility to decide on the final form of their recommendations; they would not be subject to amendment by governments. In multicultural societies, recommendations would be published in as many languages as necessary. They would be published also in forms assimilable by children of appropriate comprehension capacities, with further adaptations expected by particular departments of education, always with the approval of the Commission to prevent distortion of intentions. The media would be used extensively for explanation. Although legislation on recommendations would be a formality, governments would be free to debate the recommendations if they chose, and to advise Commissions of their views, but would not have the power of veto. The Commission would consider their reactions, as it would all other reactions, without any obligation to reach agreement with them. Similarly, it would not be necessary that Commission recommendations be approved by the public in their various representative groups, since each of these would have sectional interests and values, and conflict among them would be expected. Because of the nature of the political system and the state of public education (before substantial reforms could be introduced), the Commission's steady view of the common good would give its recommendations a moral quality above political pressures, compromise and one-sided interests.

It is to be expected that some of the major policy decisions would be made by the Commissions in the first term or two of office: policies on land use, for instance, including conservation of natural resources in their relation to quality of life; on the rate of population growth, on conservation for future generations as a question of practical morality. But decisions would be reviewed by subsequent Commissions in the light of changing circumstances: the population growth rate may have to be further checked; external aid may need to be increased. The degree of detail in a Commission's recommendations would also depend on circumstances: in the matter of nuclear warheads or of conventional weapons, some specificity may be needed. There would always be clear direction to governments with respect to legislation.

Two major practical difficulties are acknowledged, each requiring thorough investigation. The first is in the demarcation of responsibilities between the Commission and the legislature; the second is in achieving international accord for a uniform system of national Commissions. The provisional suggestions are at least sufficient to dispel preconceptions in the meantime of total impracticability.

On the first major difficulty, it is acknowledged that policies formulated by the Commission from its single-minded perspective on the common good might on some questions be so wide as to leave room for politicians still to turn them to political advantage. To take an extreme and improbable example, if the Commission were to decide that the common good of present and future generations is best served by a land-use policy which preserves wildernesses 'in so far as they are not urgently needed by the state for other purposes', such a policy would have little practical value in serving the common good. Different governments could place their own interpretations on the policy, and irreparable damage might be done before the Commission had an opportunity to rectify the situation. Similarly if the Commission were to formulate a policy which declared that defence preparations are to be 'gradually scaled down', politicians would be given opportunities to manipulate people's emotions for political advantage, while legislating against the intention of the Commission's policy, and contrary to the common good as the Commission perceived it to be. It is a fundamental requirement that Commissions would assume precedence over governments in all areas of decision-making allotted to them by the constitution, as well as over heads of governments and military advisers. From their moral perspective on the common good, Commissioners would not allow themselves to be influenced by vested interests.

The second major difficulty foreseen is in gaining international accord for the kind of political reform suggested, with elected governments given minimal powers in policy-making, though retaining wide responsibilities for 'managing the affairs of the nation',[10] to use Thomas Paine's expression, on matters of short-term objectives; and with large issues of the long-term common good left exclusively to Commissions. There would be occasions for national Commissions to meet to discuss their respective recommendations. It is expected that evidence of good intentions with respect to arms control or international aid, for instance, would lead to wide publicity in the various countries and to an influence on the people's moral attitudes and values, supported by continuing national education programmes.

The establishment of national Commissions would probably not proceed simultaneously in all countries: in some an educational lag would require that further time be allowed for acceptance of political change, until they too were influenced by world opinion.

Because of their moral perspective on the common good, all Commissions would be a-political. It is possible that because of the centralism of socialist governments a different kind of relationship would need to be worked out between their Commissions and their governments; but whatever the administrative organization, Commissions would not be under the influence of political leaders, and their recommendations would be given the widest national and international publicity. The one appreciable hope there as elsewhere is in public education, for socialist governments no less than those of free enterprise societies are subject to the will of the people and not beyond the influence of *world opinion*.

The separation of long-term moral perspectives and short-term political perspectives is not clear-cut, but decision-making by governments is characterized much more frequently by the second than by the first. There is no doubt at all on the direction which political reform needs to take, even if the suggested means are no more than preliminary thoughts on practicabilities. It is fundamentally towards reduction of responsibility to elected governments, not as a concession to liberal ideals which from the time of Locke have aimed to protect self-interest, but rather because the high moral demands on governments are now beyond the capacities of professional politicians to handle with consistent perspicacity, integrity and regard for quality of life.

## SOCIAL AND LEGAL REFORM

Quality of life is not an objective bundle of goods to be won by hard work or inherited by privilege. It is largely an attitude of mind to one's social conditions which are seen as contributory to one's well-being; it is the prospect of life being enjoyed, present life being worth living, and in that sense being valued for its own sake. Its satisfactions may come in many ways: perception of social justice, for instance; appreciation of material comforts; aesthetic appeal of environment; opportunities for intellectual or artistic activity. Like all injustices, social or distributive injustice bites deep: the understanding that suffering is not universal, that some do not have to endure suffering at all in their social circumstances. By engaging in a practical morality which considers others' interests, and not only one's own – perceiving all as persons – one can see that social reform is needed in all countries, in the developed as well as in the developing, before the end of social justice as a widely and fairly distributed benefit is achieved.

### Social Contradictions

It is quality of life which gives many the will to live, its depressing absence which weakens the will, leads some to desperation, without concern for conservation of natural resources or for any other contribution to a quality of life enjoyed by others but still denied to themselves. Between the opportunities and social conditions of the privileged in developed countries, and those of the underprivileged at the opposite pole of social advantage, there is an enormous space, tending one way towards greed and overconsumption, the other way towards acute insufficiency and suffering. Extremes of social contradiction are not a recipe for a successful resolution of problems of conservation, including related problems of controls on population growth and on war preparations, and for willing concessions to those of our kin in future generations. Social underprivilege means that many human potentialities remain frustratingly unfulfilled, and that developing intellectual and moral powers give way to apathy. The resolution of social problems such as conservation depends heavily on the active participation of many, and the moral support of all. It is an experienced quality of life that gives people the will to care whether or not a nuclear war eventuates, for instance, and to take an intelligent interest in serious social problems that might in any way impair or destroy that way of life. *Vast contradictions* tend the other way.[11]

From the moral standpoint, with all persons considered worthy of a quality of life within their variable capacities, the situations of developing countries in contrast with those of the developed is a social contradiction on a global scale. Those tormented by hunger who scratch the earth for isolated grains of food are not given the moral consideration they deserve as persons. Helpless and bewildered, their degradation of the earth loses all meaning in their day-to-day struggle to survive. Nowhere are conservation and morality conjoined more poignantly than here. Economically and socially incapacitated, the acutely impoverished become morally incapacitated too with respect to the needs of their children and their children's children.

Another point of convergence of social contradictions is in the slum dwellings of cities. It is estimated that by the end of the century the number of people in the cities of developing countries will be twice that in the cities of developed countries,[12] but there are substandard human settlements in each as indicators of inequities in the distribution of social goods. Particularly in developing countries there is evident an ineffectualness of governments to alleviate the worst of these situations. In Bombay, as elsewhere, Commissions would probably be recommending urgent international aid,[13] and formulating policies to check the widespread migrations of people to cities, especially in developing countries. Children born into environments without playgrounds, parks and gardens, without open spaces of any kind, are generally unaware of a better quality of life elsewhere, or of one that suitable conservation might put within their reach. It is a convenient rationalization to perceive them as entirely satisfied with a life of squalor, as though they were not persons but members of an inferior subhuman species. Such people are not pursuing alternative lifestyles, because they have never known an alternative. By contrast, those who *have*, in developed countries, and who choose to withdraw from it in a life of greater simplicity, are usually careful to select an environment of aesthetic appeal. To have a choice is itself a luxury of developed countries. Social and moral contradictions remain.

## Legal Reform

Legal reform has a potential for contributing to social reform in specific ways, though still only superficially. Possibilities of reform in land tenure have been suggested in Chapter 3, associated with questions of conservation of natural resources and a practical morality which allows public access to all land, regardless of tenure, on conditions which safeguard the interests of legal occupants.[14] From a moral standpoint the natural resources of the earth can scarcely be defended as belonging absolutely to any particular individuals by right of seizure, or inheritance, or the means to purchase it; even less so to particular nations. The concept of common ownership confers common responsibility, including responsibility for restoration and prevention of serious, especially irreversible, degradation. There may be a need to return to the central notion of the land as belonging to the folk, as in Anglo-Saxon England, extended outwardly to encompass ever-widening communities and eventually the community of the world: the conservation of the earth's resources has become an urgent global responsibility through changing social and economic circumstances. Since one of the interests a community might have is an enjoyment of nature away from cities, those given rights in land under a system of public land ownership, with the qualification that the right is for *use* under certain conditions, would be accountable for any action which destroyed or impaired natural resources except land approved for cultivation. Those in whom rights to use were vested would themselves need to be educated towards an understanding of the interrelationships of plant and animal life in those areas used by them, as well as in ways of protecting uncultivated land from erosion or other degradation. Although in strict legal theory individuals do not own the land to which they possess title in some common law countries such as England, this has become no more than a legal quibble; in practice the land is inheritable by heirs indefinitely, as it is under the English fee simple,[15] giving *absolute* title to property.

Legal and social reform in land tenure and use need to be decided by a Commission with a view of the common good above that of any individual's self-interest. For a long time English law was equivocal on the problem of land ownership. In the eighteenth century, Blackstone was well aware of a tension between a morality of common ownership of all natural resources, and the practicability of continuing with any system of open access which conflicted with changing economic circumstances (such as had occurred in the period of enclosures). Under the influence of landowners who in some countries have protected their interests while in government, and of liberal philosophers in the Hobbes–Locke tradition (kept alive in our time by Nozick),[16] private land ownership has tended to produce political and social power structures, sometimes self-sustaining in their fabric of social privileges and influences. The consequences of an understandable defensiveness in the family retention of any land made productive by resourcefulness and arduous toil, as in USA, Canada, Australia, South America and elsewhere, have been that natural resources of potential enjoyment to many have been reserved for a few, and in some cases exploited destructively. Legal reform of the conditions of land tenure has therefore become a social, political, economic and moral question, raising subordinate questions of the conservation of natural resources, and of equity and distributive justice.

*Standing to sue* is part of social reform inasmuch as it facilitates and encourages public participation in those large questions of conservation which lie beyond the appropriate area of political decision-making because of a potential challenge to the long-term common good. Before political reform takes place, and while piecemeal and compromising decisions are made by governments on conservation, it is a matter of social justice that the public have access to the courts to resist developments which, on thoroughly investigated and well-reasoned grounds, appear to threaten the common good.

Once Commissions were established they would invite and welcome submissions, so that public participation in decision-making would be a regular feature of their determination of matters affecting the common good. Following the demarcation of responsibilities of Commissions and elected governments, *standing to sue* might still be necessary with respect to relatively minor conservation matters left to government jurisdiction. In their general land-use policy Commissions would ensure against any possibility of political interference to vitiate their plans for the common good. Conservation has a moral orientation in so far as it can be justified as contributing to quality of life or the well-being of present and future generations. It has been stressed that, in the light of present empirical evidence, this must be taken as an assumption. But in the light of some empirical evidence, it is a reasonable inference that both the natural and the cultural heritage offer satisfactions to some which may be broadly generalized by appropriate educational programmes. The *potential common good* refers exactly to this kind of improvability of quality of life by means of education. Another consideration noted earlier is that if decision-making on large conservation questions were to wait always for confirmatory empirical evidence on a connection with general quality of life, irreversible destruction of natural resources might in some cases nullify the evidence if or when it did become available. Therefore in some circumstances a rational–moral Commission would need to decide on action, or no action, on the incomplete evidence it had before it, particularly with the interests of posterity in mind.

## PRIORITIES FOR ACTION

The following priorities are proposed on the assumption that national Commissions are established. Each will be explained in turn. The first is educational reform; the second social reform; and the third political reform, including establishment of Commissions. Following political reform there would be the foundational reforms of Commissions – social and economic; and then additional reforms on matters of global concern, by agreement among national Commissioners.

**Educational Reform**

Educational reform is given precedence over others because it is fundamental to all the succeeding steps: it is very unlikely that social and political reform, and other reforms dependent on them, would be achieved without an improvement in some aspects of secondary and tertiary education, a universalization of secondary education at least, and a wide extension of continuing education into adulthood. The reform needed is vast, in principle it is practicable, though at present prospects are limited by acknowledgement of the violence, passions of hatred and aggression, and frequent exhibitions of irrational excesses which show no signs of abatement with extensions of formal educational provisions. If education is seen as a *developing* of individuals' potentialities, including improvements in rational and moral conduct, the troubling question remains as to whether *sufficient* improvement can be sustained to serve a potential common good of a distinctly improved quality of life, to which conservation education may make a clear contribution. It seems likely that something more than formal schooling is needed. Apart from that, the greatest hope comes probably not from educational reform alone, but from its interaction with social and political reform. While education is justified as demanding consideration before and above all else, since it is largely a means to other necessary reforms, it would be on-going and supported in many ways itself by concurrent social and political reforms. Educational reforms would necessarily include all sections of society, the underprivileged as well as the privileged, yet for the underprivileged some of the most urgently needed educational improvements – notably in modification of attitudes and values – cannot be adequately achieved without substantial social reforms. Similarly the will to learn some things relevant to conservation, even the will to learn skills of discussion for effective public participation, depend largely on a perception that these are not ineffectual once they are learned, but are made meaningful and relevant in the context of *political* reform by which Commissions are approachable, open and even dependent on close public cooperation on matters of the greatest social and moral concern of all, the common good. By contrast governments tend in opposite directions of remoteness and inaccessibility. There is not much point in learning that conservation is a worthwhile objective if it is realised too that decisions made by governments are difficult to change, even by Environmental Impact

Statements, especially when compromises are made by governments or their agencies with development interests; or when governments simply legislate to overrule decisions made by environment courts which have been set up specially by them for environmental protection. Motivation in education flourishes in an atmosphere of trust and integrity: both social and political reform induce changes in individual attitudes and values which in turn motivate continuing social and political reform. The first three priorities then are only initially sequential: subsequently they are concurrent, interactive and mutually beneficial.

Educational reform will be considered first with reference to widespread ignorance and the problem of illiteracy, relevant mostly but not exclusively to developing countries; second to more specific aspects of a general education; third to education of moral attitudes and values; fourth to education of relevant skills, especially in critical thinking and self-mastery for public participation.

Programmes which have as one of their objectives a sensitive appreciation of the relationship between conservation and morality obviously pass over the heads of the illiterate. The extent and complexity of the problem are not so obvious, including the initial steps that simply have to be taken before social and political reform can develop from the people's own initiatives. Statistics compiled by UNESCO indicate that in 1982 there were over 824 million illiterates in the world, aged fifteen years and over, and that in this total over 800 million were from developing countries.[17] But the situation is aggravated by the fact that illiteracy is associated with depressed social conditions. Generally the most destitute of the population are those who are also illiterate, those whose outlook on life, including a capacity for caring about conservation and caring about others, is already undermined by inadequacies in food, health and housing. In this instance, some initial improvement in social conditions, which could come only from resources of more affluent countries, seems to be a necessary priority to initiating educational improvement, though preferably aid would be concurrently social and educational. What is most disturbing in making practical judgements from the standpoint of developed countries, all of which have social problems of their own to attend to, including substantial pockets of poverty, is the *size* of the total problem. At present the constant increase in population is frustrating attempts to reduce illiteracy in absolute numbers, even though the world illiteracy rate has fallen slightly over the last few decades.[18] The social problem of population growth rate is an integral part of the problem. Even in Europe, including the USSR, there is an illiteracy rate of 2.8 per cent of the adult population, which indicates that with all efforts at achieving compulsory primary education at least, some are illiterate in societies in which an understanding of the printed word is almost a universal need for active social interaction. The situation of illiteracy is a moral one in so far as quality of life is restricted by it: it is an associated conservation problem in so far as relevant education for environmental protection is hampered by it. In brief, illiteracy frustrates the power and freedom every individual requires to participate in social life and in the determination of social and political policy according to community aspirations and needs, including a policy on conservation of natural resources. For adequate communication, as well as for participation, the Commissions would depend upon a *literate* public.

Both the subjects and the objects of practical morality are individuals *as persons*. Similarly conservation is for everyone's understanding and contribution. Illiteracy rates in various countries, developed and developing, overlook the fact that even within developed countries there are serious regional disparities. Although in relatively affluent industrialized countries about 2.5 per cent of the population are illiterate, in certain regions, such as southern Europe, the illiteracy rate is in excess of 20 per cent.[19] In some countries where primary education is a compulsory provision for all, primary schooling is not effectively supervised: in 1980 a total of 121 million children between six and eleven years of age did not attend school.[20] Included among these were a significant number from the countryside where a knowledge of conservation procedures and the will to follow them are most needed. It has always to be acknowledged that though education is given first priority in a plan for improvement of the associated moral and conservation problem, the people of impoverished countries have the overriding problem of how to keep alive, which fails understandably to initiate any motivation to learn. Thoughts of education are a far-off secondary consideration to the 200 million people in African countries south of the Sahara who face famine or the threat of famine.[21]

It is not knowledge alone which will succeed in raising the intelligent awareness of people to a potential common good within their grasp. Interest, purpose, favourable attitudes and values are all significant. The most general knowledge needed from formal

schooling into adulthood is a progressive and critical understanding
of ourselves as persons; of political systems and social institutions;
of the nature of attitudes and values; of selected aspects of natural
science, including ecosystems; of the social and economic condition
of seriously underprivileged people both in one's own country and
elsewhere in the world; of the likely impact on conservation of
nuclear and of conventional war (including the use of biological and
chemical weapons); of the effects of industrialization in polluting
air, soil and water; of the effects of agricultural overuse of the soil,
including forms of degradation; of nuclear energy for peaceful
purposes and the problem of radiation and high-risk waste disposal;
of population growth rates in the world; of methods of restoring the
earth; of conflicts between political, industrial and conservation
interests.[22] But all this knowledge has to be actively and purposely
used by individuals, and that depends more than anything on an
understanding of the nature of practical morality as it has been
outlined in Chapter 1, and the development of personal moral
values which effectively unite a concern for conservation of natural
resources with a concern for the interests of other people, including
the kind of earth and the kind of society which future generations
will inherit. A concern for quality of life may be enjoyed
emotionally, intellectually and aesthetically, but it is not merely a
cultural norm to be acquired by social interaction. From the
standpoint of practical morality, it is possible to formulate universal
standards for a quality of life for persons everywhere.[23]

The learning of moral attitudes and values requires special
mention because of its central importance in educational reform.
Certainly knowledge will be relevant to this learning, such as a
knowledge of the characteristics of sentient animals, specifically of
their capacity for suffering; and in higher forms for an enjoyable
emotional life in caring for their young, in free movement, play and
so forth. The personal valuing of natural resources in nature
reserves of various kinds, including wildernesses, is also largely
dependent on knowing something about them, but such values are
not moral values unless they are related in some way to a practical
consideration of the interests of others, whether or not this leads to
a concern for the common good. Other knowledge already noted
which is directly relevant to both practical morality and to
conservation concerns degradation of the earth, the suffering and
helplessness of those people contributing to it, the moral responsibility of others to rescue both the people and the natural resources.

From the detached and benevolent stance, becoming aware of such human predicaments transforms sociological knowledge to moral knowledge, provided that there is already a structure and understanding of moral principles. In moral terms the world is one people, and the earth is one resource.

Environmental education, like environmental ethics, is sometimes based on a non-moral value of respect for (or love of) nature. In that form its fundamental weakness for wide relevance to other persons is that it does not lead compellingly to action except self-justifying action for those who experience the valuing. Moral ought statements or conclusions do not follow from it. The action schema for this kind of valuing of nature is the same as for valuing nature out of scientific curiosity, or from a scientific standpoint alone: desire and emotion – non-moral attitude and value – self-rewarding action. Reports on some environmental education, in secondary schools in particular, suggest that it is too heavily informational, failing frequently to motivate students towards any personal moral and emotional involvement in conservation as something they should be caring about. The total number of persons visiting national parks (in some countries reported to be declining) may be related to the kind of conservation education that is given. So too may be the incidence of vandalism in national parks. In educational curricula a fundamental change of emphasis seems to be needed. Certainly the non-moral value of scientific curiosity needs to be fostered as widely as possible, but what is potentially universal is rather a moral valuing of other persons. This is the *lingua franca* which has an appeal to all students, and from this moral principle of a consideration of the interests of others moral oughts *do* follow. Conservation education has to show that some conservation questions are moral questions too, not merely personal preferences based on aesthetic or intellectual inclinations, as in the case of personal love of nature or of scientific curiosity, each of which is a non-moral value.

In the secondary school, and in the last year or two of elementary education, methodology is all important for a connection to be made between conservation and morality. As in all moral education at these periods of formal schooling, the most beneficial method is group discussion, led by carefully selected, sensitive and unobtrusive teachers able to guide without forcefully directing. The interaction among peers is a moral education in itself, each learning to listen to and to respect others' views as well as to contribute. It is that understanding which provides the motivation and the reason to view all other persons similarly, wherever they may live, appreciating that they have interests, values, viewpoints, beliefs, aspirations or goals as all others have, that there is indeed a moral unity of people everywhere, as there is a unity of natural resources. In general, information on conservation questions would be learned incidentally in this procedure, not formally by teacher instruction; and so would moral principles of considering others' interests and respecting others as persons, treating all fairly and without prejudice or discrimination. Values of equity in distributive justice would be expected to develop from repeated discussions of appropriate situations of acute underprivilege and the associated degradation of the earth. The teacher's own example of compassion, expression of personal values in various ways, and skill in stimulating students to think through problem situations themselves, would demand high professional competence. On teachers' complete suitability for the role they would play, the educational success of the activity largely depends, supported by a carefully devised programme of conservation problems or situations with moral connections. Many such discussion topics are to be found, with appropriate research material for students themselves to explore, best left to the professional judgement of those in daily touch with students' capacities and interests. Some might become intellectually and morally involved, for instance, by considering the kind of earth their grandchildren might inherit, if they are to have a suitable quality of life; or by considering the consequences of an overpopulated earth; or by planning to make national parks more accessible to poor people; or by discussing the effects on sentient animals of a destruction of their habitats by forest-clearing. Many discussion possibilities are to be found in connection with the nuclear threat, the peaceful uses of nuclear energy and its dangers, industrial pollution and moral obligations to assist impoverished people, each conjoining conservation and a practical morality of considering others' interests.

The methodology of group discussions would be varied by imaginative exercises on experiences of isolated survivors of nuclear conflict; outdoor activities such as visits to natural areas or holiday camps to observe plant and animal life; carefully selected visual aids, such as on Ethiopia or the devastation of Hiroshima. If suitable funds could be organized, in some cases exchange visits by students of various countries to some of the most distinctive natural features of each, with students selected without regard to social or economic circumstances, would help to foster the idea of the earth as one of common ownership and common responsibility.

Developing moral attitudes and values would be expected to have a much clearer orientation towards *action* than would values of personal love of nature or scientific curiosity. Moral values are universalizable, while non-moral values of this kind are not. The action-schema for practical morality presupposes rational–dispositional deliberation prior to action, the dispositional component comprising mainly moral attitudes and values.[24]

Guided group discussions provide opportunities also to develop the first skills in critical thinking on which practical moral thinking partly depends, uniting efforts at clarity of understanding and statement with a moral purpose of integrity and directness. In these circumstances leadership would demonstrate impartiality and fairness by example, as well as self-mastery and resistance to self-enhancing impulses.

## Social, Political and Economic Reform

Social and educational reform are closely related in ways already explained: those who resent their social conditions may have unfavourable attitudes to education, which may be something they see as serving the interests of the advantaged rather than their own; similarly, willingness to participate in public affairs may be inhibited by dissatisfaction with social conditions and the society which tolerates contradictions. In the case of reform of land ownership so that it is vested in the people, attitudes and values towards objects related to conservation may be favourably modified by reform.

The most sensitive link between social and educational reform is the first of these, which is expressed in the problem of equality of educational opportunity. Though in developed countries there is usually a universal provision of elementary and secondary education at least, what are provided are equal schooling opportunities rather than equal *educational* opportunities, because of the unfavourable attitudes to learning commonly associated with extremes of poverty.[25] Social reform to eliminate all such extremes is therefore a prerequisite to educational reform by which all children would have approximately equal opportunities in developing their selected potentialities, regardless of home background.

Both educational and social reforms are needed before political reform has a chance of succeeding by means consistent with the moral principles explained in Chapter 1. To achieve a Commission with responsibilities for the common good would first require a much higher level of education than is general in communities throughout the world at present, with much better understanding of political systems and their limitations, much greater capacities for critical thinking, and much better moral attitudes and values so that people themselves, and not only the Commission, would become personally involved in the common good. Similarly, political reforms would require societies with much better distributive justice than at present, so that extremes of social disadvantage would no longer be impediments to a total willingness to work for the common good. In the last resort the social and political reforms which could be introduced by the establishment of a Commission would find their support and justification in the minds of citizens made more rational and more moral by prior educational and social reforms.

The first task of national Commissions would be to institute early reforms on matters of the common good, free entirely of political bias: population growth policy, land-use policy, defence policy; each of them from fundamental moral perspectives. By that time the people would be ready to reject conspicuous disparities between military spending and defence spending of the kind now familiar.[26]

Since large economic changes affecting production, employment and many social adjustments cannot be made by unilateral national policy and action, their success would be dependent very largely on international agreement. That itself would be dependent on acceptance of a principle of political self-determination for the managerial functions of government, given agreement on Commissions' functions. The Commissions would have neither the will nor the means to interfere in the internal political situation of nations. Yet there are some *economic* features with worldwide moral implications: overproduction in some commodities, duplication of national production efforts to capture world markets. Conferences of Commissioners would probably direct their attention to the possibilities of international regulation of production, while ensuring that there is no unfair burden on any nation, recommending production of some goods to those countries better fitted than others to produce them, and opening up possibilities for developing countries to establish secondary industries, rather than being locked out by the industrial strength of more affluent trading nations.

Conservation has clear connections with economic development, and the two would be considered within the total social, political and moral complex.

Because of the ingrained self-interest of human nature and its conspicuous political and economic manifestations, especially among affluent nations in the extent of their preparedness to assist developing countries to become established as industrial competitors, sacrifices which would be involved in any economic rationalization on a world scale would be one of the greatest hurdles confronting Commissions. Sacrifices could not be expected to come readily at the present level of individual practical morality, even in the knowledge that they were needed to help a country to become slowly self-supporting, though dependent on continuing aid for years ahead; or to help save the earth from irreversible degradation in acutely impoverished countries, especially for younger and future generations. The crucial test of a global practical morality is whether benevolence in impartially considering others' interests belongs to moral theory, or whether it can be translated to practice of a kind that calls for personal sacrifices. Only a groundswell of public moral concern is likely to shake the most entrenched self-interests and self-indulgence, but there can be no bland optimism for prospects of success. If reason and morality do not prevail, with Commissions' recommendations given wide support by a public made ready for change by education, the present world trend towards an ultimate degradation of the earth, either by war or by increasing industrial-ization in vain efforts to sustain ever larger world populations, will pose a continuing threat to quality of life. The interests of future generations are particularly at risk.

Commissions would themselves decide on the kind of economies best suited to conservation from moral standpoints. There seems little doubt that a curbing of industrial growth in developed countries would be a serious consideration, and that it would be morally preferable to divert some industrial energy away from the production of unnecessary luxury items to necessities for some parts of the world. There seems little doubt too that the world's population growth rate is excessive, creating an increasing demand for goods, putting ever heavier strains on natural resources, exacerbating the problem of polluting industries and the capacity of impoverished people to help themselves. But the solutions of complex social, economic, political and moral problems are much more difficult to perceive than the need for change, and

Commissions would probably confer many times before reaching policy conclusions. One of the possibilities is that, when in possession of all relevant information and apprised of the social effects of economic adjustments, Commissions might recommend that for a specified period each of the developed nations should adjust to a zero production growth or a steady-state economy. In circumstances of an increasing emphasis on moral education, it is expected that social values would change gradually, with a disciplined reduction in consumer demand becoming largely self-imposed, while preserving individual freedom as much as possible. Whenever social justice prevails, with each sharing the same opportunities and the same burdens, it seems likely that ostentatious displays of wealth in the accumulation of unessential consumer goods would become as unpopular and as intolerable as they were in some countries immediately after the Second World War. And during war, people generally show that they are prepared to do entirely without luxury goods, even to make the most of privation on restricted rations, *as long as conditions are the same for all.*

Vague notions of changes from consumer to conserver societies underestimate the complexity and extent of the moral and educational transformation needed, without jettisoning the obvious benefits to quality of life of particular technological discoveries, as in diagnostic medicine. A change in social values will be apparent when money-making is as distasteful throughout the world as it was to Plato, and when respect for intellectual and moral quality replaces appetite, envy, greed and one-sided self-interest. Both education and experience suggest that people's values are not as rigidly unmodifiable as is sometimes supposed: the overriding need is non-discrimination, a social order that is seen by all as fair, as Plato had explained in the *Republic.*

With evidence of a change of social values towards acceptance of fairness in the treatment of all persons as a common principle of justice, changes in the moral attitudes and values of governments would almost certainly follow, influenced by the general standard of moral awareness in the community. At that stage there would be no reason for governments to be in conflict with Commissions. Governments on their part could be expected to support the notion of Commissions making decisions on the large moral questions as indicated, and their support (rather than any initial resistance from envy) would be needed. Commissions in turn could be expected to acknowledge the demanding role of governments in their very responsible management of the nation's affairs, mindful of the complex and difficult nature of contemporary societies.

Conservation depends ultimately on moral cooperation and understanding between Commissions, governments and the people in the political organization proposed. With the establishment of a just society, it would be much more likely than now that the earth and its resources would be cared for as a joint moral responsibility of persons.

## CONCLUSION

In this final statement the purpose is to reconstruct the main conceptual framework in order to show the progression of the argument and the complexity of the relationship between conservation and practical morality. The foundation of this structure are the two primary concerns of practical morality: first, a perception of *personhood* with relevance to people everywhere on earth, in total disregard of political or national boundaries, and within a comprehensive morality of an *equal consideration* of the interests of persons; second, the common good of people wherever they may live. The concept of the *common good* as the proper end of government widens from national concerns to global concerns and a moral concern for the *quality of life* of all people. From historical concerns among philosophers for security as the main feature of the common good, Bentham's generalized notion of *well-being* (happiness or satisfaction) is a significant development, because it provides the bridge between the limited common good of most English empirical philosophers from Hobbes and Locke onward and the concept of quality of life, with wide application to conservation and other social problems of contemporary societies, particularly in view of their marked social contradictions. *Individual interests* are central to the practical morality proposed, referring to acts which aim to benefit others or to promote their well-being. The common good generalizes these interests.

Quality of life is the conceptual bridge between the common good and *conservation*. Not all conservation questions are moral questions inasmuch as some of these have no clear connection with quality of life as a common good, or with any consideration of the interests of others, including interests of sentient animals. There is no indubitable evidence that all persons derive benefit from the natural and cultural heritage, but for a practical morality which is based on moral acts (or on restraint in relevant circumstances) a case may be made for disregarding the necessity for conclusive evidence on the following grounds.

First, the interests of future generations need to be considered. Continuing destruction of natural areas such as wildernesses and rainforests leads to a less diversified environment, thereby reducing the scope for benefit from intellectual and aesthetic satisfactions. The view of the welcome colour of the earth from space, in contrast with the barrenness elsewhere, is the often-repeated experience of astronauts. It is probable that future generations will have increasing opportunities to observe this contrast. If it becomes less marked as time goes on, it will probably indicate that the earth's habitability is being impaired beyond its capacity for recovery. It is a reasonable assumption that our grandchildren's grandchildren (looking ahead as far as we normally can by using a living chain of kinship) will not be radically different in nature from ourselves. They too will have a variety of *interests*, and perhaps an increasing technological capacity to bring the life of the rainforest and the wilderness visually into the home or the study centre. Once awarenesses are heightened by education and appropriate social conditions, it is probable that they too would derive a universal *aesthetic* satisfaction at least from contact with a green and colourful earth of diversified living things rather than one that is bare, or covered extensively with man-made works. Yet to ask for their preferences under *any* social conditions, and without appropriate education, would probably yield the same result as it would at present. That is why Preference Utilitarianism does not provide reliable guidance in practice towards an improvement in quality of life: the preferences elicited would often be ill-informed and influenced by actual social conditions. (Ask slum-dwellers of cities such as Bombay, or any of the increasing number of city-dwellers in the world, if they would prefer a green earth or an earth of man-made cities, and the results might be disturbing to those conservationists who are unaware of the complexity of the social questions involved.)

Second, population increases are very probable, even to three or four times the present world levels, at a time when the sustainability of the earth is already under serious stress in some regions. The increase is anticipated even if, in the next decade or so, decisions are made to check population growth throughout the world. There may therefore be an increasing desire of future generations – especially with the benefit of improved education and social conditions – to seek relief from the density of urban settlements where most people will live.

Third, interest in natural areas may be developed much more widely by improved educational programmes. There is no reason to assume that natural or cultural resources have the potential for contributing to quality of life only when the initial interest is already strong. Much of the task of educators is to *develop* interests, often from unpromising beginnings. There is always a potential common good to be attained by education, and the area of conservation has not been found unproductive.

The notion of *education* is fundamentally an *improving* notion, one of developing potentialities in various selected directions. While education emphasizes individual potentialities, the notion of the *potential common good* generalizes these for a whole community, and even for a community that is worldwide.

The potential common good is dependent for attainment on conditions of social justice. Social injustices, expressed conspicuously in extremes of poverty and underprivilege, and in any discrimination between individuals on irrelevant grounds, affect the individual's attitude to other persons, to society and to conservation. Social injustice has an effect on the very motivation to learn, to take advantage of formal educational opportunities offered. International cooperation on conservation is dependent largely on a common perception of a just society of world people. It is unlikely to be promoted by paternalistic aid, or by any other failure to give an equal consideration to the interests of persons wherever they might live.

The potential common good is also dependent on *political reform*. Conservation is one of a small number of large issues which are of the deepest moral concern inasmuch as they affect future generations as well as present ones. The nuclear threat is a conservation issue as well as a moral one; so too are degradation of the earth through abject poverty and the imperative to alleviate the suffering in such places, and the threat of world population outstripping the capacity of the earth to sustain it. Such far-reaching moral questions must be decided by *exceptional* persons of every nation, given constitutional responsibilities and functions separated from those of governments, and meeting in international conferences to decide on matters directly concerned with the habitability of the earth and the quality of human life on it, as well as on the preservation and protection of sentient animals. The *common good* is the people's good, but generally it is not the people's perception of their good, or the *public interest* as seen by them or by their political leaders. It is a long-term moral and rational view which is seen by the most exceptional persons selected from every community.

On the notion of *Commissions* as it has been presented there are several points to be stressed. First, they are symbolic of rational–moral thought. The views attributed to them are not attempts to preempt what they would decide in practice (after thorough deliberations), but simply to point to what is a rational–moral point of view on first thoughts at least, in contrast with one that is not. Second, Commissions are presented as part of practical theory, not of ideal theory, for they are themselves imperfect. Restriction of membership to the most exceptional persons in the community on rational and moral criteria implies not that they are infallible, but that they are the least prone of all citizens to error in making practical judgements on the common good. More positively, they have the capacity to perceive what the common good is, in the sense that they can be *relied upon* for this capacity more than others in the community. (There is no Platonic exclusiveness of all others in this suggestion: certainly some talented persons outside the Commissions would have the required perspicacity.) Third, the preliminary proposals for their organization are not intended as an exercise in political science, but simply to emphasize that in this organization, or in some other more appropriate one, the large moral and social questions of our time, including conservation, are above party political systems. Fourth, the members of the Commissions, apart from having a rational–moral perspective on all problems before them, would also adopt an educational standpoint: that is, a perception of persons as capable of continuing improvement (given appropriate social conditions and suitable education).

The priorities of an action programme are initiation by educational reform, then immediate attention to a *just society*. Political reform succeeds educational and social reform, but when society is reformed, the three become mutually supportive and interdependent. Commissions could not be established effectively without educational and social reform, including a reform of the moral attitudes and values of citizens and of politicians: otherwise they would be in danger of becoming ineffectual pawns of government or of power groups among the people.

In short, the prospects for the habitability of the earth, and for the common good served partly by conservation, depend on *vast* educational changes, the most far-reaching changes conceivable in the knowledge, attitudes and values of the people, so that from widespread apathy and unconcern there develops moral responsibility. There is no great hope for arresting the present drift without social and political reform.

While it is impossible to dismiss the contemporary scene of violence and aggression and the never-ending warfare in some part of the world (with over 16 million deaths from war or war-related causes since the end of the Second World War),[27] a practical morality is a morality of action, not a moralistic reflection on human shortcomings. There are many contemporary checks on optimism, and a rational–moral standpoint would take full account of our poor record over the last 100 years since Mill saw that the capacity for rational conduct is the only hope for humanity. The ultimate check to optimism must be the nuclear threat and the immoral and irrational political leaders who propagate it. T. S. Eliot once called Dante, the creator of the Inferno in his *Divine Comedy*, 'the most universal of poets in the modern languages'[28] for the quality of his visual imagination (and the lucidity of his style). What Dante's imagination would conjure up now to give mankind a universal picture of a *nuclear* inferno, nearly seven centuries after his own vivid imagery of a much more limited scene, would undoubtedly help to arouse many from their intellectual and imaginative torpor. Without such a stimulus, all efforts must now be bent towards raising the level of awareness of potential horrors that are much less improbable than the apathetic choose to believe.

In more general terms, to counteract pessimism and apathy on moral and social questions, Plato's thought needs to be added to Mill's, with an educational perspective on man's potential for improvement both morally and rationally. Superficial impressions may still seem to confirm that the large majority of the human population are incorrigible creatures of appetite, quarrelsome as Hobbes thought they were, dominated by self-interest as even Hume thought too – with all his generous understanding of human nature. But competent educators are insistent on man's capacity for improvement. The great difficulty is that improvability can *not* be assured under *any* conditions. That is why reform of social conditions in all countries must, in practical terms, be linked with education as the first priority for action in solving problems of the common good, including conservation.

If Dante is the universal poet, in some respects Plato is the universal political philosopher. In two fundamental ways he has shown what is necessary for political reform towards the attainability of a common good: first, a *just society*, second, government by the very *best persons* in the community – best in the capacity for rational decision-making, best dispositionally in the capacity for practical morality. But it is only the common good which is reliably perceptible by exceptional persons, and generally not by others; the second and universal moral capacity – that of understanding personhood and the significance of an equal consideration of the interests of others – is within reach of ordinary persons with an appropriate moral education. That second perception was denied to Plato, making it difficult to acclaim him as the universal *moral* philosopher. And the perception of the improvability of all persons rationally and morally (within their individual capacities) was also denied him, making it difficult in turn to acclaim him as the universal *educational* philosopher.

As there is no need for any special conservation morality, so there is no need for a philosophy of conservation as a special branch of philosophy. That is the task of general philosophers with a perspective on knowledge which comprehends conservation's complex moral face – made complex not by the principles of practical morality itself, but by its own many social, scientific, political, economic, legal and administrative involvements.

# Notes

## CHAPTER 1

1 Anthropologists have become conspicuous at times for misperceiving the personhood of those of different cultures, those sometimes presumed to be 'primitive' or in other ways inferior. The presumption of some academics to lecture to indigenous students in the rudiments of the students' own culture (their information gathered largely from informers of the culture, only minimally from direct observation) has been noted by students themselves, as in Papua-New Guinea.

   Imposed treaties in the nineteenth century left sensitive persons humiliated for generations – treaties such as the Nanking Treaty of 1842, affecting the alienation of Hong Kong. See *Beijing Review*, vol. 7, no. 52 (Dec.1984) p.4.

   In day-to-day administrative situations the threat to personhood is very common. For instance, judgements of preference may be made by selection committees for recruiting or promoting staff (as in universities) often without clear or consistent criteria, and on a presumption of infallibility from the committee's own perception of their status and experience.

2 UN, *Declaration on Race and Racial Prejudice*, Article I, 1 (1978).

3 'I fully subscribe to the judgement of those writers who maintain that of all the differences between man and the lower animals the moral sense or conscience is by far the most important.' *The Descent of Man* (London: Watts & Co., 1930). Page references are to this edition.

4 The strong didactic and moralistic impulse in the eighteenth century was evident in political and religious thought. See, for instance, Shaftesbury's 'An Essay on the Freedom of Wit and Humour' in *Characteristics of Men, Manners, Opinions, Times etc.*, various editions; and Joseph Butler's *Fifteen Sermons* (1726) in *Works*, vol.II (Oxford, 1850).

5 D. Hume, *A Treatise of Human Nature*, ed. L. A. Selby-Bigge, bk.III, pt.I, sect. II, p.495 (Oxford: Clarendon Press, 1888). Hume was careful to attempt an analysis of the various senses in which 'nature' and 'natural' are used (474). Sentiments of morality are certainly 'natural', he explained, inasmuch as they are not rare or unusual among us. It was sympathy that was in Hume's mind more than any other aspect of the moral sense. Later, and after publication of the *Treatise*, Hume had much more to say on benevolence as a moral sentiment. In his *Enquiry Concerning the Principles of Morals* he considered benevolence as the principal social virtue. See *Enquiries Concerning Human Understanding*

*and Concerning the Principles of Morals*, reprinted from the posthumous edition of 1777, and edited by L. A. Selby-Bigge, 3rd edn, revision by P. H. Nidditch (Oxford University Press, 1975) pp.176–82 and 184.

6 Apart from natural disasters, there are also man-made disasters which raise moral questions, such as that at Bhopal in India – questions of respecting the interests of developing countries in suitable safety standards of industries, as well as in proximity of settlements to them. The world sensitivity to the moral implications of this disaster are expressed, for instance, in *Beijing Review*, vol.27, no.51 (Dec.1984). The Economic Commission for Africa has now listed twenty-one countries facing famine in the sub-Saharan region, with rapidly deteriorating social and economic conditions. See *UNDRO News*, Office of the UN Disaster Relief Coordinator (Jan/Feb 1984).

7 For these see Kant's *Critique of Practical Reason and Other Works on the Theory of Ethics*, trans. T. K. Abbott, 6th edn (London: Longmans, Green, 1909) pp.38–9; 47. The references are to 'Fundamental Principles of the Metaphysic of Morals', second section.

8 H. Sidgwick, *The Elements of Politics* (London and New York: Macmillan, 1891) ch. XIII, p.191. In contrast with true morality, positive morality was relatively indefinite and inconsistent (contrasting with the law too in these respects), p.195.

9 A British court recently upheld a defendant's plea that suppression by the government of the circumstances relating to a particular incident in a recent war was not in the public interest. Government interest and the public interest were seen to be at variance, indicating that a government's perception of the public interest may be in conflict with some others' perceptions of it, or of the common good.

10 *The Republic*, various editions. Page references are to the Everyman edition, trans. A. D. Lindsay (London: Dent, 1935; New York: Dutton, 1935).

11 L. S. Hsii, *The Political Philosophy of Confucianism* (London: Routledge, 1932) pp.105, 127. Although when Confucius wrote in approx. 500 B.C. China's feudal system was disintegrating, there were still widespread tyranny and exploitation of peasants.

12 Aristotle, *Politics*, various editions and translations. The translation used here is by Benjamin Jowett.

13 From 'The First Philippic Against Marcus Antonius', in *Selected Political Speeches of Cicero*, trans. M. Grant (Harmondsworth: Penguin Books, 1969) p.298.

14 *Julius Caesar*, Act V, sc.v,lines 71–2. With dramatic licence, Shakespeare gave rather more honour to Brutus than he deserved historically, but in so doing expressed both the Roman love of state and the republican ideal of the common good.

15 For a comprehensive survey of seventeenth-century writers on this and related matters concerning individual property rights, see J. A. W. Gunn, *Politics and the Public Interest in the Seventeenth Century* (London: Routledge and Kegan Paul, 1969) pp.324ff.

16 T. Hobbes, *Leviathan* (Harmondsworth: Penguin Books, 1968). Page references are to this edition (first published in 1651).

17 *De Cive* was translated into English from the original Latin and published in the same year (1651). Its English title was *Philosophical Rudiments Concerning Government and Society*. Page references are to the first collected edition of Hobbes' works, edited by Molesworth in 1841. See *The English Works of Thomas Hobbes* (London: John Bohn, 1841) vol.II, ch.V.

18 J.-J. Rousseau, *The Social Contract*, trans. M. Cranston (Harmondsworth: Penguin Books, 1968). Page references are to this edition. Originally published in 1762.

19 Despite the difficulties of justifying the notion of a general will, some have sought to defend it as a convenience of usage. One such defence of its linguistic utility argues that it provides a metaphorical explanation of social intention and action, emphasizing social unity even though it is individuals who have intentions and who act. The will shows the individual as a unit in action, and the general will shows the society or state as a unit in action. See B. Mayo in P. Laslett (ed), *Philosophy, Politics and Society* (Oxford: Basil Blackwell, 1956) pp.92–7. First series.

20 *The Works of Jeremy Bentham*, published under the superintendence of his executor, John Bowring (Edinburgh: William Tait, 1843). See vol.2: 'An Examination of the Declaration of the Rights of Man and the Citizen', comment on Article VI, p.507. Page references to this edn.

21 D. Hume, *A Treatise of Human Nature*, bk.III, sect.VI.

22 *The Works of Jeremy Bentham*, vol.I, *Principles of Morals and Legislation*.

23 Ibid., vol.III, ch.I.

24 For a selection of these, see L. A. Selby-Bigge, *British Moralists* (Oxford: Clarendon Press, 1897). For criticism of Hobbes in this work see Samuel Clarke, 'Discourse Upon Natural Religion', pp.38–9. Page references to Shaftesbury and Hutcheson are to this edn.

25 J. Rawls, *A Theory of Justice* (Oxford University Press, 1972). 'Justice as Fairness' is published in P. Laslett and W. G. Runciman (eds), *Philosophy, Politics and Society*, pp.132–57. Second series.

26 Rawls explains an institution as 'a public system of rules which defines offices and positions with their rights and duties, powers and immunities, and the like' (p.55).

27 For Rawls' controversial *difference principle* see pp.75–83. The significance of the *original position* is explained on pp.17–22. It is an intellectual position taken by contracting parties behind a 'veil of ignorance' concerning what their actual interests are, all parties adopting a position of equality and rationality as they work out together the terms of their future association.

28 Public interest groups, or lobby groups, have been prominent in most industrialized societies in the last two decades or so. For an account of their structure and objectives see J. M. Berry, *Lobbying for the People. The Political Behavior of Public Interest Groups* (Princeton University Press, 1977). (The perspective is sociological rather than philosophical.)

29 Mill's *Utilitarianism* is in various editions. Page references are to *Mill's Ethical Writings*, ed. J. B. Schneewind (New York: Collier Books;

188 *Notes*

London: Collier-Macmillan, 1965).
30 Cf. S. I. Benn, 'Interests in Politics', *Proceedings of the Aristotelian Society*, vol.60 (1960) p.129: an interest 'is no more than a claim with reasons offered in support of it'.
31 The demands on the individual in perceiving the common interest have been stated in ideal theory in this way: 'the public interest may be presumed to be what men would choose if they saw clearly, thought rationally, acted disinterestedly and benevolently'. W. Lippmann, *The Public Philosophy* (London: Hamish Hamilton, 1955) p.44. Here the 'public interest' is identified with the *common good*.
32 K. Marx and F. Engels, *The German Ideology* (London: Lawrence and Wishart, 1976) pp. 246–7 (Progress Publishers, Moscow, pp. 263–4) vol.I,III (written 1845–6). The authors are replying to the views of Stirner. The former view is illustrated in T. Nagel's, *The Possibility of Altruism* (Oxford: Clarendon Press, 1970). In this the challenge to altruism is largely from 'the manner in which human beings have conducted themselves' (p.146), rather than from any serious consideration of what man might become by education.
33 See n.31. For Rawls' original position, see n.27.
34 Bentham explained that the method of summing pleasure, or of determining a balance of pleasure over pain, was one of simple arithmetic (*Introduction to the Principles of Morals and Legislation*, ch.I, V, p.16). See also his reference to political arithmetic in his *Codification Proposal*, vol.IV, pt.I, sec.3, p.540.
35 *Utilitarianism*, from *Mill's Ethical Writings*. It is noteworthy that Mill substituted *interest* for *happiness*.
36 G. E. Moore, *Principia Ethica* (Cambridge University Press, 1962). For Sidgwick's views on utilitarianism see his *The Methods of Ethics*, 7th edn (London: Macmillan, 1907).
37 For various views on this question see A. Quinton, *Utilitarian Ethics* (London: Macmillan, 1973), especially p.43 for the adequacy of a *general impression* of pleasure and pain; and J. J. C. Smart and Bernard Williams, *Utilitarianism For and Against* (Cambridge University Press, 1973), where Smart (pp.44–5) commends *spontaneity* as opposed to the utilitarian calculation.
38 For instance, E. F. Carritt charged utilitarians with neglecting justice and individual rights as they look solely to a totality of good results. *Ethical and Political Thinking* (Oxford: Clarendon Press, 1947) p.145.
39 Hare, *Moral Thinking. Its Levels, Method, and Point* (Oxford: Clarendon Press, 1981).
40 R. M. Hare, 'Reply to J. M. Mackie' in *Utility and Rights*, ed. R. G. Frey (Oxford: Basil Blackwell, 1985) p.111.
41 A suggestion of Karl Popper's in *The Open Society and its Enemies*, 5th edn (London: Routledge and Kegan Paul, 1966) vol.I, ch.5, n.6.
42 One philosopher with apprehensions about the effects on personal morality of a utilitarian, public-reaching orientation, is B. Williams in *Utilitarianism For and Against*, p.136.
43 Ibid., p.147. Bernard Williams refers to the simple-mindedness of Preference Utilitarianism.

44 Williams attributed 'simple-mindedness' to Preference Utilitarians with respect to social decisions, which might be misleadingly applied to their findings on individual preferences. See ibid., p.149.

45 J. L. Mackie, 'Rights, Utility, and Universalization', in Frey, *Utility and Rights*, p.87.

46 In *Justice, Morality and Education* (London: Macmillan, 1985), I have suggested this as the formal notion of justice, with wide distributive applications especially to equality of educational opportunity.

47 For the rights-based position advanced by J. L. Mackie, opposing utilitarianism, see his 'Rights, Utility, and Universalization', in Frey (ed.), *Utility and Rights*, pp. 86–105. See also, 'Reply to J. L. Mackie', in the same, by R. M. Hare, pp.106–20, especially pp.108–9. For other views on rights, see J. Griffin, 'Towards a Substantive Theory of Rights', ibid., pp.137–60.

48 From Kant's *Critique of Practical Reason and other Works on the Theory of Ethics*. The practical imperative that followed was: 'So act as to treat humanity, whether in thine own person or in that of another, in every case as an end withal, never as a means only' (*Fundamental Principles of the Metaphysic of Morals*, pp.46–7).

49 C. Fried, *Right and Wrong* (Cambridge, Mass.: Harvard University Press, 1978) p.85.

50 Ibid., p.7.

51 A fuller explanation of these is given in *Justice, Morality and Education*, ch.4.

## CHAPTER 2

1 Fragment 21 in P. Wheelwright, *Heraclitus* (Princeton University Press, 1959). Cf. Fragment XLI in I. Bywater, *Heraclitus of Ephesus* (Chicago: Argonaut Publishers, 1969) p.94.

2 Aldo Leopold, *Sand County Almanac* (New York: Oxford University Press, 1949) p.207. Leopold's enthusiasm motivated widespread interest and concern, especially in the USA. (He was not a moral philosopher.)

3 In *Man's Responsibility for Nature*, 2nd edn (London: Duckworth, 1974, 1980), John Passmore's aim is different: it is to show that there is a fundamental *Western ethic* applying over the centuries to Western civilization, and that there is no need for any special environmental ethic, for questions of conservation are adequately resolvable within that ethical tradition. For a critical review of this book by V. Routley see *Australian Journal of Philosophy*, vol.53, no.2 (August 1975) pp.171–85, in particular for a restrictive view of preservation as distinct from conservation (pp.179–80), a viewpoint on moral obligations to posterity (p.180), and for an attitude to wildernesses (pp.182–3).

4 These three examples are from the agreed management objectives of the International Union for the Conservation of Nature and Natural Resources, the UN Environmental Programme and the World Wildlife Fund, in *World Conservation Strategy* (1980). See Executive Summary, p.VI.

5 From General Principles of the UN World Charter for Nature (Oct 1982).
6 From 'Observations on the Beautiful and the Sublime' (1764). See A. Biese, *The Development of the Feeling for Nature in the Middle Ages and Modern Times* (New York: Burt Franklin, n.d. (published in London, 1905)).
7 J. S. Mill, *Autobiography* (London: Longmans, Green, Reader and Dyer, 1875) pp.146–50. For one such reference to Mill and an implied instrumental value in nature's inspiration see H. Rolston, 'Can and Ought We to Follow Nature', in *Environmental Ethics*, vol.I, no.1 (Spring 1979) p.30. For the second view that contact with nature provides general psychological benefits see, for example, E. Partridge, 'Nature as a Moral Resource', *Environmental Ethics*, vol.6, no.2 (Summer 1984) pp.101–30.
8 For a biographical background and its connection with Wordsworth's attitude to nature see M. Lacey, *Wordsworth's View of Nature* (Cambridge University Press, 1948). One of the strongest expressions of Wordsworth's personal feeling for nature is in his 'Lines Composed Above Tintern Abbey', describing his impression of sublimity.
9 This refers to Garrett Hardin's 'The Tragedy of the Commons', *Science*, vol.162 (1968) pp.1243–8. See also his *The Limits of Altruism: An Ecologist's View of Survival* (Bloomington and London: Indiana University Press, 1977), in which the altruism of internationalism is discredited from a limited view of the dominance of self-interest.
10 The reference to 'major philosophies' refers to those argued for and defended in academic publications, and of sufficient intellectual rigour to command respect among those who pursue philosophy as a discipline, particularly in universities, where not only arguments, but also assumptions, are examined critically.
11 In some environmental ethics there may be a concealed premiss that God as creator is to be held with reverence. In those cases where such a premiss is concealed rather than openly stated, the form of the reasoning does not lead clearly to the conclusion that therefore all God's work (that is, all nature) is an object of reverence.
12 *Sand County Almanac*. Leopold's love of nature is evident in his writing, sometimes with a lyrical nostalgia for the past: 'No living man will see again the long-grass prairie, where a sea of prairie flowers lapped at the stirrups of the pioneer' (p. 189).
13 An argument used by C. Stone in *Should Trees Have Standing?* (Los Altos, California: Kaufman, 1974). See also *Environment Law Review* (1973) pp.553–604 (reprinted from *The Southern California Law Review*, vol. 45. no. 2, pp.450–501).
14 Page reference is to John Locke, *Works* (London: Tegg, 1823) Book II.
15 *Leviathan*. See Chapter 1, ref.16 above.
16 From *Enquiries Concerning Human Understanding and Concerning the Principles of Morals*.
17 Land Values Publication Department, Glasgow etc., 1909, ed. E. Wedgwood. Tolstoy strongly supported the views which Henry George had expressed against private property in *Social Problems*

(London: Kegan Paul, 1884), and *Progress and Poverty* (London: Reeves, 1880).

18 Page references are to the 9th edn (London: Longmans Green, 1886), vol.I, bk.II, ch.II.

19 J. Dymond, *Essays on the Principles of Morality*, 2nd edn (London: Hamilton, Adams, 1830) vol.I, ch.II, p.184.

20 *Principles of the Civil Code*, pt.I, ch.VIII, 'Of Property', p.309. From *The Works of Jeremy Bentham*. See Chapter 1 above, ref.20.

21 Published by T. Cadell and J. Butterworth and Son, 16th edn (London, 1825). Page references are to this edn. The work was originally published in the previous century.

22 The lack of clear definition of land rights is not confined to England. It applies in most countries which have been influenced by English common law, including the USA. See L. K. Caldwell on land use in *Environment Law Review* (1975) pp.409–25.

23 The World Heritage List is the responsibility of the World Heritage Convention of the UN, or the International Convention for the Protection of the World Cultural and Natural Heritage.

24 The diversity of interests in monuments is reflected in the open legal definition of 'monument' in England, applying not only to structures or works, caves and excavations, but even to traces of previous works such as soil discoloration. See F. A. Sharman, 'The New Law on Ancient Monuments', *Journal of Planning and Environment Law* (Nov. 1981) pp.785–6.

25 Moral thinking and political thinking mix, for instance, in the allocation of government funds to UNESCO. While this UN agency aims morally at improving the quality of life, such as by increasing the literacy rate, it is dependent on funds from member nations which may withhold or reduce them for political reasons.

26 B. Johnson, *International Environmental Law* (Stockholm: Liber Förlag, 1976) p.22. The author refers to Principle 21 of the Stockholm Conference, 1972, reflecting the morality of international relations with respect to damage by one state to the environment of another, and Principle 22 on compensation. The Draft Declaration at the Stockholm Conference refers to the morality of states advising neighbouring states of any of their activities likely to cause damage across their borders.

27 Rawls believes that 'with more capital and better technology it will be responsible to support a sufficiently large population'. *Social Justice*, p.287 (see Chapter 1 above, n.25). A contrasting view, from which the quotation is taken, is contained in the *Eleventh Annual Report of the Council on Environmental Quality*, Summary Report (Washington, D.C.: US Govt Printing Office, 1980) p.1.

28 One of the most dependable sources is the *World Conservation Strategy* (1980). This was the product of three years of research by the International Union for Conservation of Nature and Natural Resources (IUCN), in which a number of scientists from various contries participated.

29 Among contemporary philosophers one of the pioneers in drawing attention to the morality of sentient animals, and the moral obtuseness

of some towards animal suffering, is Peter Singer, in *Animal Liberation* (London: Granada Publishing, 1977).

30 Page references are to *Autobiography of Charles Darwin* (London: Watts & Co., 1929) (The Thinker's Library, no.7).

31 *Politics*. Translation by Benjamin Jowett.

32 For one criticism of the 'responsible dominion' view see V. Routley's review of John Passmore's *Man's Responsibility for Nature*, n.5.

33 *Leviathan*. Page reference is to the Penguin edn.

34 A. Schweitzer, *Civilization and Ethics* (London: Adam and Charles Black, 1946) p.239 (3rd edn; first edn, 1923). His basic principle of ethics was 'devotion to life resulting from reverence for life'.

35 S. Schwartz, *Wildlife Areas of Washington* (Seattle, Washington: Superior Publishing, 1976) p.7. Foreword by Ira Spring. The statement is made in the context of a plea that visitors should not frighten animals, warning that animals can be harmed by non-hunters at least as much as by 'people with guns'.

36 For various views on animal rights see P. Singer, *Animal Liberation*; T. Regan and P. Singer (eds), *Animal Rights and Human Obligations* (Englewood Cliffs, New Jersey: Prentice-Hall, 1976); H. J. McCloskey, 'Moral Rights and Animals', *Inquiry*, vol.22 (1979) pp.23–54; ibid., 'The Right to Life', *Mind*, vol.LXXXIV (1975) pp.403–25; R. Watson, 'Rights of Nonhuman Animals and Nature', *Environmental Ethics*, vols 1–2 (1979–80) pp.101–29.

37 It has been described as 'an exercise of the imagination involving self-consciousness and comparison'. H. B. Acton, 'The Ethical Importance of Sympathy', *Philosophy*, vol.XXX, no.112 (Jan 1955) p.66.

38 The vaccines and antibiotics on which medical science relies to safeguard public health have developed from the experimental use of animals such as rats and mice. Crippling diseases such as poliomyelitis have been eradicated in many countries following animal experimentation. It is estimated that there are still 700 million people in the Third World suffering from parasitic diseases for which vaccines are not yet available: to develop these, animals still need to be used in medical research. Since animals generally suffer in experiments (sometimes minimally), the ethical issue is controversial. A strong case may be made for carefully regulated animal experiments in medical research on the grounds that humans have reason, a much more complex set of relationships both within and outside the family, a capacity for much greater mental suffering associated with physical illness, whether in the person or in another family member, and in general the potential for a quality of life beyond the reach of animals. But it is difficult to dismiss the issue even on these grounds, or on a consideration of the totality of suffering among humans, using some of Bentham's principles such as *intensity* and *duration*, without some moral uneasiness on the question of the level of *moral detachment* of which we are capable. (Can we judge our own situation? Or are we bound by anthropocentricity when we view ourselves in relation to sentient animals?)

CHAPTER 3

1 J. Rawls, *A Theory of Justice*, pp.12–13 (see Chapter 1 above, n.25).
2 The need for this is explained more fully in *Justice, Morality and Education*, ch.4.
3 In the *Republic* Socrates says to Glaucon: 'In the world of knowledge the Form of the good is perceived last and with difficulty, but when it is seen it must be inferred that it is the cause of all that is right and beautiful in all things, . . . and this Form of the good must be seen by whosoever would act wisely in public or in private' (p.210). In Books VI and VII, Plato explains the Form of the good in terms of ideal knowledge, a way of showing how the Forms which are the objects of knowledge are related to one another and to a higher knowledge.
4 For certain aspects of legal rights see J. Raz, 'On the Nature of Rights', *Mind*, vol.XCIII, no.370 (April 1984) pp.194–214.
5 For a development of this argument see *Justice, Morality and Education*, ch.8.
6 Jowett's translation is again followed.
7 Cf. F. A. Nigro and L. G. Nigro, *Modern Public Administration*, 5th edn (New York: Harper and Row, 1980) p.81. The authors refer to Watergate, quoting Senator Erwin's comment that certain persons loyal to the Nixon administration 'resorted to evil means to promote what they considered to be a good end'.
8 Translation by W. D. Ross.
9 From Kant's *Principles of Politics*, ed. and trans. W. Hastie (Edinburgh: T. & T. Clark, 1891). All page numbers are to this edn. Kant's thoughts on politics and morality were incomplete, but the unity of the two in his mind is indicated in his intention to end his philosophical career with a System of Politics, only part of which was completed. For another translation of these political views see Carl J. Friedrich (ed.), *The Philosophy of Kant. Moral and Political Writings*, The Modern Library (New York: Random House, 1949). (See pp.116–31 for the 'Idea For a Universal History with Cosmopolitan Intent'.)
10 *Principles of Politics*.
11 In Theodore Roosevelt's administration, the system of national parks was extended to include national monuments as well. One of the schemes planned for the practical common good was proposed by the Secretary of the Interior in 1970, to 'bring parks to the people', within easy access of cities so that more might visit them. It was frustrated by the Vietnam War and inflationary trends. See *Environment Law Review* (1977) pp.452, 460.
12 In Britain there are statutory declarations of 150 National Nature Reserves whose purpose is to conserve key areas representing characteristic ecosystems. As well as the key areas there has been a notification of some 3500 Sites of Special Scientific Interest. See D. Ratcliffe, *A Nature Conservation Review*, The Nature Conservancy Council (Cambridge University Press, 1977) p.1.
13 The Federal Republic of Germany has legislated to license all industrial plants for this purpose. For politics and statutes on air pollution control

as a contributor to the common good, see J. McLoughlin, *The Law and Practice Relating to Pollution Control in Europe* (London: Graham and Trotman, 1976) pp.96–7.

14 *A Treatise of Human Nature.* Hume's observations on the status of international treaties must be related to eighteenth-century attitudes. In our time they are fundamental to international law (Hume's italics).

15 A comment by Elizabeth I, who added that 'hardly a faithful or virtuous man may be found'. Quoted from J. Nichols, *The Progress . . . of Queen Elizabeth* (1823) vol.III, p.552. From J. Hurstfield, *Freedom, Corruption and Government in Elizabethan England* (London: Jonathan Cape, 1973) p.137.

16 In *The Prince* Machiavelli wrote: 'A prince who wishes to do great things must learn to deceive.' (See the edition by J. Plamenatz, London, Collins, 1972, p.231.) He explained that even cruelty, murder, deception and betrayal may be necessary to establish order and to maintain it. Taken out of context Michiavelli has been used through the centuries to suit a variety of purposes. See Felix Raab, *The English Face of Machiavelli. A Changing Interpretation 1500–1700* (London: Routledge and Kegan Paul, 1964), for the changing attitudes to Machiavelli, from abuse in Elizabethan times as an atheist, to acceptance after 1642 as a critic of kings and of *de facto* power. For an Elizabethan translation of *The Prince* see the edition, with introduction by H. Craig, published by the North Carolina Press (1944). For comment on the disparate interpretations of Machiavelli, See M. Fleisher, *Machiavelli and the Nature of Political Thought* (New York: Atheneum, 1972) pp.114–47.

17 Page reference is again to the 9th edn.

18 See *Justice, Morality and Education*, ch.5, pp.185–9, for a comparison of a moral decision-making model with one where motives and ends are entirely institutional, and another where the institutional and the moral are combined.

19 Pressure groups have been variously defined. E.g. G. C. Moodie and G. Studdart-Kennedy, *Opinions, Publics and Pressure Groups* (London: Allen and Unwin, 1970) p.60: 'By "pressure group" we mean, simply, any organized group which attempts to influence government decisions without seeking itself to exercise the formal powers of government' (in this way distinguishing them from political parties or conspiratorial groups).

20 *The Social Contract*, for page reference.

21 See A. C. Fisher, J. V. Krutilla and C. J. Cicchetti, 'Alternative Uses of Natural Environments', in J. V. Krutilla (ed.), *Natural Environments. Studies in Theoretical and Applied Analysis* (Baltimore and London: Johns Hopkins University Press, 1972).

22 The Second World Conference on National Parks was held in September 1972, and its recommendations were published by the International Union for the Conservation of Naure, Morges, Switzerland, 1974. *Biomes* refer to the major ecological communities of plants and animals such as those of tropical rainforests and coral reefs. Agreement was reached by a large majority that the highest priority for national parks is the preservation of their *natural* state, noting that some nations such as

the USSR do not permit tourism or recreation in their nature reserves (p.81). Delegates agreed that parks are for people 'for all time and not just for the present generation' (p.82). Recommendations included conservation of ecosystems of tropical rainforests, north and south polar regions, and the establishment of an Antarctic World Park (pp.443–4).

23 The moral consequences extend far beyond conservation issues. See D. Spurgeon, 'Nobel Prize Chairman Warns of Nuclear Weapon Threat', *Features*, no.792 (1983) UNESCO, pp.1–2.

24 Recent information is available in *Jane's Weapon Systems 1984–5*, *Jane's Armour and Artillery 1984–5*, and *Jane's Military Vehicles and Ground Support Equipment, 1984* (London and New York: Jane's Publishing Co.). See also R. L. Sivard, *World Military and Social Expenditures, 1983* (Washington, D.C.: World Priorities) which gives nuclear capabilities, comparative figures on military and social expenditures and casualty figures for conventional warfare.

25 J. R. M. Cobo, 'The Tlatelolco Treaty: an Update', *International Atomic Energy Agency Bulletin*, vol.26, no.3 (Sept 1984) p.25. The author commented (p.26) on the increasing number of countries in the world aspiring to become nuclear powers. The Tlatelolco Treaty is a treaty for the prohibition of nuclear weapons in Latin America, with twenty-six signatories, effective from April 1969.

26 Ibid. Cobo commented that 'the world has become a hostage of the superpowers and is bound to serve their interests'.

27 'Law' has various references, with different applications to conservation problems. *Common law* in England developed out of *customary law* which was simply the custom in the community on such matters as land rights as they pertained under feudalism. When King's justices began to take control of the courts they decided cases according to custom by and large, but when novel situations developed they were obliged to make rules that seemed to them fair and reasonable, and in so doing gradually built on common law. Thus a law that was *common to* the whole country developed. Judge-made law was distinct from *statutes* which were enacted by parliaments. *Common law* is used variously: sometimes to apply broadly to the English system of law; sometimes to the law created by the courts, or case-law, as distinct from statutes; sometimes to common-law courts in England prior to the development of equity courts. In the eighteenth century Blackstone divided municipal law (or the national law of England) into *lex non scripta*, the unwritten or common law; and the *lex scripta*, the written or statute law (*Commentaries on the Laws of England*, bk.I, III, p.63). When newly promulgated statutes were unclear, judges always needed interpretative powers, and still do. Once cases have been decided, judges' powers are usually limited by precedent. *Customary law* still applies in some English-speaking countries, quite distinct from common law and statutes: among some Australian aborigines, for instance, customary law still stipulates the rules by which the tribes shall live. Since conservation has worldwide relevance, it is important to note that *common law* applies to England and to other countries whose legal systems have been derived (though with modifications) from it, including USA and

Australia. *Civil law* applies in France and in most other European countries, as well as in Japan and some other Asian countries. A modified Roman–Dutch system applies in Holland and South Africa.

28 C. Stone, *Should Trees Have Standing?* (see Chapter 2 above, n.13). Blackstone had explained what was then a traditional legal division of persons into 'either natural persons or artificial'. Artificial persons 'are such as are created and devised by human laws for the purpose of society and government, which are called corporations or bodies politic'. *Commentaries on the Laws of England*, bk.I, ch.I, p. 123.

29 J. Austin, *The Province of Jurisprudence Determined*, ed. H. A. L. Hart (London: Weidenfeld and Nicolson, 1954) p.126. See the editor's introduction for the reference to the Natural Law Theorists. In Bentham's own time there were repeated observations of the gap between the law and morality: e.g. J. Dymond, *Essays on the Principles of Morality*, p.245. H. A. L. Hart discusses 'Positivism and the Separation of Law and Morals' in R. M. Dworkin (ed.), *The Philosophy of Law* (Oxford University Press, 1977) pp.17–37. R. M. Dworkin replies to Hart in 'Is Law a System of Rules?', ibid., pp. 38–65, pointing out that the higher courts in both USA and England sometimes reject established rules of law.

30 The latter is the view of R. Pound, in *Social Control Through Law* (New Haven: Yale University Press, 1942) pp.64–5.

31 A standard work is K. Llewellyn's *The Common Law Tradition* (Boston: Little, Brown, 1960). Llewellyn himself seems to have had excessive confidence in judges' rationality in claiming that, in their common experiences and capacities, they would be likely to reach similar decisions in cases before them of a similar nature.

32 Environment law refers to the many kinds of rules governing human relationships with the natural environment. Its sources are almost entirely statutes (such as those referring to pollution control). Unlike English common law, which after centuries of rules for man's common use of the natural environment became strongly protective of the interests of landowners, environment law has taken the focus from private interests to the larger interests of the community, relating them to quality of life. It is emerging and still very imperfect, as in matters of access.

33 Hence the statement by Ch. Perelman of the formal idea of justice as 'observing a rule which lays down the obligation to treat in a certain way all persons who belong to a given category'. *The Idea of Justice and the Problem of Argument*, trans J. Petrie (London: Routledge and Kegan Paul, 1963) p.40.

34 It has to be acknowledged that the influence of common law is not nearly as strong as it was with respect to precedent. In both USA and England it is not unusual for common law rules to be overturned or to be radically amended. Statutory rules too are frequently given fresh interpretations, even to the extent of inconsistency with the 'bonum' or the good intended by the legislators. On this point see R. M. Dworkin (ed.), *The Philosophy of Law*, p.57.

35 Britain's constitution is encapsulated in various acts of Parliament and

other documents which express its traditions of limited monarchy and representative government. A Select Committee of the House of Lords in 1978 expressed the view that human rights protection in England would not be significantly improved by a formal Bill of Rights. In some countries such as Australia, a Bill of Rights is being considered by government (1985).

36 From the Constitution of the People's Republic of China, 1982. Published in English translation in *Beijing Review* (27 Dec 1982).

37 *EPA Journal*, United States Environmental Protection Agency, vol.6, no.1 (Jan 1980) p.34.

38 J. McLoughlin, *The Law and Practice Relating to Pollution Control in Europe*, p.78.

39 Blackstone's explanation is relevant to the original white occupation, referring to all 'plantations or colonies in distant countries'. He explained in his *Commentaries on the Laws of England*, vol.I, introduction, sect.4, that these are 'claimed by right of occupancy only, by finding them desart and uncultivated, and peopling them from the mother-country; or where, when already cultivated, they have been either gained by conquest, or ceded to us by treaties'. This was the law of nature, or at least that of nations (p.107). In the Australian situation the land was 'desert' in the sense of uncultivated, but it was certainly not unused by the aborigines. There were no official government treaties.

40 Attempts to generalize the rules on the restitution principle lead to obvious inconsistencies. From a rational–moral perspective, the interests of white settlers have to be considered as well as those of the aborigines. 1. White settlers also often have a spiritual affiliation with the land (though of a quite different kind from that of the aborigines). 2. On the restitution principle there could be almost endless claims by white Australians (for 'folklands' lost by Anglo-Saxon ancestors, for example; for lands seized during the Norman Conquest, and so forth). 3. Present claimants of land rights who are of mixed European and aboriginal descent are inconsistently claiming only on the basis of aboriginal descent. 4. To be consistent, the restitution principle needs to be applied to present descendants of Europeans who wrongfully seized other Europeans' lands (Danes who seized Anglo-Saxon lands, Normans who seized lands, and all other European conquerors who took the spoils of war in land). Again the restitution principle leads to almost endless cases, and complications of absurd proportions in deciding liability. In political hands, there is a danger that inconsistencies will be overlooked for a form of positive discrimination. (On the aborigines' mythological link with the land, see R. M. and C. H. Berndt, *The World of the First Australians*, 2nd edn (Sydney: Ure Smith, 1977) p.138.)

41 J. S. Mill, *Principles of Political Economy*.

42 Conspicuous among international documents on conservation is *World Conservation Strategy*. Its significant subtitle is 'Living Resource Conservation for Sustainable Development'. See sect.18, 'The Global Commons', on parts of the earth's surface outside the jurisdiction of states, such as the open ocean, the atmosphere and Antarctica. Here the accent is on control of living resources in such places, against

198 *Notes*

commercial exploitation or other human abuse, as well as into research
into atmospheric changes related to rapid industrialization.

43 Borobudur is a ninth-century Buddhist monument in Indonesia.
UNESCO promoted and coordinated an international effort at
restoration. See *UNESCO Review* (March 1984) pp.2–6. The US
Environmental Protection Agency has contributed substantially to
protecting buildings and statues on the Acropolis. See *EPA Journal*,
vol.6, no.3 (March 1980).

44 Apart from treaties, other sources of international law are simply
international custom, or practices accepted as law among states; and
certain general principles of law accepted in common by 'civilized
nations'. See M. Akehurst, *A Modern Introduction to International Law*,
4th edn (London: Allen and Unwin, 1982).

45 G. Delcoigne *et al.*, 'Arms-Control Treaties: Review and Revision',
*International Atomic Energy Agency Bulletin*, vol.26, no.3 (Sept
1984) p.37. Various attempts have been made to argue that international
law is legally binding: e.g. I. Detter, *Law-Making by International
Organizations* (Stockholm: Norstedt, 1965) pp. 322ff. See also
I. Brownlie, *Principles of Public International Law* (Oxford: Clarendon
Press, 1973) pp.1–2, for the contrast between statutes and the 'rules of
general application' under international law. One of the greatest legal
obstacles in international law is in the consistent failure of states to
waive their respective claims to national sovereignty. See G. Von Glahn,
*Law Among Nations. An Introduction to Public International Law*, 3rd
edn (New York: Macmillan, 1976) p.726.

46 This was eventually endorsed by the General Assembly of the UN.
For difficulties in reaching agreement see, B. Johnson, *International
Environmental Law*, p.22. See also Chapter 2, n.26.

47 From Kant's *Principles of Politics*, pp.74–6.

CHAPTER 4

1 Instances of this kind probably occur in most countries. Examples are
taken from the USA because of the availability of documentation. The
source of bias at the time of citing appears itself to be a deception:
though industry had only approximately one-third of the seats, most of
the professional officers who were included in the majority two-thirds
were themselves drawn from the offending industries. See F. Grad
*et al.*, *Environmental Control: Priorities, Policies and the Law* (New
York and London: Columbia University Press, 1971) pp.84–5. An
instance of governments legislating to circumvent judicial decisions has
occurred in one state in Australia, where the Chief Judge of the Land
and Environment Court ruled against development of an historical site
for a football stadium, only to be overruled by government legislation.
In this there may have been a conflict between local community values
and the long-term common good which only a Commission would be
able to determine.

2 Ibid., pp.85, 93.

3 *Environmental Law Review* (1972) introduction, p.x.

4 R. Carson, *Silent Spring* (Harmondsworth: Penguin Books, 1965) p.59.

5 M. P. Ryan, 'The Role of Citizen Advisory Boards in Administration of National Resources', *Environment Law Review* (1972) p.67.

6 For both strengths and weaknesses of the Environmental Impact Statements see G. E. Nahkies, *Environmental Impact Reporting in the USA and NZ* (University of Auckland: Department of Town Planning, 1976) pp.10–20. On p.44 of the author's notes, reference is made to particular research indicating that projects usually go ahead even if the EISs are adverse: although 127 out of 200 EISs were adverse, there was no case which resulted in the project's cancellation. Most of the alternative actions suggested were rejected as economically unfeasible.

7 The EIS system is not radically different in Australia. See A. Gilpin, *Environment Policy in Australia* (Brisbane: University of Queensland Press, 1980) pp.64–74.

8 One of the most controversial cases is the flooding of Lake Pedder in Tasmania in 1972 as part of a hydroelectric development plan. The Premier appointed himself Attorney-General in order to prevent a court challenge to the government decision. In the final report of a Committee of Inquiry in 1974, reference was made to 'unwise alienation of land and the loss of important recreational, scientific and aesthetic values'. See G. M. Bates, *Environmental Law in Australia* (Sydney: Butterworths, 1983) pp.32, 128. Another controversial decision was made by a minister in Queensland to construct a road through a tropical rainforest. Heavy rains have made the road unusable and, much as predicted by naturalists, muddy waters from it have threatened the health of a coral reef below.

9 *Annual Report of the Executive Director 1983* (Nairobi: UN Environment Programme, May 1984) pp.2–5.

10 See *Silent Spring*, p.28, on the failure to act on acid rain.

11 There is ample evidence of hasty decision-making and precipitate action with respect to DDT. *Silent Spring*, pp.125, 127. One consequence has been blindness in fish.

12 Administrative negligence of this kind occurred twice in NSW, Australia, in 1985. When complaints were received by the Water Resources Commission responsible, instructions were given to pump the water back into the former swamp and to build levee banks to contain it, but thousands of birds had perished.

13 *The Complete Essays of Montaigne*, trans. D. M. Frame (Stanford University Press, 1958). From Book III:13, 'Of Experience', p.819.

14 J. S. Mill, *Principles of Political Economy*, vol.2, bk. v, pp.492–3.

15 For an example of a specific statute calling for clear definition of terms before it can be implemented in any uniform way by the courts, see Yearn Hong Choi, 'Low-level Radioactive Waste Management: Federal–State Cooperation or Confusion?' *The Journal of Environmental Sciences* (July–August 1984) pp.41–6.

16 L. L. Fuller, *The Morality of Law*, revised edn (New Haven and London: Yale University Press, 1969) pp.39, 81.

17 J. McLoughlin, *The Law and Practice Relating to Pollution Control in*

*Europe*, pp.206, 514. For a more general reference to the disjunction between the law and its enforcement on conservation matters, see *World Conservation Strategy*, sect. II.

18 L. L. Jaffe, 'The Administrative Agency and Environmental Control', *Environment Law Review* (1972) p.7.

19 *Environment Law Review* (1977) p.259. See also *EPA Journal*, vol.6, no.6 (June 1980) pp.12–14. See p.13 for reference to the Reserve Mining case which lasted for many years, but eventually succeeded in ending the deposits of tacomite tailings into Lake Superior.

20 J. McLoughlin, *The Law and Practice Relating to Pollution Control in Europe*, pp.514–15.

21 G. M. Bates, *Environmental Law in Australia*, pp.191–8. The High Court has refused standing to environmental groups such as the Australian Conservation Foundation.

22 Whenever vacancies occur in the US Supreme Court, appointments are made by the President, making it possible that appointees will share many of his attitudes and values on social questions such as conservation, specifically on land-use policy. Political influence in judicial appointments is well known in many countries.

23 D. Hume, *An Enquiry Concerning the Principles of Morals* (La Salle, Illinois: The Open Court Publishing Co., 1953) p.152 (reprinted from the edition of 1777).

24 *News Feature*, Oct 1983, p.1. UN Environment Programme. The World Bank's 1975 figure of 'absolute poverty' was 550 million. This had increased by 200 million in the next eight years. World Bank's capital for development is unable to offset this trend.

25 *The State of the Environment, 1984*, UN Environment Programme, p.15. Poverty is a relative concept inasmuch as it is related to the general standard of living within the respective nations, but there are minimum moral standards for quality of life of persons, regardless of where they may live.

26 Ibid., p.13. It is estimated that over 1300 million people in the world lack safe drinking water and over 1700 million lack adequate sanitation: according to the World Health Organization together these account for 25 000 deaths a day, and for 80 per cent of world disease. WHO figures are quoted from *Water and Sanitation for All* (London: Earthscan, 1981).

27 UN Centre for Human Settlements, *Habitat* (Nairobi, 1984) p.16.

28 Figures are from the Newsletter of the UNESCO Cooperative Action Programme, no.1 (1982).

29 See for example, *Implications for the Trade and Investment of Developing Countries of United States Environmental Controls*, UN Conference on Trade and Development, Geneva (New York: UN, 1976). It is suggested that 'developing countries should consider the trade impact when establishing environmental standards', p.1, and that they should be given early warning, as exporters, of any impending regulations in the USA on product standards, p.2. The small benefits from such paternalistic suggestions are likely to be ignored when contrasted with the massive aid needed to establish some of the

developing countries in a world community of traders.

30 For examples of the attitude of developing countries to conservation, see *Development and Environment*, Report and Working Papers of a Panel of Experts Convened by the Secretary-General of the UN Conference on the Human Environment (New York: UN, 1971) pp.5–10.

31 Ibid. From a paper by Enrique Iglesias, 'Development and the Human Environment', pp.56–7.

32 D. A. Kay and E. B. Skolnikoff (eds), *World Eco-Crisis* (University of Wisconsin Press, 1971) p.310. The expression is quoted from Maurice F. Strong, Secretary-General of the Stockholm Conference, 1972.

33 There is no suggestion that nations should ignore their own interests. It is acknowledged also that underprivileged countries should do something to help themselves, as in population control. But the views of Garrett Hardin in *The Limits of Altruism: An Ecologist's View of Survival*, are not supported. Altruism is achievable from a moral perspective on common personhood.

34 In Ethiopia alone, because of overgrazing, overpopulation and inadequate farming techniques, one estimate of more than a decade ago was that the Central Highland Plateau was losing approximately 1600 million tonnes of topsoil each year. Food and Agriculture Organization of the United Nations, *Protect and Produce, Soil Conservation for Development*, p.17, no date.

35 UN Environment Programme, *The State of the Environment, 1984*, p.13.

36 It is estimated that more than 1500 million people in developing countries depend on firewood for cooking and warmth. *World Conservation Strategy*, sect.4, para.II.

37 One estimate is that one-third more may be affected by the year 2000. UN Environment Programme, *Desertification*, 'Feature' (March 1984).

38 A. Bell, 'When the Air's Carbon Dioxide Doubles', *ECOS*, no.28 (May 1981) CSIRO, Australia. See also, *The Global Environment Monitoring System* (1982) pp.18–19. *Carbon Dioxide and Climate: Scientific Assessment*, Climate Research Board, National Research Council (Washington, D.C.: National Academy of Sciences, 1979). In the last-mentioned publication it was estimated that a doubling of carbon dioxide in the atmosphere would lead to a probable global warming of approximately 3°C, with a probable error of plus or minus 1.5°C.

39 Some research has used computer models to explore interactions in the atmosphere. Research initiated in 1983 under the auspices of the International Meteorological Institute in Stockholm continues to explore the possible impact of climatic changes on ecosystems of the earth. UN Environment Programme, Annual Report for 1983, p.40.

40 'Cutting Down on Sulphur Dioxide', *ECOS*, no.3 (Feb 1975) pp.3–10.

41 Some have expressed doubts on sulphur dioxide as the major contributor to deaths in the London smog of 1952: other airborne particles such as soot may have contributed substantially. Sulphur dioxide from the burning of fossil fuels differs with the quality of the fuel. Coals vary considerably in sulphur content. Some natural gas has no sulphur content at all. Despite an increasing output of sulphur dioxide, its concentration in the atmosphere is not rising. Ibid., pp.3–6.

42 The expression 'acid rain' was first used in Manchester over a century ago, observing it close to factories. Its effects far from pollution sources were first observed in Scandinavia, and in parts of North America and Scotland, where lakes and rivers became acidified sufficiently to kill fish. The indirect effects of acid rain on health are experienced when there is acidification of soils and the possible release of metals such as lead, copper, zinc, cadmium and mercury into groundwater used for drinking purposes. UN Environment Programme, *The State of the Environment, 1983*, p.20.

43 A recent estimate is that burning of coal accounts for about 60 per cent of the emissions, and the burning of petroleum products for about 30 per cent. Ibid., p.17. For present research into pollutants such as sulphur dioxide, see *Environmental Research, An International Journal of Environmental Medicine and the Environmental Sciences*, ed. I. J. Selikoff: e.g. on the incidence of cancer near points of pollution, congenital abnormalities and chronic respiratory diseases, effects on health of living near smelters. See also *Acid Rain: the British Approach* (London: Central Office of Information, July 1984) no.244/84. Here it is claimed that the extent to which Britain is responsible for acid rain is small. Recent research suggests that because of the complexity of chemical and biological systems the damage caused by acid rain is difficult to quantify. It is no longer clear what is causing damage to forests in the Federal Republic of Germany.

44 In England a 'public nuisance' has been defined in one judicial interpretation as 'an act or omission which materially affects the reasonable comfort and convenience of a class of Her Majesty's subjects'. D. A. Bigham, *The Law and Administration Relating to Protection of the Environment* (London: Oyez Publishing, 1973) p.123. While it is a crime to create a public nuisance, and also a tort (wrong) for which an individual may claim damages, with respect to polluting industries a Commission might decide that both the government and the law are protecting industry, and not serving the common good.

45 Long-term effects of DDT and other insecticides on health of humans and sentient animals are unclear. Some insecticides are believed to be carcinogenic, with consequences of deformities in unborn children, and possible genetic mutations affecting future generations. The most prominent of the alternatives is the use of biological control, such as the use of the cochineal insect and the larvae of a moth to kill prickly pear, insect predators for lantana and, more recently, for salvinia which has choked waters in New Guinea and elsewhere.

46 Many inhabitants of Minamata died or suffered neurological disorders. Unborn children were afflicted, their brain cells destroyed by the mercury. Before any action was taken by the company, for twenty years local people had been falling ill unaccountably, fish had been seen floating dead in the bay, cats which had eaten fish had died or had developed brain disorders. Suggestion of a possible link between contamination of the rivers mentioned and a rather above-normal incidence of cancer is made by H. J. Kool *et al.*, *Organic Water Contaminants and Health Parameters* (The Hague: National Institute for Water Supply, 1982).

47 See Chapter 1, n.6.
48 *Principles of Political Economy*, vol.II, bk.IV, ch.6, sect.2.
49 *A Treatise of Human Nature*. See Chapter 1, p.9, above.
50 First published by J. Johnson (London, 1798). Page numbers are from the edition reprinted for the Royal Economic Society, published by Macmillan, London, 1926. See p.25 for Malthus's illustration of the superior power of geometrical proportion over arithmetical proportion. Demographers refer generally now to *exponential growth*.
51 G. Hardin, 'The Tragedy of the Commons'. See Chapter 2 above, n.11. (Faith in science to answer all food problems may be misplaced.)
52 In several Arab countries the infant mortality rate is such that one in every ten die in the first year of life. The general life expectancy throughout the Arab world is fifty years only, whereas the fertility rate is claimed to be the highest in the world. A.-R. Omran, *Population Problems and Prospects in the Arab World*, UN Fund for Population Activities (July 1984) pp.14–16.
53 Figures are quoted from *Population Issues – Background of the International Conference on Population*, UN Department of Public Information (July 1984). In developing countries the rate of population growth is 2.5 to 3 per cent. In developed countries the rate is 1 per cent or less. China is an exception among developing countries with a growth rate of a little more than 1.2 per cent: its policy is aimed specifically at improving quality of life. With generally improved health-care provisions and substantial reduction in malnutrition and disease, infant mortality would be reduced in developing countries, but if life expectancy increases from the average of fifty-seven years at present (compared with seventy-three years in developed countries), population growth rates will rise correspondingly unless steps are taken to reduce fertility rates.
54 In particular, the use of global models in research has been shown to lead to conclusions consistent with the assumptions originally used. The most conspicuous of recent research findings is that population trends are leading human life eventually to total self-destruction, or at least in that direction unless there are radical changes in man's behaviour. See, for instance, P. R. Erlich and A. H. Erlich, *Population, Resources, Environment. Issues in Human Ecology* (San Francisco: W. H. Freeman, 1972). In 'Paying the Piper', *New Scientist*, vol.36, pp.652–5, Paul Erlich forecast disaster between 1970–85, with hundreds of millions of people dying from famine. See also D. H. Meadows *et al.*, *The Limits to Growth* (New York: Universe Books, 1972). Here the authors argued that the interaction between five variables – world population trends, industrialization, pollution, food production and resource depletion – were highly dangerous unless man's behavioural patterns changed. The argument relied heavily on preconceptions and on a methodology now widely challenged. Different sets of initial assumptions lead to quite different conclusions. See *Environment Law Review* (1977) p.34.
55 For this and other information on the International Conference on Population at Mexico City in 1984, see *Populi*, Journal of the UN Fund for Population Activities, vol.II, no.4 (1984) pp.24ff. The Mexico City Declaration on Population and Development stressed in its articles the

continuing concern at population growth, high mortality and migration problems, etc., noting that in the decade to 1984 world population had increased by 770 million, with 90 per cent of the increase in developing countries, and in most countries urban populations increasing far more rapidly than total populations.

56 Ibid., pp.46–53.

57 Research has shown that 50 per cent of Algeria and 75 per cent of Nigeria are at risk from wind erosion, while water erosion threatens nearly all of Sierra Leone and about 50 per cent of Liberia. *Global Environmental Monitoring System*, p.20.

58 It is probably true that in a state-imposed policy of one-child families as in China, individual suffering occurs at least temporarily as sharp breaks are made with cultural traditions. The government sees quality of life of the people generally as of prior importance. For this party viewpoint see Xiao Mu and Yang Xiaobing, 'Rural Child-rearing Outlook Changes', *Beijing Review*, vol.28, no.16 (22 April 1985) pp.19–20.

59 For one such explanation see R. Peterson in *The Human Environment. Action or Disaster*, UN Environment Programme (1982) p.56 (a report of a public hearing in London).

60 The Yearbook of the UN, 1961, pp.30–1, records this resolution. For an explanation see M. Akehurst, *A Modern Introduction to International Law*, p.200.

61 Political judgements during war are not necessarily unsound. The judgement of President Truman to order the first bomb to be dropped on Hiroshima is controversial. The Japanese mood was to continue fighting on their islands without surrender: this itself might have led to equal casualties at least, roughly as MacArthur had estimated. This is a quite different problem from that of initiating war.

62 *Environmental Quality*, the Third Report to Congress of the Council on Environmental Quality, 1972, Washington, D.C., Appendix 2, pp.105–7. This agreement was signed in Moscow on 23 May 1972. The statement of purpose is contained in the Preamble.

63 See Chapter 3, n.25 on the Tlatelolco Treaty. Morality and prudence probably combined in the purpose of this treaty.

64 In the twenty years to 1982 global military expenditure doubled: in the same period it increased fourfold in the *developing* world. The developed countries spent nearly 5 per cent of their gross national product in 1981 on defence, and less than one-third of 1 per cent on aid to developing countries. *World Development Report* 1983. Published for the International World Bank, July 1984 (Oxford University Press) p.150.

65 In the context of military spending in developing countries, it is significant that two-thirds of all terrestrial species live there, and that these include most of the world's endangered species. About 40 per cent of all terrestrial species live in tropical forests, and it is the destruction of these habitats that threatens the extinction of many species. *The State of the Environment 1984*, UN Environment Programme, p.23.

66 For basic information see R. L. Sivard, *World Military and Social Expenditures, 1983*, pp.13–14.

67 Ibid., p.23.
68 It is expected that smoke and dust from nuclear explosions would be compounded by burning cities, forests and grasslands, oil-wells and storage tanks. Scientists from both USA and USSR have projected the following consequences from an anticipated drop in temperature over the earth's surface of 10°C to 40°C: destruction of tropical rainforests and all the life they support (two-thirds of all animal species in the world); death of plankton near the surface of oceans on which the entire fish food-chain depends; destruction of much plant and animal life away from the tropics, unable to accommodate to sudden lowering of temperature; destruction of food crops; radiation fall-out reaching all parts of the earth.
69 One explanation is by J. H. Kittel, 'The Status of Nuclear Waste Management', *The Journal of Environmental Sciences* (Sept–Oct 1980) pp.28–30.
70 Nuclear energy for peaceful purposes is now supported by the UN. See UN Conference for the Promotion of International Cooperation in the Peaceful Uses of Nuclear Energy. UN Department of Public Information, 26 April 1983. The Joint Division of Atomic Energy in Food and Agriculture has conducted research into use of radiation to induce mutations in plants, producing new varieties of wheat, rice and other crops with a higher yield, or better nutritional value, or greater resistance to disease, or earlier maturity. Benefits may be high to developing countries especially.
71 A. Gilpin, *Environmental Policy in Australia*, p.318.
72 Like people the world over, the Chinese are viewing economic and social development partly in terms of the production and distribution of consumer goods. See Xiao Mu and Yang Xiaobing, n.58 above, 'single-child families have 10% more TV sets, 28% more electric fans and 60% more washing machines, than the average local level'. Beyond these, an increasing number of non-essential goods are becoming available.
73 F. Grad *et al.*, *Environmental Control: Priorities, Policies, and the Law*, pp.158–9. The authors illustrate with the Delaware Compact, involving both the State of New York and the State of Delaware – the latter smaller in terms of population, industrial development, use of the river basin and capacity to contribute to its development; yet with power to delay projects, and to influence decisions out of proportion to its contributory strength simply through the exercise of the equal state sovereignty principle.

## CHAPTER 5

1 In Benjamin Jowett's translation, 'the mean, the possible, the becoming'.
2 This formal idea of education is further developed in the author's *Justice, Morality and Education*, Chapters 1 and 8.
3 Among the strongest supporters of the idea were Mill and Newman. In the nineteenth century it contributed to intellectual and social élitism in

England, especially through university education, with ideals of intellectual culture as distinct from vocational preparation.

4 Hume explained that 'reason alone can never produce any action'. *A Treatise of Human Nature*, Part III, bk.II, p.414. Page references are again to the edition by Selby-Bigge.

5 One of those taking the view that naturalism leaves out the apparent authority of ethics is J. L. Mackie in *Ethics. Inventing Right and Wrong* (Harmondsworth: Penguin Books, 1977) p.33. But Mackie refers to the desire satisfactions of those being guided, not to the complexity of moral attitudes and values involved when a person makes a moral judgement. It is these that give moral authority. The common antithesis between *reason* (leading directly to morality) and the *natural tendencies* of desire, was expressed in Locke's account of the 'foundation of all Virtue and Worth': 'That a Man is able to *deny himself* his own Desires, cross his own Inclinations, and purely follow what Reason directs as best, tho' Appetite lean the other way.' *Some Thoughts Concerning Education*, ed. R. H. Quick (Cambridge University Press, 1898) p.21.

6 R. M. Hare, *Moral Thinking*. For comment see Chapter 1.

7 Plato, *Republic*, Everyman edn, trans. A. D. Lindsay.

8 Page references are to the Penguin edition, trans. T. J. Saunders (Harmondsworth, 1970).

9 Page references are again to the 9th edn (London: Longmans, Green, 1886).

10 Thomas Paine, *Rights of Man* (Secaucus, New Jersey: Citadel Press, 1974) p.145 (first English edition, 1791).

11 'We travel together, passengers on a little spaceship. . . . We cannot maintain it half-fortunate, half-miserable, half-confident, half-despairing, half-free. . . . No craft, no crew, can travel safely with such vast contradictions.' Adlai Stevenson, Geneva, 1965.

12 UN Information Centre (UNIC), *Urban Land Policies and Land-use Control Measures*, vol.VII (New York: Global Review, 1975) p.2.

13 UN Centre for Human Settlements (HABITAT), June 1982, *Problems in Greater Bombay*, p.10.

14 A similar system still operating in some countries is that of communal tenure, whereby rights in land are not held exclusively by those who use the land, but rather by members of a community, which may be a family or a village or a collective: an individual has a right of use, but not a right to decide how the land is to be used by him. See A. W. Ashby, *Public Lands. An FAO Land Tenure Study* (Rome: UN Food and Agriculture Organization, 1956).

15 See Chapter 2, n.22, for reference to *Environment Law Review* (1975).

16 R. Nozick, *Anarchy, State and Utopia* (Oxford, Basil Blackwell, 1974). For Nozick's entitlement theory, see ch.7, p.151.

17 UNESCO Office of Statistics, *Revised Estimates and Projections of the Number of Illiterates and Illiteracy Rates* (Paris, 1982). Included in the world total are over 600 million in Asia and over 156 million in Africa.

18 If the present trend continues of an increase of approximately 100 million illiterates per decade since 1970, by the year 2000 there are expected to be 900 million illiterates in the world.

19 These rates compare with a 40 per cent to 60 per cent illiteracy rate in developing countries, but regional rates in some so-called developed countries are still abnormally high.

20 UNESCO Office of Statistics, *Reflections on the Future Development of Education* (Paris, 1981).

21 UN Disaster Relief Organization (UNDRO), *L'Afrique en Détresse* (Jan–Feb 1984) p.3.

22 A number of curriculum plans have been devised to suit the needs of particular students at both secondary and tertiary levels, some more scientifically-based than others. For one such course at tertiary level see G. C. Gupta, 'Introduction to Environmental Science: A Course for Nonscience Majors', *The Journal of Environmental Sciences* (July–August 1982) pp.27ff.

23 The Belgrade Charter which was adopted at the International Workshop on Environmental Education at Belgrade in October 1975 made very general recommendations, most of which were of little practical value in guiding educators. The first of its preliminary objectives was: 'For each nation, according to its culture, to clarify for itself the meaning of such basic concepts as "quality of life" and "human happiness" in the context of the total environment, with an extension of the clarification and appreciation to other cultures . . . ' But quality of life and human well-being (or happiness) are not culture-bound from a moral standpoint. Recommendation 4 on a global environmental ethic is made without a basic understanding of moral philosophy.

24 For a fuller explanation of the learning of moral attitudes and values see the author's *Justice, Morality and Education*, ch.5 on aspects of moral education.

25 For the problem of equality of educational opportunity see ibid., ch.8.

26 *World Development Report 1984*, International World Bank, p.150. See also *World Military and Social Expenditures*, pp.22–3.

27 In this world total the greater number of deaths have been among civilians. *World Military and Social Expenditures, 1983*, p.21.

28 T. S. Eliot, *Dante* (London: Faber and Faber, 1929) p.17. (Dante's description of his rapid flight from the Inferno to Purgatory, led by his companion Virgil, is an instance of this imaginative quality.)

# Select Bibliography

## BOOKS

Note: The particular editions or translations cited, when there are others available, are those used in the text.

Akehurst, M. *A Modern Introduction to International Law*, 4th edn (London: Allen and Unwin, 1982).

Aristotle. *Politics*, trans. B. Jowett.

Asamoah, O. Y. *The Legal Significance of the Declarations of the General Assembly of the UN* (The Hague: Martinus Nijhoff, 1966).

Attfield, R. *The Ethics of Environmental Concerns* (Oxford: Basil Blackwell, 1983).

Austin, J. *The Province of Jurisprudence Determined* (London: Weidenfeld and Nicolson, 1954).

Barry, B. *Political Argument* (London: Routledge and Kegan Paul, 1965).

Bates, G. M. *Environmental Law in Australia* (Sydney: Butterworths, 1983).

Bentham, J. *Works* (Edinburgh: William Tait, 1843).

Berry, J. M. *Lobbying for the People. The Political Behavior of Public Interest Groups* (Princeton University Press, 1977).

Bigham, D. A. *The Law and Administration Relating to Protection of the Environment* (London: Oyez Publishing, 1973).

Blackstone, W. *Commentaries on the Laws of England*, 16th edn (London: T. Cadell and J. Butterworth, 1825).

Brown, L. M. *Justice, Morality and Education* (Basingstoke and London: Macmillan, 1985).

Brownlie, I. *Principles of Public International Law* (Oxford: Clarendon Press, 1973).

Butler, W. E. *Soviet Law* (London: Butterworths, 1983).

Carritt, E. F. *Ethical and Political Thinking* (Oxford: Clarendon Press, 1947).

Carson, R. *Silent Spring* (Harmondsworth: Penguin Books, 1965).

Cicero, *Selected Political Speeches*, trans. M. Grant (Harmondsworth: Penguin Books, 1969).

Commoner, B. *The Closing Circle. Nature, Man and Technology* (New York: Alfred A. Knopf, 1972).

Darwin, C. *Autobiography* (London: Watts, 1929).

——. *The Descent of Man* (London: Watts, 1930).

Dressner, H. R. *The Search for the Public Interest* (New York: Ford Foundation, 1969).

Dworkin, R. (ed.) *The Philosophy of Law* (Oxford University Press, 1977).

Dymond, J. *Essays on the Principles of Morality*, 2nd edn (London: Hamilton, Adams, 1830).

Erlich, P. R. and A. H. *Population, Resources, Environment. Issues in Human Ecology* (San Francisco: W. H. Freeman, 1972).

Findlay, J. N. *Values and Intentions* (London: Allen and Unwin, 1961).

Fleisher, M. *Machiavelli and the Nature of Political Thought* (New York: Atheneum, 1972).

Frey, R.G. (ed.) *Utility and Rights* (Oxford: Basil Blackwell, 1985).

Freid, C. *An Anatomy of Values* (Cambridge, Mass.: Harvard University Press, 1970).

——. *Right and Wrong* (Cambridge, Mass.: Harvard University Press, 1978).

Friedrich, C. J. (ed.) *The Philosophy of Kant. Moral and Political Writings* (New York: Random House, 1949).

——. *The Pathology of Politics* (New York: Harper and Row, 1972).

Fuller, L. L. *The Morality of Law*, revised edn (New Haven and London: Yale University Press, 1969).

Geiger, G. R. *The Theory of the Land Question* (New York: Macmillan, 1936).

Gilpin, A. *Environment Policy in Australia* (Brisbane: University of Queensland Press, 1980).

Grad. F. *et al. Environmental Control: Priorities, Policies and the Law* (New York and London: Columbia University Press, 1971).

Gunn, J. A. W. *Politics and the Public Interest in the Seventeenth Century* (London: Routledge and Kegan Paul, 1969).

Hampshire, S. (ed.) *Public and Private Morality* (Cambridge University Press, 1978).

Hardin, G. *The Limits of Altruism: An Ecologist's View of Survival* (Bloomington and London: Indiana University Press, 1977).

——. *Population, Evolution and Birth Control*, 2nd edn (San Francisco: W. H. Freeman, 1964, 1969).

Hare, R. M. *Moral Thinking. Its Levels, Method and Point* (Oxford: Clarendon Press, 1981).

Hart, H. A. L. *The Concept of Law* (Oxford: Clarendon Press, 1961).

Held, V. *The Public Interest and Individual Interests* (New York and London: Basic Books, 1970).

Hobbes, T. *Leviathan* (Harmondsworth: Penguin, 1968).

——. *Works*, ed. W. Molesworth (London: John Bohn, 1841).

Hsii, L. S. *The Political Philosophy of Confucianism* (London: Routledge, 1932).

Hume, D. A. *A Treatise of Human Nature*, ed. L. A. Selby-Bigge (Oxford University Press, 1888).

——. *Enquiries Concerning Human Understanding and Concerning the Principles of Morals*, 3rd edn, ed. L. A. Selby-Bigge (Oxford University Press, 1975).

Hurstfield, J. *Freedom, Corruption and Government in Elizabethan England* (London: Jonathan Cape, 1973).

Johnson, B. *International Environmental Law* (Stockholm: Liber Förlag, 1976).

Kant, I. *Critique of Practical Reason and Other Works on the Theory of Ethics*, trans. T. K. Abbott, 6th edn (London: Longmans, 1909).

——. *Principles of Politics*, ed. W. Hastie (Edinburgh: T. and T. Clark, 1891).

Kay, D. A. and Skolnikoff, E. B. (eds) *World Eco-Crisis* (University of Wisconsin Press, 1972).

Krutilla, J. V. (ed.) *Natural Environments. Studies in Theoretical and Applied Analysis* (Baltimore and London: Johns Hopkins University Press, 1972).

Lamont, W. D. *The Value Judgement* (Edinburgh University Presss, 1955).

Laslett, P. (ed.) *Philosophy, Politics and Society* (Oxford: Basil Blackwell, 1956). Series 1–3.

Leopold, A. *Sand County Almanac* (New York: Oxford University Press, 1949).

Lippmann, W. *The Public Philosophy* (London: Hamish Hamilton, 1955).

Llewellyn, K. *The Common Law Tradition* (Boston: Little, Brown, 1960).

Locke, J. *Some Thoughts Concerning Education*, ed. R. H. Quick (Cambridge University Press)

——. *Works* (London: Tegg, 1823).

Luttwak, E. N. *Strategic Power* (Beverly Hills, London: Sage Publications, 1976).

Machiavelli, *The Prince, Selections from the Discourses and Other Writings*, ed. J. Plamenatz (London: Collins, 1972).

McCaffrey, S. and Lutz, R. E. (eds) *Environmental Pollution and Individual Right* (Netherlands: Kluwer Deventer, 1978).

Mackie, J. L. *Ethics. Inventing Right and Wrong* (Harmondsworth: Penguin, 1977).

Malthus, T. R. *First Essay on Population* (London: J. Johnson, 1798). (Reprinted for the Royal Economic Society, London: Macmillan, 1926.)

Meadows, D. H. *et al. The Limits to Growth* (New York: Universe Books, 1972).

Marx, K. and Engels, F. *Collected Works* (London: Lawrence and Wishart, 1976). (For *The German Ideology*.)

McLoughlin, J. *The Law and Practice Relating to Pollution Control in Europe* (London: Graham and Trotman, 1976).

Mill, J. S. *Autobiography* (London: Longmans, Green, 1875).

——. *Ethical Writings*, ed. J. B. Schneewind (London: Collier-Macmillan, 1965).

——. *Principles of Political Economy*, 9th edn (London: Longmans, 1886).

——. *Utilitarianism, Liberty, Representative Government*, ed. H. N. Acton (London: J. M. Dent, 1972).

Montaigne, M. *Works*, trans. W. Hazlitt (London: C. Templeman, 1865).

——. *The Complete Essays*, trans. D. M. Frame (Stanford University Press, 1958).

Moodie, G. C. and Studdart-Kennedy, G. *Opinions, Publics and Pressure Groups* (London: Allen and Unwin, 1970).

Moore, G. E. *Philosophical Studies* (London: Routledge and Kegan Paul, 1922).

——. *Principia Ethica* (Cambridge University Press, 1962).

Nagel, T. *The Possibility of Altruism* (Oxford: Clarendon Press, 1970).
Nahkies, G. E. *Environmental Impact Reporting in the USA and New Zealand* (Auckland University Press, 1976).
Nozick, R. *Anarchy, State and Utopia* (Oxford: Basil Blackwell, 1974).
Orloff, N. *The Environmental Impact Statement Process. A Guide to Citizen Action* (Washington D.C.: Information Resources Press, 1978).
Osborne, H. *Foundations of the Philosophy of Value* (Cambridge University Press, 1933).
Paine, T. *The Rights of Man* (1791) (Secaucus: Citadel Press, 1974).
Passmore, J. *Man's Responsibility for Nature*, 2nd edn (London: Duckworth, 1974, 1980).
Perelman, Ch. *The Idea of Justice and the Problem of Argument*, trans. J. Petrie (London: Routledge and Kegan Paul, 1963).
Plato, *The Republic*, trans. A. D. Lindsay (London: J. M. Dent, 1935).
——. *The Laws*, trans. J. Saunders (Harmondsworth: Penguin, 1970).
Pound, R. *Social Control Through Law* (New Haven: Yale University Press, 1942).
Quinton, A. *Utilitarian Ethics* (London: Macmillan, 1973).
Raab, F. *The English Face of Machiavelli. A Changing Interpretation 1500–1700* (London: Routledge and Kegan Paul, 1964).
Ratcliffe, D. *A Nature Conservation Review* (Cambridge University Press, 1977).
Rawls, J. *A Theory of Justice* (Oxford University Press, 1972).
Regan, T. and Singer, P. (eds) *Animal Rights and Human Obligations* (Engelwood Cliffs, N.J.: Prentice-Hall, 1976).
Rousseau, J.-J. *The Social Contract*, trans. M. Cranston (Harmondsworth: Penguin Books, 1968).
Schweitzer, A. *Civilization and Ethics*, 3rd edn (London: Adam and Charles Black, 1946).
Selby-Bigge, L. A. *British Moralists* (Oxford: Clarendon Press, 1897).
Sidgwick, H. *The Elements of Politics* (London and New York: Macmillan, 1891).
——. *The Methods of Ethics*, 7th edn (London: Macmillan, 1907).
Singer, P. *Animal Liberation* (London: Granada, 1977).
Sivard, R. L. *World Military and Social Expenditures 1983* (Washington D.C.: World Priorities, n.d.).
Smart, J. J. C. and Williams, B. *Utilitarianism For and Against* (Cambridge University Press, 1973).
Stone, C. *Should Trees Have Standing?* (Los Altos, California: Kaufman, 1974).
Tolstoy, L. *On Land and Slavery* (Glasgow: Land Values Publication Department, 1909).
Von Glahn, G. *Law Among Nations. An Introduction to Public International Law*, 3rd edn (New York: Macmillan, 1976).

PERIODICALS AND REPORTS

*Australian Journal of Philosophy*, vol.53 (1975).

*Council on Environmental Quality (Annual Reports)*, First Report, 1970, Third Report, 1972, Eleventh Report, 1980 (Washington D.C.: US Gov. Printing Office).

*Earth Law Journal* (International and Comparative Environmental Law)

*Environmental Comment*

*Environmental Ethics*

*Environment International*

*Environment Law Review*

*Environmental Research, An International Journal of Environmental Medicine and the Environmental Sciences*

*EPA Journal*, United States Environmental Protection Agency.

*Ethics*, vol.88, no.2 (1978).

*Harvard Law Review*, vol.76 (1969).

*Inquiry*, vol.16 (1973); vol.22 (1979).

*International Atomic Energy Agency*, Bulletin.

*Journal of the History of Ideas*, vol.36 (1975).

*Journal of Planning and Environment Law*

*Macro-Economic Evaluation of Environmental Programmes*, Organization for Economic Cooperation and Development (1978).

*Mind*, vol.LXXXIV (1975); vol.XCIII (1984).

*Proceedings of the Aristotelian Society*, vol.60 (1960); supplementary vol.38 (1964).

*Second World Conference on National Parks, 1972* (Morges, Switzerland: International Union for Conservation of Nature, 1974).

*Sinews for Survival*. A Report on the Management of Natural Resources (London: HMSO, 1972).

*The Problem of Chemical and Biological Warfare* (Stockholm International Peace Research Institute, Stockholm: Almqvist and Wiksell, 1973).

*The Human Environment. The British View* (London: HMSO, 1972).

*The International Journal of Environment Studies*

*The Journal of Environmental Sciences*

*United States Attorneys' Symposium on Environment Litigation and Land Use Planning* (Department of Justice, 1974).

*World Development Report 1984*, for the International World Bank (Oxford University Press, 1984).

UNITED NATIONS PUBLICATIONS

*Protect and Produce. Soil Conservation for Development* (Food and Agriculture Organization).

*Public Lands. An FAO Land Tenure Study* (Rome: 1956).

*Habitat* (UN Centre for Human Settlements).

*Implications for the Trade and Investment of Developing Countries of US Environmental Controls*, UN Conference on Trade and Development (New York: 1976).

*Development and Environment*, UN Conference on the Human Environment (1971).

*Population Issues – Background of the International Conference on*

*Population, 1984*, UN Department of Public Information.
*Stockholm and Beyond*, Report of the Advisory Committee on the 1972 UN Conference on the Human Environment (1972).
*International Law and the United Nations*, Address by U Thant to the International Bar Association (1968).
*UNDRO News*, Office of the UN Disaster Relief Coordinator.
UNDRO, *L'Afrique en Détresse* (1984).
UN Environment Programme, *Annual Report of the Executive Director, 1983*
——. *UNEP News*
——. *The Global Environment Monitoring System, 1982*
——. *The Human Environment. Action or Disaster, 1982*
——. *The State of the Environment, 1984*
——. *World Conservation Strategy, 1980* (UNEP with International Union for the Conservation of Nature and Natural Resources, and the World Wildlife Fund).
UNESCO Office of Statistics, *Revised Estimates and Projections of the Number of Illiterates and Illiteracy Rates* (1982).
UNESCO *Features* Bulletin
——. *Co-Action* Newsletter
——. *Reflections on the Future Development of Education* (1981).
UNESCO–UNEP, *The International Workshop on Environmental Education* (Belgrade: 1975).
UN Fund for Population Activities, *Population Problems and Prospects in the Arab World, 1984*.
——. *Populi*, vol.II, no.4 (1984).
UN Information Centre, *Urban Land Policies and Land-use Control Measures*, vol.VII (New York: 1975).
*UN World Charter for Nature*, Resolution of General Assembly, 37/6 (Oct 1982).

# Author Index

# Subject Index